POLITICAL GEOGRAPHY

POLITICAL GEOGRAPHY
APPROACHES, CONCEPTS, FUTURES

RACHAEL SQUIRE & ANNA JACKMAN

S Sage

1 Oliver's Yard
55 City Road
London EC1Y 1SP

2455 Teller Road
Thousand Oaks, California 91320

Unit No 323-333, Third Floor, F-Block
International Trade Tower, Nehru Place
New Delhi 110 019

8 Marina View Suite 43-053
Asia Square Tower 1
Singapore 018960

Editor: Natalie Aguilera
Editorial assistant: Daniel Price
Production editor: Sarah Sewell
Copyeditor: Christine Bitten
Proofreader: Fern Bryant
Marketing manager: Fauzia Eastwood
Cover design: Francis Kenney
Typeset by: KnowledgeWorks Global Ltd.

© Rachael Squire and Anna Jackman 2024

Apart from any fair dealing for the purposes of research, private study, or criticism or review, as permitted under the Copyright, Designs and Patents Act, 1988, this publication may not be reproduced, stored or transmitted in any form, or by any means, without the prior permission in writing of the publisher, or in the case of reprographic reproduction, in accordance with the terms of licences issued by the Copyright Licensing Agency. Enquiries concerning reproduction outside those terms should be sent to the publisher.

Library of Congress Control Number: 2023936410

British Library Cataloguing in Publication data

A catalogue record for this book is available from the British Library

ISBN 978-1-5264-9884-7
ISBN 978-1-5264-9885-4 (pbk)

CONTENTS

About the Authors	vii
Acknowledgements	ix
1 Political Geography: Approaches, Concepts, Futures	1
2 Situating Political Geography: Tracing the Emergence of the Sub-discipline	7
3 Feminist Geopolitics: Sites, Spaces, Scales	23
4 Decolonising: Dismantling Architectures of Privilege	41
5 Non-human Worlds: From Objects to Animals	59
6 Popular Geopolitics: Shaping Geopolitical Imaginations	79
7 States and Territory: Heights, Depths, Thinking 'Volume'	97

8 Borders: From State Lines to the Body	115
9 Nationalism: Flags, Fears, Fictions	133
10 Mobilities: Geopolitics in Motion	149
11 Violence: Practice and Experience	167
12 Peace and Resistance: Decentring War	185
13 Surveillance: Geographies of Digital Space and Life	203
14 Crisis and Hope: Thinking with Geopolitical Futures	221
Index	241

ABOUT THE AUTHORS

Dr Rachael Squire is a Lecturer in Human Geography at Royal Holloway, University of London. Her research draws on feminist geopolitics to explore questions relating to the sea, territory, volume, and, most recently, earth futures and Anthropocene geographies. Rachael has published in a range of journals in addition to her monograph *Undersea Geopolitics: Sealab, Science, and the Cold War*. Her most recent work explores the political, cultural, and social geographies of public aquariums in a time of environmental crisis.

Dr Anna Jackman is a Lecturer in Human Geography at the University of Reading. Anna is a feminist political geographer interested in technological visibilities, volumes, relations and futures. Her current research approaches these issues through the lens of the drone, exploring the 'unmanning' of everyday, urban and military life in the drone age. Anna's Economic and Social Research Council (ESRC)-funded research project 'Diversifying Drone Stories' engaged with a range of stakeholders (including emergency services, lawyers, industry, local authorities, pilots, and members of the public) to explore the diverse use, perception, and impact of drones in changing UK airspace. Anna is on Twitter @ahjackman.

ACKNOWLEDGEMENTS

Our collective thanks go to Daniel Price and the team at Sage for their guidance, support, and patience, and for making the process a smooth and enjoyable one. We would also like to thank the amazing scholars who contributed to the 'In the field' boxes. We really appreciate your time and willingness to share your insights and experiences – these have enriched the book. Finally, our thanks to the reviewers of our initial proposal. The feedback from this was extremely generous and it has been formative in shaping the pages that follow.

Rachael: My personal thanks firstly go to my co-author, Anna. It was a pleasure to co-design a political geography course together and it's wonderful to see that the spirit of this has found a home here. As always, I'm very grateful for you as both a colleague and friend. More broadly, I am indebted to the wider political geography community and specifically, to the work of the many feminist political geographers who changed/are changing the discipline for the better. This broader community also includes students. I'm extremely grateful to all those I've had the pleasure of working with on GG2052 Political Geography. They have taught me a lot and are always a source of inspiration and constructive critique! My thanks to colleagues at Royal Holloway and beyond. The list is long but a special mention here to Katy Flowers, Laura Shipp, Harriet Hawkins, Katherine

Brickell, Vandana Desai, Jay Mistry, Katie Willis, Peter Adey, Oli Mould, Kim Peters, Alex Jeffrey, Johanne Bruun, Paul Lincoln, and Dan Webb. Finally, thank you to my incredible family and friends for your love, care, championing, and cheerleading. You are the very best of (many) reasons not to work evenings and weekends.

Anna: After co-teaching a module on political geography, we imagined what our own textbook could look like, what it might do. Both to bring our idea to life and to share it with students and peers is a great privilege. My first thank you goes to my brilliant co-author and friend, Rachael Squire. It has been, and continues to be, a pleasure and privilege to think and write with you. Of course, I also owe much to fellow political geographers, who have shaped my career and from whom I have learned a great deal. It is my hope that this textbook both meaningfully engages with and celebrates their diverse and powerful work. I'd also like to thank my partner, Chris, for listening to (over-enthusiastically delivered) ideas and offering encouragement. Too often do academics fail to recognise or slow down to enjoy an accomplishment. Thank you for creating pause and raising a glass. Lastly, thank you to my family – Andrew (dad), Jeanne (mom), Kate, Hope, and Monty (the dog) – who have offered support and good humour in equal measure.

ONE

POLITICAL GEOGRAPHY: APPROACHES, CONCEPTS, FUTURES

Chapter Overview

From the everyday to the global, political geography matters. It equips us with the tools to help make sense of a tumultuous world – a world convulsing under the pressures of a Climate Emergency, straining amidst the effects of war, and emerging from the devastation of the worldwide Covid-19 pandemic. As an approach, political geography enables us to locate the geopolitical in unexpected spaces, placing the spotlight on the space of the bedroom as much as the battlefield; the body as much as the border; the school as much as the state. Political geography teaches us that the geopolitical is located in the ordinary and the extraordinary, the mundane and the dazzling expressions of state power. It also asks of us to think critically about the geopolitical world, to challenge and resist dominant ideas, and to open out multiple ways of seeing, engaging, and being. When surrounded by such profound, catastrophic, and uneven change, such an imperative is more important than ever.

Whether hopeful, hopeless, or somewhere in between, geopolitics underpins and shapes the world around us. But what is it and how is it different from political geography? In this book we understand 'geopolitics' in simple terms as the relationship between power and space. This is not to ignore the complex and fraught histories of geopolitics as a term and practice – we turn to these in the next chapter. It is also not to say that the effects of this relationship are straightforward; on the contrary, this definition opens up a world of complexity and it is our job as political geographers to critically examine these complexities. How, for example, is power situated in the world around us? How does this relationship unfold across multiple scales and contexts? How does power move and travel? How is power resisted and how does this manifest itself spatially? In short, as students of political geography, we want to explore where power lies, who and what holds and experiences it, and how it might be thought and distributed differently. In exploring these intersections, political geography helps us to make sense of the world, to think critically about pasts, presents, and futures and to challenge hegemonic or dominant geopolitical understandings that tell us how the world should be. In order to do this effectively, political geography should be understood as a vibrant sub-discipline of human geography. The key concepts and concerns of space, place and scale are central to political geography, as are the critical thinking skills of the human geographer more broadly. In this sense, political geography also benefits from its close associations with other offshoots of human geography including cultural, historical, social, and urban geographies.

What Does it Mean to Us?

For both of us, political geography has been instrumental in shaping our perspectives as academics and geographers. For me (Rachael), this began with my undergraduate degree in Geography, Politics and International Relations. This was formative in helping me to understand what it means to think critically and to challenge settled assumptions. Moreover, it brought home that the geopolitical is not just something that exists 'out there'. On the contrary, the geopolitical and spatial dynamics of power course through our everyday lives and characterise everything from our interactions in the home to the social and legal norms that dictate how we navigate everyday spaces around us. More broadly, my experiences as a political geographer have taught me that, as a sub-discipline, political geography has the capacity to prompt thinking about more just and equitable futures, to unsettle hegemonic and privileged sites of power, and to fundamentally and radically reimagine what politics might look like at multiple scales. Whilst there is a way to go to realise this, feminist and decolonial thinkers provide hope that such re-scripting is possible and these are ideas we'll be exploring in the following pages.

For me (Anna), I too came to encounter political geography as an undergraduate. Here, in lecture halls and seminar rooms, geography opened up critical ideas, voices, and questions about the world around me. Through its focus on the spaces, processes, and practices of power, political geography invited and enabled me to see the familiar anew, with a greater awareness, attention, and care to uneven relations, and, as Rachael notes, the spaces, encounters, and experiences of resistance that can destabilise and challenge these too. From thinking anew about the politics of the toys I played with as a child, to reflecting on my experiences and privileges as a dual national travelling through sites and spaces of bordering, political geography acted as an invaluable toolkit to understand and seek intervention into a world that is at once changing and uneven, resistant, and hopeful. Later in my career, I was also fortunate enough to apply my research expertise into a policy context, acting as a Specialist Adviser to an inquiry led by the Science and Technology Committee. This experience offered a glimpse into the spaces of politics I had read and taught about, while reinforcing the idea that, as political geographers and citizens, we play an active role in the composition and (re)shaping of geopolitical worlds.

The Structure of this Textbook

To explore these ideas and themes further, this textbook begins with a contextual chapter that engages with the deeply problematic histories of political geography. It traces these histories through to the present day, using contemporary critiques as a springboard to better understand the chapters that follow. The remaining chapters are organised around three key sections. This isn't necessarily designed to neatly encapsulate different components of the discipline. The lines and boundaries around any particular idea or theme are never neat, and nor should they be. On the contrary we see the complexity and messiness of political geography as something to be celebrated. What the following three sections do, however, is to provide framing and structure for the book to help shape your engagement.

Approaches

The opening 'approaches' are designed to help you get to grips with some of the key lenses *through* which to engage with political geography. They draw on key thinkers to provide entry points to the geopolitical world, and to unsettle preconceptions of what geopolitics is, and how we locate it across various scales and contexts. We identify four key approaches in the following chapters:

- (Chapter 3) Feminist Geopolitics: Sites, Spaces, Scales
- (Chapter 4) Decolonising: Dismantling Architectures of Privilege
- (Chapter 5) Non-human Worlds: From Objects to Animals
- (Chapter 6) Popular Geopolitics: Shaping Geopolitical Imaginations

Each of these chapters and approaches make the geopolitical present in different ways and provide an opportunity to reflect on both where we locate the geopolitical and how it is experienced, sensed, and made meaningful. Each can also be applied to section 2, *Concepts*. You might, for example, explore the border through an intersectional approach drawing on and applying decolonial and feminist approaches. Or perhaps you want to explore it through the lens of objects or non-humans, or a mixture of all three. Whichever you engage with, the approaches detailed here offer related and interconnected ways to broaden understandings of key geopolitical ideas, and to critique and reimagine settled and dominant assumptions.

Concepts

Having established key approaches within the discipline, the *Concepts* section offers an opportunity to introduce a number of key themes and ideas that have shaped political geography as a sub-discipline. This section is organised around seven chapters:

- (Chapter 7) States and Territory: Heights, Depths, Thinking 'Volume'
- (Chapter 8) Borders: From State Lines to the Body

- (Chapter 9) Nationalism: Flags, Fears, Fictions
- (Chapter 10) Mobilities: Geopolitics in Motion
- (Chapter 11) Violence: Practice and Experience
- (Chapter 12) Peace and Resistance: Decentring War
- (Chapter 13) Surveillance: Geographies of Digital Space and Life

These seven ideas are designed to provide an entry point into key debates, and to enable us to reimagine concepts that we may otherwise take for granted or presume to be part of some sort of 'natural' world order – such as the 'state'. These chapters engage with the geopolitical at and across multiple scales, drawing on the key approaches outlined above to try and make sense of geopolitical processes and practices, and to think through how these are experienced, resisted, and challenged.

Futures

The final chapter of the book offers a moment to pause and reflect on emerging and potential geopolitical futures, and the futures of political geography as a discipline:

- (Chapter 14) Crisis and Hope: Thinking with Geopolitical Futures

The final chapter explores geopolitical thinking around 'futures'. Turning to the contexts of data, outer space, and climate change futures, it applies futures thinking to examine how different practices of imagining and anticipating futures unevenly impact different people and spaces. From direct action to storytelling, it also explores reactions and responses to these imagined and anticipated futures, highlighting the agencies of diverse and hopeful peoples in the face of future crises.

Cross-Cutting Considerations

There are a number of overarching principles that cut across each of the three sections above. You might, for example, have expected to see a chapter on the Climate Emergency. Climate change represents the most profound challenge to humanity and is an issue that cuts across, and through, every aspect of the geopolitical. It is therefore incorporated across the following pages, and is not confined to a set chapter. Similarly, woven throughout each section is an openness to a wide range of geopolitical thinking. Whilst, in an Anglophone context political geography has two flagship journals – *Political Geography* and *Geopolitics* – it remains a lively sub-discipline informed by a whole range of approaches and scholarship from different areas of geography (e.g. cultural geography), sociology, anthropology, Latin American studies, and history, to name but a few. The textbook thus proceeds on the premise that rather than diluting the discipline, an openness to different ways of thinking 'geopolitically' has enriched political geography and worked to make the tent of political geography bigger and better (see Hyndman 2019).

Finally, we wanted to make clear that whilst we have aimed to do some of the work of bringing together different research, writings and ideas, the textbook is of course inspired by the work we cite and the incredible diversity of thinking by scholars in and beyond this field. Whilst acknowledging the significant contributions of the dominant White male thinkers that were formative in shaping political geography (see Chapter 2), we are particularly inspired by the work of early career scholars, feminist, and decolonial thinkers who have pushed, and continue to push, for a more expansive and diverse political geography, as well as both undergraduate and postgraduate students undertaking rich and varied work. We have sought to foreground these approaches in the pages that follow. In reality, no single (or pair) of political geographers can claim intellectual authority over a rich and varied field. This book therefore points to the exciting work that is emerging and defining the discipline across a range of themes and concepts.

How to Use this Book

In an ideal scenario, we would recommend reading this textbook like you would any other book – from start to finish. This is because no one theme sits in isolation from another, they all interlink to form part of the rich tapestry of the geopolitical world, and therefore reading the book in sequence gives you the best chance of grasping and thinking across key approaches and ideas. In reality, we also realise your reading of this book might take other forms. You might dip in and out, read in conjunction with themes as they come up in your courses, or read as you are planning for an essay. For this reason, each chapter also functions as a standalone intervention, enabling you to get to grips with a key approach, concept, or idea about the future. To help you navigate this process, each chapter contains a number of features:

Overview: Each chapter starts with an 'overview'. This will offer a brief introduction to the chapter, outline the directions it will take, and highlight any key conclusions.
Read with: You'll find 'read with' at the beginning of each chapter. It will flag any other chapters that are directly relevant or particularly helpful to read in conjunction with the one you are currently on.
Key terms: You'll find 'key terms' in boxes in each chapter. They provide definitions and explanations of key terms.
Case studies: Examples will be embedded throughout the chapters, but specific case study boxes in each chapter highlight work that is particularly relevant to and applying the concept or idea being discussed.
Over to you: These are activities designed to take your learning off the page. They provide an opportunity to put what you'd learned into practice and to develop your own critical thinking skills on key geopolitical issues.
In the field: Each chapter will contain a short interview with a political geographer to give you a sense of *how* political geography is done in practice, and the kinds of considerations researchers grapple with in their work. Each interview will relate back

to the chapter theme to give you an insight into real world research and how this informs our geopolitical knowledge.

Follow-on resources: At the end of each chapter, you'll find both a list of references and a short selection of 'follow-on resources'. These might be films that would be helpful to watch in conjunction with the chapter, podcasts, or other media that will support your engagement with the subject.

The textbook provides an overview of some of the key themes, ideas, and concepts of political geography. Needless to say, no single book can cover everything, and we suggest you see this as a springboard for your learning. In this sense, each chapter is an introduction to a key approach or concept, but also an invitation to you to explore further, delve deeper, and to run with the ideas you're reading about. Moreover, we also believe that knowledge is not just constituted through reading, so as you go through each chapter, think about the geopolitics of your own worlds and how you experience these through all of your senses, whether that be sight, sound, touch, or even smell. In short, integrate this textbook into your ways of understanding, navigating, and experiencing the world and be open to having those understandings stretched in different directions.

References

Hyndman, J. (2019). Unsettling feminist geopolitics: Forging feminist political geographies of violence and displacement. *Gender, Place & Culture, 26*(1), 3–29.

TWO

SITUATING POLITICAL GEOGRAPHY: TRACING THE EMERGENCE OF THE SUB-DISCIPLINE

Chapter Overview

This chapter provides an opportunity to reflect on political geography's troubled and violent past. It briefly traces the evolution of Anglophone political geography as a sub-discipline, exploring its troubled beginnings through key thinkers such as Halford Mackinder, interrogating its evil applications in the British Empire and Nazi Germany, and ending on the present day. These histories are by their nature inherently and overwhelmingly White and male, so too is much of the writing on these histories. This history is also complex and fraught, and in many ways, beyond the scope of a chapter in a textbook (see Agnew 2016 and Kuus 2010 for fuller accounts). The proceeding pages are thus an introduction rather than a comprehensive overview to the disgraced ideas that laid the foundation of the discipline, and its resurgence back to a mainstream, lively, and vital lens through which to understand the world.

Learning Objectives

1. To explore the evolution of political geography in the UK.
2. To understand its troubled and violent past and the implications of this today.
3. To situate today's lively and vibrant sub-discipline.

Read with: Chapter 3 (Feminist Geopolitics), Chapter 4 (Decolonising Geopolitics), Chapter 6 (Popular Geopolitics).

Troubled Beginnings

> It is our sad but necessary duty to make space in our disciplinary accounts for the morally bankrupt ends to which geographical ideas have been put. (Keighren 2018: 774)

As the quote above by Innes Keighren suggests, it is imperative that as students of geography, we do not turn a blind eye to the violent and, at times, abhorrent histories and intellectual lineages of our discipline. Political geography is no exception to this. The histories of geopolitical thought are fraught, deeply problematic, and rooted in practices of empire and colonialism in the late 1800s. As Toal et al. (1998: 15) state, 'geopolitics as a form of power/knowledge was born in the era of imperialist rivalry', and it finds its inception in a time characterised by 'colonial expansionism' under the dominant structure of the British Empire, and amidst great anxiety from British circles about the rise of the German state.

A key protagonist in shaping and defining early political geography was Halford Mackinder (1861–1947). A zoologist by training in his undergraduate degree (Blouet 2004), Mackinder is often understood to be one of the first and founding political geographers, concerned as he was with developing a 'new way to seeing international politics as a unified worldwide scene' (Toal et al. 1998: 16). In other words, Mackinder viewed the world from above – adopting the God's Eye View, or 'divine gaze' to develop geopolitical strategies and ideas that could be applied to the world as a whole. Mackinder's (problematic) way of thinking was important as he became an influential figure both in British politics and in academic geography. Whilst he founded the Oxford School of Geography in 1899 and later became the director of the London School of Economics in 1903, Mackinder was also a Member of Parliament and widely involved in policy-making circles. Adamant in his belief that both policy makers and the British public must be educated into becoming loyal imperial citizens, he was also a member of the Colonial Office's Visual Instruction Committee, playing a major role in the shaping of 'educational materials for schools and the wider reading public' (Dodds 2007: 121).

KEY TERMS: ENVIRONMENTAL DETERMINISM

This is the idea that geopolitics and political action are determined and directly shaped by geographical location or the physical environment. This idea was prominent in Mackinder's writing and it remains problematically prominent in writings today (see for example Tim Marshall's *Prisoners of Geography*).

As political geographers today we should be critical of this idea. While the environment might be a factor in geopolitical processes, it is certainly not the determinant as humans, rather than the environment, construct geopolitical phenomena such as the state, borders, and territory.

For Mackinder, the discipline of geography was a powerful tool and he articulated his ideas through a series of addresses and lectures at the Royal Geographical Society. 'The practical requirements of the statesman' argued that with no new lands to conquer, geography could aid statecraft by engaging with foreign policy and by 'training children to become fierce imperial citizens' (Kearns 2010: 191). Geography, for Mackinder, should both inspire and instruct. In the words of Toal et al. (1998: 16) it was to be 'a discipline that *disciplined*', teaching 'uneducated masses to think in a political way that experts like Mackinder wanted them to think'. In another address in 1887, he spoke on 'The scope and methods of geography', arguing that with the end of the Age of Exploration and the last of the great 'discoveries', the world had now become a closed and locked political system. Geography could find new relevance by serving and promoting the cause of empire (Kearns 2010: 187). Within this framework, geography was not just a discipline that would describe the world, it was one that could aid statecraft both through education but also through directing politics. This 'new geography' should aspire to be a science of environmental causation and spatial arrangement, a discipline that, through experts like Mackinder, could 'play God by claiming to see objectively, perceive the real, and explain all' (Toal et al. 1998: 17).

These ideas plugged into Mackinder's wider thinking which we might understand through five interrelated and interlocking belief systems (see Kearns 2013: 918–921):

1. **Resources**: Mackinder's ideas were often premised on the idea that the environment determined political realities (see environmental determinism). He understood resources to be clustered in particular spaces, meaning that some states might have access to various resources, and others may not. This, for Mackinder, meant that there were inequalities across the globe in the capacity for development and in the ability to express geopolitical and military power.
2. **Interconnectedness**: Mackinder argued that with the decline of discovery and colonisation, and with the spread of technology, the world was becoming so interconnected that distance no longer provided any defence against events happening elsewhere. This meant that British national interests must extend well beyond the shores of the UK. Moreover, this connectedness meant that influence and power can spread.
3. **Spatial units**: Mackinder saw the world as a patchwork of distinct spatial units, 'comprising large territories that could be coloured differently: black or white, red or blue, yellow or brown' (Kearns 2013: 919). Within these state units, Mackinder believed populations to be 'relatively homogeneous while being radically different from their equally homogeneous neighbours'. These units were believed to be so different from each other that conflict would be inevitable.
4. **Exceptionalism and racial supremacy**: In Mackinder's eyes, these spatial units and civilisations were not equal. Within this system, the British were the flag bearer of universal values and stood above all other nations. Describing the British tradition as the 'happiest and highest in mankind', he understood Britain to be the 'intricate product of a continuous history, geological and

human' (Mackinder 1902: 229–230) with a precious bloodline that needed protecting. The natural environment provided the context for 'the struggle of the races' (Kearns 1984: 30).

5. **Strength, force, and masculinity**: For Mackinder, the environment shaped cultural identity in ways that produced a 'patchwork of mutually hostile peoples' (Kearns 2010: 188). States (or spatial units) could thus only survive through strength, force, and victory in conflict. Britain was not just motivated by territorial gain but by preventing the 'selfish aggression of others' (Kearns 2010: 1880). Ideals and practices of masculinity underpinned this process. The British, wrote Mackinder, had to be taught to 'value the Empire as the protection of their manhood' (Mackinder 1905: 143). Mackinder opposed women having the vote, arguing 'that extending the franchise to a weaker sex obscured the fundamental relation between force and decision making' (Kearns 2010: 193).

The Geographical Pivot of History (1904)

Mackinder's belief systems culminated in his most influential grand strategy and theory about world politics – the Geographical Pivot of History. Initially, Mackinder had been concerned that if the British race failed, Germany would rise to power. But with the demise of sea power, and the spread of technologies like the railway, other power centres were emerging around the Russian landmass. The resource potential in this land mass was vast, with unknown potentials of wheat, cotton, fuel, metals, and possibilities for population expansion (Toal et al. 1998). This area became known in Mackinder's geopolitical imagination as the 'Pivot Area', or the 'Heartland'. Beyond this Pivot Area lay the 'Inner Crescent', including states such as Germany, Austria, India, and China. Beyond this lay the 'Outer Crescent', which included the UK, South Africa, Canada, the US, and Japan (see Figure 2.1). For Mackinder, the significance of these spheres could not be understated. As Mackinder asserted:

> Who rules East Europe commands the Heartland; Who rules the Heartland commands the World Island; Who rules the World Island commands the World. (1919: 150)

Beyond eliminating 'the tremendous geographical diversity and particularity of places on the surface of the earth' (Toal et al. 1998: 17), Mackinder's vision of the world generated a lot of attention. His ideas and strategies, premised on environmental determinism and the authority granted from expertise and the God's Eye View, reshaped the geopolitical map, with legacies that continued into the Cold War. Crucially, we see that in the early twentieth century, geopolitics was a 'form of power/knowledge concerned with promoting state expansionism and securing empires' (Toal et al. 1998: 4). Mackinder's ideas still hold power in the present day, with notions of the 'Heartland' or 'Pivot Area' forming crucial components of Russian geopolitical thinking, among others. Mackinder's ideas, whilst later disgraced, are by no means dead (see Kearns 2006, 2013).

Figure 2.1 Heartland–Mackinder map

Credit: This scanned document has been provided by the wikimedian-in-residence at the National Macedonian Academy of Arts and Sciences (MANU) as part of a cooperation project with Shared Knowledge (Creative Commons Attribution-Share Alike 4.0 International license) https://commons.wikimedia.org/wiki/File:Heartland-Mackinder-map.jpg

Source: Mackinder, 1904:435.

Evil Applications and the Downfall of Political Geography

Mackinder was not alone in generating grand theories about the world along the lines of race and environmental determinism. Geopolitics was gaining traction in America through the likes of Alfred Mahan, and in Germany, Friedrich Ratzel (1844–1904), a zoologist and geologist by training (Klinke and Bassin 2018: 55), who developed ideas that brought together land and space with political projects. Often cited as being the founding father of political geography (Klinke 2019: 2), Ratzel stressed the importance of the relationship between a state's territory and soil, in the development of national strength and power, and in the development of an empire (Toal et al. 1998: 4). As Klinke (2018: 1) writes, Ratzel was preoccupied with understanding the 'causal influence that a nation's position, climate or access to natural resources had on its rise and fall'. His thinking was very much anchored in wider nineteenth century debates about the interactions and relationships between human societies and the environment. For Ratzel, much like Mackinder, 'geographical conditions were not passive, but rather played a direct role in shaping human activity' (Klinke and Bassin 2018: 55). Within this context, Ratzel, heavily influenced by Darwinism and the principles of natural selection, imagined the state as being like an organism that naturally seeks to grow and expand, and that is intricately connected and rooted to the soil on which it stands. German soil was, for Ratzel, 'superior to all others' (Toal et al. 1998: 4).

Lebensraum

A key tenet of Ratzel's thinking was that in this world of overlapping state spaces or organisms, there would always be a tension between the expanding movements of life and the 'always stable and infinite world on which they dwelled' (Klinke 2018: 26). The state was therefore always locked in a struggle for survival. To counter this, Ratzel argued that the state must always seek to expand. He believed that Europe was politically saturated, advocating instead for colonialism and slavery in Africa (Klinke and Bassin 2018: 55) so that 'true German culture could be recreated and preserved' (Klinke 2018: 26). These ideas were popularised in an essay, *Lebensraum* (Living Space), authored by Ratzel in 1901. It argued that humans and their political and social lives were 'but an effect of the natural world and therefore subject to nature's law in much the same way as the animal and plant kingdom' (Klinke and Bassin 2018: 53). In comparing the actions of the state and population to that of the natural world, Ratzel naturalised territorial expansion. Within the framework of Lebensraum, this was an inevitable and unavoidable consequence of the relationship between humanity and the environment. Lebensraum is still used commonly today as a term to describe aggressive territorial actions by one state to another (Klinke and Bassin 2018).

Ratzel's ideas and the beginnings of German geopolitics 'would have perhaps remained a footnote in world history' were it not for one of Ratzel's followers, Karl Haushofer (1869–1946) (Klinke 2018: 2). Haushofer had influence among German policy circles. He was a scholar of geopolitics, and devotee of Mackinder and Ratzel. Writing between the First World War and the Second World War, he detailed the significance of the Heartland and argued for the need for Lebensraum (Fettweis 2000: 58), understanding geopolitics to be a science of political lifeforms and their natural living spaces (Klinke 2018). This idea was extremely popular in German political discourse. Its appeal lay in its capacity to rehabilitate Germany after it had lost overseas colonies and territory within Europe after the end of the First World War. The perception that more living space was needed to accommodate Germany's population and ambition 'that was already palpable in Ratzel's day, grew ever more widespread and acute' (Klinke and Bassin 2018). Political geography and geopolitics as a discipline laid the foundation for this ideology, a problem that was cemented when, in 1924, Haushofer was introduced to a then relatively unknown Austrian politician, Adolf Hitler (Klinke 2018). As Keighren (2018: 774) highlights, Haushofer, though the intellectual descent of Ratzel, has 'long been characterised as Hitler's intellectual inspiration', having provided the language and vocabulary with which Hitler's manifesto, *Mein Kampf* (1925), was peppered. In reality, there is considerable debate about the extent of Haushofer's influence over Hitler, yet he has been unequivocally cast as the geopolitical mind behind Nazi ideology, and the 'scholarly plotter of German world domination' (Keighren 2018: 774).

We can clearly see how these ideas rippled through the German state. This might be through works like *Mein Kampf*, but also in public propaganda material. As demonstrated in Figure 2.2, the Nazi Party adopted Lebensraum with great gusto. Figure 2.2 depicts a German postcard from 1933–1936. The large text reads 'Here lies our living space' whilst the text at the bottom quotes Adolf Hitler (1933): 'There is a great deal that Germany

Figure 2.2 Nazi Germany postcard

Credit: Wikimedia (Creative Commons Attribution-Share Alike 4.0 International license) https://commons.wikimedia.org/wiki/File:Auch_hier_liegt_unser_Lebensraum_Die_deutsche_Kolonialausstellung_Berlin_Postkarte_Ansichtskarte_farbige_Propagandakarte_des_Reichskolonialbundes_Afrika_Kolonien_Fahnen_1930s_934370_Nazi_Germany_postcard_No_known_copyright.jpg

needs to get from the colonies, and we need colonies as much as any other power'. As Klinke and Bassin (2018: 57) write, the idea of Lebensraum suited the purposes of the Nazi party 'perfectly':

> It captured quite neatly the spirit of their political programme of territorial expansion and conquest, and helpfully legitimized this programme by characterizing it as a natural and organic imperative necessary for the healthy growth of the German nation ... By the early 1920s, Adolf Hitler was using the term repeatedly in his manifesto Mein Kampf to describe and justify his call for Germany to reclaim the territories it had lost in the war and to expand beyond them.

These understandings of the relationship between the people, state, and the land and the soil became fundamental to the expression and discourse propagated by the Nazi Party (Keighren 2018). Whilst Ratzel died when Hitler was a child and would have certainly objected to his work being appropriated by Hitler, his work was nonetheless used to bolster this particular expression of the German state, 'whose unity and ultimate expression was to be cemented through territorial expansion' (Keighren 2018: 773). Ratzel's work, refracted and distorted along the way, laid 'a foundation upon which Nazi ideology was built' (Keighren 2018: 773).

In the Field with Ian Klinke: The History of Political Geography

Ian Klinke teaches at the University of Oxford. He is the author of *Life, Earth, Colony: Friedrich Ratzel's Necropolitical Geography* (University of Michigan Press, 2023).

What drew you to researching Friedrich Ratzel?

When researching German nuclear bunkers a few years ago, I wanted to understand how these sites were framed by military strategists and civil defence planners in the 1950s and 60s. I soon realised that they were dealing with nuclear war in a vocabulary which was indebted to a Ratzelian brand of geography. I wanted to find out more about Ratzel – but nobody had written a decent book on him. Given the impact of his ideas on a range of political thinkers (from W.E.B. Du Bois to Carl Schmitt) and political figures (including Augusto Pinochet and Adolf Hitler), this seemed a real opportunity.

How did you go about doing this in practice?

I had to do a fair amount of reading to get to grips with Ratzel's published work: over 30 books and over 1,000 shorter pieces on topics that ranged from panpsychist philosophy to alcohol-fuelled misbehaviour at German railway stations. I also had to familiarise myself with Ratzel's influences and his reception, i.e. those on whom he drew and those who drew on him. Finally, I had to study his correspondence and diaries and sift through some unpublished material. Most of the archival material I drew on for my book was held in two archives in Germany but I also ventured to archives in Britain and the United States. I found all of this very rewarding to do.

Why is it so important we continue to engage with political geography's troubled past?

Whether we like it or not, a Ratzelian geopolitics still matters to the world around us. It lives on in Russian imperial blueprints for Ukraine, German far right politics and in US billionaire fantasies of space colonisation. If we don't understand why these ideas continue to find followers, we will struggle to find solutions to today's problems.

Needless to say, the discipline of political geography and geopolitics as a way of thinking could not survive in the wake of the Second World War and the atrocities committed by Hitler and the German state. Both the concept of Lebensraum, and Ratzel as an intellectual thinker, remain disgraced within political geography. The entangling of geopolitical thinking and the lives and legacies of early political geographers meant that geopolitics was 'fundamentally discredited' due to its association with the Nazi regime (Klinke and Bassin 2018: 57). The degree to which geographers were really complicit in this is, again, up for debate. Regardless, geopolitics became associated with 'evil geographies' (Keighren 2018: 722). The early beginnings of political geography were thus deeply entangled within imperialist discourse, ideas of evolutionary biology, and atrocities of unimaginable scale propagated by a cast of 'elite White men' who believed themselves to be masters and purveyors of the globe (Toal et al. 1998: 4).

A New Kind of Geopolitical Thinking: Towards Critical Geopolitics

In many ways, it is difficult to imagine how political geography as a sub-discipline has rehabilitated itself to the extent that it has. In the wake of its history, it largely disappeared as a subject. In order for this rehabilitation to take place, political geography and geopolitical ideas had to be radically uprooted and reimagined, to become something very different. Early geopolitical thought had been premised, in part, on developing 'scientific' grand strategies and narratives that simplified a complex world. Reducing state behaviour to that of a natural organism is a prime example of this, a strategy that helps to create the illusion of understanding the world and thus being able to control it, prescribing pre-determined outcomes (Flint 2021: 1). Such pronouncements are, however, a mirage. As this textbook explores, the world around us is socially constructed, it is complex, and it is driven by human behaviour rather than environmental conditions. If geopolitics were to survive, grappling with these complexities, rather than resting on grand and totalising statements, was a necessity. And it was a pressing necessity too. Just because geopolitics as a discipline had fallen out of favour does not mean that the geopolitical world stopped spinning.

As we know in hindsight, the Cold War was geopolitics writ large. On every scale, geopolitical sensibilities coursed through the world. From the superpower politics that shaped the relationship between the US and the Soviet Union, to everyday fears about nuclear warfare, the Cold War was, for many, all encompassing. The spatial politics of this were also vast. From submarine warfare in the depths of the sea, to the Space Race to the stars, the geopolitics of this period touched every dimension on earth (see Turchetti and Roberts 2014, Squire 2021). Within this context, the term 'geopolitics' became widely used within US policy. It meant something quite different to the way it had been deployed by the likes of Ratzel and Mackinder. As Agnew (2016: 20) demonstrates, geopolitics served as a 'convenient sign under which to classify disparate policies' and helped to make sense, and communicate, the place of the US in the wider world.

In the 1990s, intellectual thought about geopolitics within the discipline of political geography was also changing. There was an increasing recognition that political geography was needed. With tumultuous events unfolding the world over, and the geopolitical upheaval of the Cold War, a language and discourse were needed to try and make sense of the world. The answer came largely in the form of *critical* geopolitics. The word 'critical' is pivotal here. This was to be a geopolitical model designed to provide opportunities to analyse and critique *how* the world works rather than adopting the God's Eye View to project models and strategies *onto* the world (Agnew 2016). The word critical was used to signal to readers, academics, and policy makers alike that this was not the next iteration or continuation of Mackinder et al., but that it was something else – an analytic designed to deconstruct configurations, imaginaries, and projections about the world produced by so called 'intellectuals of statecraft'.

▓▓▓ KEY TERMS: INTELLECTUALS OF STATECRAFT ▓▓▓

'Intellectuals of statecraft' refers to a community of state bureaucrats, leaders, foreign-policy experts and advisors throughout the world who comment upon, influence and conduct the activities of statecraft. (O'Tuathail and Agnew 1992: 193)

This meant that rather than understanding the world as being constructed through natural scientific facts and processes, critical geopolitics would understand the world as a social construction, laden with historical and social complexities. Within this critical framework, geopolitical phenomena emerge as 'anything but simple reflections of a natural geopolitical order' (Agnew 2016: 20). On the contrary, these phenomenon are actively brought into being, constructed, represented, actualised, and legitimised through a range of social practices and processes. The role of the political geographer is to deconstruct these elite practices and processes, rather than to reproduce them (see Massaro and Williams 2013). This means destabilising and challenging the God's Eye View, brought into being through maps, surveys, and more recently, satellite images, to better understand where power is located, how it operates, and how it shapes international relations (Dodds and Sidaway 1994).

Early critical geopolitics thinkers (for example, Gerard O'Tuathail, Simon Dalby, John Agnew, Klaus Dodds) saw this unfolding in a number of ways. For O'Tuathail and Agnew (1992), for example, discourse was key with critical geopolitics serving as a tool to analyse how the world is scripted. This might, for example, involve undertaking discourse analysis on political speeches and policy documents, and deconstructing the vocabularies, narratives, and pronouncements of intellectuals of statecraft and the hegemonic state to better understand how the world was being spatialised. During the Cold War (and beyond) this might take the form of language that draws upon words like 'us' and 'them' to create bounded and oppositional geopolitical communities or which represent the world 'out there' in certain ways in order to secure what particular states might 'hold dear "over here"' (Agnew 2016: 23).

For O'Tuathail, in his seminal work, *Critical Geopolitics* (1996), whilst discourse is key, critical geopolitics might also be expanded to 'expose the plays of power involved in grand geopolitical schemes' (see Dodds and Sidaway 1994: 517). Drawing on a range of theoretical perspectives, the book sought to 'render strange the geographical constructions of the world map' (Koopman et al. 2021: 1). It was an approach that opened up possibilities for the unravelling and deconstructions of expressions of power and which expanded to include analyses of a wide range of phenomena, including matters related to 'identity, economy, resources, development, fear, and emotional geopolitics' (Massaro and Williams 2013: 568). As critical geopolitics demonstrated, the relations of modern states are not a natural given determined by mountains, rivers, seas, and other physical geographical features.

Three key tenets of critical geopolitics emerged as a result of this early scholarship in the field. To borrow the diagram from Dodds (2007, see Figure 2.3), critical geopolitics could be described as understanding how geopolitical representations of the self and 'other' are formed through representations and practices that spatialise the world in particular ways. These spatialisations occur through three key spheres:

1. **Practical geopolitics:** This refers to the actions, discourse, and geopolitical imaginations of those who we would traditionally think of as intellectuals of statecraft. This includes policy makers, the institutions of the state, foreign-policy makers and diplomats.
2. **Formal geopolitics:** This refers to the work of those seeking to engage with and deconstruct the world of practical geopolitics. This refers to academics (including students of political geography), alongside strategic institutes and think tanks.

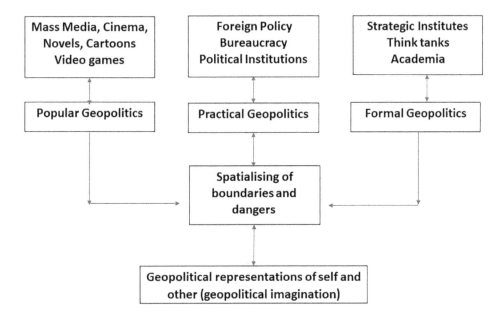

Figure 2.3 A diagram of critical geopolitics (Dodds 2007) (permission granted)

3. **Popular geopolitics:** This was an important addition to the study of geopolitics. It recognises that geopolitical imaginations are shaped in the everyday and not just in elite circles. As Chapter 6 explores in much greater detail, popular geopolitics refers to how imaginaries of the world are produced through films, TV, video games, and other popular media.

The inclusion of popular geopolitics was important here as it recognised that the political world is produced in the everyday as well as at national and international levels. In doing so, it offered much more 'sophisticated understandings of the ways in which knowledges of the world are circulated' but also how they are received at different scales, and thus opened the door to explore how everyday perceptions of the geopolitical world were shaped (Dowler and Sharp 2001: 166–167, see also Dodds and Sidaway 1994). Critical geopolitics thus offered a marked departure from its intellectual predecessors. Leaving behind delusions of grandeur associated with the God's Eye View, it sought to offer a lens and analytical approach to deconstruct geopolitical phenomenon. As the next section explores, however, it was not without its critics.

Conclusions: With and Beyond Critical Geopolitics

Whilst critical geopolitics pushed political geography and geopolitical thinking in new directions, there was still more work to be done to enliven and diversify the discipline. Firstly, we might be critical in the first place of the distinctions made by O'Tuathail and others between formal, practical, and popular geopolitics (Sharp in Koopman et al. 2021: 2). The personal is, after all, inherently political (see Chapter 3), and such distinctions arguably belie the messiness of the geopolitical world, which cannot be so neatly categorised and defined into neat groupings. Secondly, and perhaps the most searing critique, is the gendered and masculinist underpinnings of critical geopolitics (see Massaro and Williams 2013). As Jo Sharp (2000) highlighted in a review of O'Tuathail's *Critical Geopolitics* (1996), it offered a view of geopolitics about elite White men, written by elite White men. You may have noticed in the list of early critical geopolitical thinkers, all of them are White males, serving to reproduce the highly gendered logics of geopolitical thinking. As Jo Sharp also highlighted, this was not because of a shortage of women writing on the subject, but rather oversight of the work of scholars such as Cynthia Enloe, who were writing from feminist traditions about international relations at the time. Subsequently, write Massaro and Williams (2013: 569), the 'masculinist tradition of geopolitics is perpetuated rather than challenged'.

Thirdly, alongside gender, Dowler and Sharp (2001: 167) noted that critical geopolitics failed to account for the intersectional issues of race, class, sexuality, and differentiated physical needs and abilities. The narrative, they argued, was instead 'reduced to a genealogy of heroic men' both in the histories critical geopolitics accounted for and also in the interventions of political geographers themselves (Dowler and Sharp 2001: 167).

In many ways, this reproduces the very logics that critical political geographers sought to avoid. It situates the critical political geographer 'at an ironic distance' whereby they critique the representations and discourses they engage with from afar. The critical geographer does not have to 'disclose their own location' (Dowler and Sharp 2001: 167) or their own position in the world. Their Whiteness and masculinity is seen as irrelevant. As geographers we know that our own positions in the world matter enormously in shaping the kinds of knowledges that are produced about the world around us, and which we produce. 'The language of critical geopolitics is', as Dowler and Sharp (2001: 167) write, 'presented as universal' when in reality it is far from this. It is situated, multi-scalar, and multi-dimensional. In failing to acknowledge these 'spaces of knowledge production and contestation' critical geopolitics runs the risk of reproducing the abstracted 'view from nowhere' (Massaro and Williams 2013: 569).

Finally, while critical geopolitics offers a useful lens to deconstruct and critique dominant geopolitical discourse, it often offers 'little sense of alterative possibilities' (Dowler and Sharp 2001: 167). How could the world be otherwise? How might alternative geopolitical realities be understood and ushered in? Is it possible to enact a more radical politics? The often White, Western underpinnings and reasoning that inform critical geopolitics is part of the problem here and one which the following pages seek to grapple with. In many ways, this textbook takes off where these critiques end. It stands on the shoulders of feminist scholars who have sought to reimagine critical geopolitics, to push it further, to stretch in new directions and to ultimately make the tent of political geography bigger. Building on the work of critical geopolitics, it engages with a more inclusive, more diverse, political geography that is more agile in its approach to grappling with the complexities of the geopolitical world (see Hyndman 2019, Squire in Koopman et al. 2021).

Over to You

Having read this chapter, spend some time creating your own statement about what the discipline of political geography is, or could be. Use the following questions as a guide:

1. How might political geography avoid the pitfalls of its past?
2. How might it build on the work of critical geopolitics?
3. How can it better account for more diverse approaches and knowledge systems? How can the tent be made bigger?
4. Can current frameworks account for the challenges of the twenty-first century?

Once you have finished reading this textbook, revisit your statement. Is there anything you would change?

Summary

- Political geography has a troubled, problematic, and evil history, associated as it was with both empire and colonialism, and Nazi ideologies.
- Because of this, political geography effectively disappeared as a discipline after the Second World War.
- There was recognition, however, that something was needed to analyse the subsequent geopolitical upheavals of events such as the Cold War. This saw the beginnings of critical geopolitics.
- Critical geopolitics laid the foundation for the modern discipline of political geography and has since been extended and re-imagined in various ways to shape the field as we know it today.
- Key critiques of critical geopolitics unfold in the following chapters.

Follow-on Resources

Geopolitics and Empire: This book by Gary Kearns provides important insights into the enduring legacies of Mackinder's ideas and writings in the present day (Kearns, G. (2009). *Geopolitics and empire: The legacy of Halford Mackinder*. Oxford: OUP).

Critical histories of the Royal Geographical Society (with IBG): A reading list for critically exploring the Royal Geographical Society's past at: www.rgs.org/research/higher-education-resources/criticalrgs/

The Historical Geography Research Group: The HGRG are one of the largest research groups of the Royal Geographical Society. Find out more about what they do, and activities they may be running at: https://hgrg.org.uk/

References

Agnew, J. (2016). The origins of critical geopolitics. In K. Dodds, M. Kuus and J. Sharp (eds), *The Ashgate research companion to critical geopolitics* (pp. 19–32). London: Routledge.

Blouet, B. W. (2004). The imperial vision of Halford Mackinder. *Geographical Journal, 170*(4), 322–329.

Dodds, K. (2007). *Geopolitics: A very short introduction*. Oxford: Oxford University Press.

Dodds, K. and Sidaway, J. (1994). Locating critical geopolitics. *Environment and Planning D: Society and Space, 12*(5), 515–524.

Dowler, L. and Sharp, J. (2001). A feminist geopolitics? *Space and Polity, 5*(3), 165–176.

Fettweis, C. (2000). Sir Halford Mackinder, geopolitics, and policymaking in the 21st century. *US Army War College Quarterly: Parameters, 30*(2), 58–71.

Flint, C. (2021). *Introduction to geopolitics*. London: Routledge.

Hyndman, J. (2019). Unsettling feminist geopolitics: Forging feminist political geographies of violence and displacement. *Gender, Place & Culture, 26*(1), 3–29.

Kearns, G. (1984). Closed space and political practice: Halford Mackinder and Frederick Jackson Turner. *Environment and Planning D, 2*, 23–34.

Kearns, G. (2006). Naturalizing empire: Echoes of Mackinder for the next American century? *Geopolitics, 11*, 74–98.

Kearns, G. (2010). Geography, geopolitics, and empire. *Transactions of the Institute of British Geographers, 35*, 183–207.

Kearns, G. (2013). Beyond the legacy of Mackinder. *Geopolitics, 18*(4), 917–932.

Keighren, I. (2018). History and philosophy of geography II: The excluded, the evil, and the anarchic. *Progress in Human Geography, 42*(5), 770–778.

Klinke, I. (2018). *Cryptic concrete: A subterranean journey into Cold War Germany*. Oxford: John Wiley & Sons.

Klinke, I. (2019). Vitalist temptations: Life, earth and the nature of war. *Political Geography, 72*, 1–9.

Klinke, I. and Bassin, M. (2018). Introduction: Lebensraum and its discontents. *Journal of Historical Geography, 61*, 53–58.

Koopman, S., Dalby, S., Megoran, N., Sharp, J., Kearns, G., Squire, R., Jeffrey, A., Squire, V. and Toal, G. (2021). Critical Geopolitics/critical geopolitics 25 years on. *Political Geography, 90*.

Kuus, M. (2010). Critical geopolitics. In *Oxford Research Encyclopaedia of International Studies*. Available at: https://oxfordre.com/view/10.1093/acrefore/9780190846626.001.0001/acrefore-9780190846626-e-137 (accessed 11 September 2023).

Mackinder, H. J. (1902). *Britain and the British Seas*. London: Heinemann.

Mackinder, H. J. (1904). The Geographical Pivot of History. *Geographical Journal, 23*(4), 421–437.

Mackinder, H. J. (1905). Man-power as a measure of national and imperial strength. *National and English Review, 15*, 136–145.

Mackinder, H. J. (1919). *Democratic ideals and reality: A study in the politics of reconstruction*. New York: H. Holt.

Marshall, T. (2015). *Prisoners of geography*. New York: Scribner.

Massaro, V. A. and Williams, J. (2013). Feminist geopolitics. *Geography Compass, 7*(8), 567–577.

O'Tuathail, G. (1996). *Critical geopolitics: The politics of writing global space* (Vol. 6). Minneapolis: University of Minnesota Press.

O'Tuathail, G. and Agnew, J. (1992). Geopolitics and discourse: Practical geopolitical reasoning in American foreign policy. *Political Geography, 11*(2), 190–204.

Sharp, J. P. (2000). Remasculinising geo-politics? Comments on Gearoid O'Tuathail's critical geopolitics. *Political Geography, 19*(3), 361–364.

Squire, R. (2021). *Undersea geopolitics: Sealab, science, and the Cold War*. London: Rowman & Littlefield.

Toal, G., Dalby, S. and Routledge, P. (1998). *A geopolitics reader*. London: Routledge.

Turchetti, S. and Roberts, P. (2014). *The surveillance imperative: Geosciences during the Cold War and beyond*. New York: Springer.

THREE
FEMINIST GEOPOLITICS: SITES, SPACES, SCALES

Chapter Overview

If critical geopolitics helped to revitalise the sub-discipline of political geography, feminist geopolitics transformed it. Perhaps no other branch of thinking has had a bigger impact on shaping geopolitical understandings than feminist scholarship. Feminist geopolitics asked radical questions of political geography, questioning the 'who', 'where', and 'what' of geopolitical thought. For feminist scholars, geopolitics is embodied, situated, and located in the everyday spaces of our lives alongside big state buildings and spaces of elite policy making. This chapter takes you through some of the key tenets of feminist geopolitics. It begins by questioning the sites and scales of geopolitics before exploring how we might understand the home, body, and emotions within this framework.

Learning Objectives

1. To gain an understanding of what feminist geopolitics is and why it matters.
2. To develop understanding of the key actors, scales, sites, and spaces of feminist geopolitics.
3. To facilitate the application of feminist geopolitics to case studies.

Read with: Chapter 4 (Decolonising), Chapter 11 (Violence), Chapter 12 (Peace and Resistance)

It is not an understatement to say that feminist geopolitics has transformed political geography. It has expanded the tent of the geopolitical and radically refocused attention on actors, scales, and contexts otherwise neglected in critical geopolitical discourse. In simple terms, feminist geopolitics seeks to challenge the focus of traditional geopolitics on the state and political elites. It does this by reimagining the actors, scales, and contexts at the centre of geopolitical accounts. As Jennifer Hyndman (2007: 36) writes, for feminist geopolitics, 'people as much as states are the subjects of geopolitics'. In other words, feminist geopolitics is underpinned by the idea that 'the personal is political' (Sundberg in Dixon et al. 2019: 163); it is interested in people, in us and our everyday lives, and the ways that we experience and practise geopolitical power.

========= **KEY TERMS: FEMINIST GEOPOLITICS** =========

Feminist geopolitics places the bodies, practices, and experiences of everyday people at its centre. Traditional geopolitics focuses on the state and political elites. Feminist geopolitics re-approaches geopolitics at different scales and sites, and through the perspectives of people often marginalised in traditional accounts.

Feminist geopolitics was a necessary intervention on earlier critical geopolitical approaches (outlined in Chapter 2) for two key reasons. The first, and 'unavoidable point of entry to these debates was the continued lack of women in political geography' (Dowler and Sharp 2001: 165), and the fact that the discipline was being defined by the perspectives and voices of elite White men (Koopman 2011). The second critique centred upon the subject matter of political geography. For a long time, nation states, strategic narratives, and grand theorising dominated geopolitical discourse (Sharp 2020). For Koopman (2011: 274), at this time, the practice of geopolitics was being imagined as 'big men moving big guns across a big field'. Whilst such narratives are important to deconstruct, they represent a limited view of what the political is. Moreover, this view was always situated 'from above'. It was a God's Eye View, where political geographers (White and male) would make pronouncements over the world. Feminist geopolitics presents a radical challenge to this approach. It decentres the grand and elite as the primary modes and scales of analysis and instead seeks to make geopolitics accountable to everyday experiences, to bodies, to people, situating the geopolitical from the ground up rather than the top down. For Hyndman (2007: 37), feminist geopolitics traverses scales, from 'the macrosecurity of states to the microsecurity of people and their homes; from the disembodied space of neorealist geopolitics to a field of live human subjects with names, families, and hometowns'.

Within this framework, individuals and everyday experiences matter and are read as being inherently geopolitical. Feminist geopolitics explores how power unfolds within these contexts and how power is experienced and projected differently based on positionality (Massaro and Williams 2013: 567). Take a moment to think about your own *position* – your location, nationality, gender, race, and class. These markers afford you different forms of privilege and hardship and can result in different knowledges, understandings, and experiences of geopolitical issues (Hyndman 2004). Climate change is a useful example here. It is a pressing global issue, often narrated through international summits, the Intergovernmental Panel on Climate Change (IPCC) reports, government policy (or a lack of) and carbon metrics. Yet it is also intensely personal, traversing a range of scales, as Hyndman (2007) suggests. Experiences of climate change vary from person to person (Suliman et al. 2019). Exposure to the risks and effects of climate change are uneven, and rooted in deep societal and structural inequalities such as gender, race, and class (Sultana 2014). The 'view from below' shifts the focus to people's differing lived and everyday experiences of geopolitics (Williams 2013: 233). It re-routes fundamental geopolitical questions through everyday sites and contexts to understand geopolitics as something that is 'characterised at both global and intimate scales' (Hyndman 2019: 8). Importantly here, feminist geopolitics does not 'dismiss the state' but instead urges us to think about the 'multiple scales of geopolitics' and the ways it is 'forged and contested' by a range of state and non-state actors (Naylor 2020: 3, Williams and Massaro 2013: 751). The following sections unpack these complexities, beginning with the space of home, before turning to the body, and finally emotion.

The Home

The United Nations (UN) general assembly meeting room, parliamentary buildings of the White House (US), Red Square (Russia), Sansad Bhavan (India) or The Hague (Netherlands) might come to mind when thinking about the spaces of geopolitics. Feminist geopolitics reminds us, however, that geopolitics takes place beyond the board rooms of political buildings (Smith 2020). Traditional geopolitical analysis tends to focus on the 'public' arena of geopolitics. Feminist geopolitics argues that this focus creates an 'artificial' divide between this 'public' political space and 'private' 'seemingly unpolitical' spaces (Blunt and Dowling 2006; Brickell 2012a; Williams and Massaro 2013: 752). This matters, because private spaces, such as the home, have been 'designated as feminine', while public spaces have been 'determined as masculine' (Dowler and Sharp 2001: 173). Feminist geopolitics challenges these divisions by re-focusing our attention on 'supposedly non-political spaces' which are commonly overlooked as 'outside of politics' (Sharp 2020: 2). After all, everyday life is a 'site where power relations, inequalities, and social differences are played out, lived, and experienced' – a site where 'small-scale actions' connect to 'larger-scale inequalities' (Hall 2020: 813).

In developing discussions of the spaces of geopolitics, feminist work has engaged with the home, arguing that the homes we live in are crucial spaces in the creation, flows, and functioning of geopolitical power (Brickell 2020). From examples as varied as domestic violence and drone strikes on homes, to forced evictions, this work argues that geopolitics is both 'influenced by, and emerges from, the home' (Brickell 2012a: 585). Challenging the idea that the home is a 'haven' and universal site of safety and belonging, feminist geopolitical approaches diversify the 'lived realities' of these spaces (Brickell 2012b: 226). For some, homes are spaces of safety, protection, warmth, while for others home can be unsafe, sites of anxiety and fear, mould and cold. Experiences of home vary and can depend on a 'range of social coordinates' and privileges (Brickell 2012b: 227). The Covid-19 pandemic made this all too clear. While Covid-19 was experienced in diverse ways, many experienced 'lockdown' or 'stay at home' orders (Figure 3.1), with work and education moved 'online' and travel limited (Reuschke and Felstead 2020, Rose-Redwood et al. 2020: 99).

Figure 3.1 Stay at home times three, Newport city centre

Credit: Jaggery (Creative Commons Attribution-Share Alike 2.0 Generic license) https://commons.wikimedia.org/wiki/File:STAY_AT_HOME_times_three,_Newport_city_centre_(geograph_6437309).jpg

The lockdown or 'stay at home' policies issued by a number of governments powerfully illustrate how the 'nation and international are reproduced' in everyday life and space (Dowler and Sharp 2001: 171). In other words, politics enters our homes and lives through these policies. In reflecting on geopolitics across these scales, the geopolitical complexities of the everyday are laid bare.

One key issue highlighted in the pandemic lockdown, and in scholarship on the home and the geopolitical, was that of domestic violence. While it was once remarked that 'geographers have little to say about domestic or sexual violence' (Pain 2015: 64), domestic violence is receiving growing attention within political geography. Taking seriously the idea that the 'personal is political' (Brickell and Cuomo 2020), domestic violence highlights the link between bodies, homes, and wider political questions in profound ways. Domestic violence can be understood as a 'pattern of coercively controlling behaviour' by an abuser who uses 'a variety of tactics' to inflict 'emotional, psychological and physical violence' (Cuomo 2019: 61). Through the lens of home, geographers have sought to understand how women (as well as men) can become 'bound into webs of emotional abuse and physical violence', spatially as well as physically entrapping them (Warrington 2001: 369). Whilst this may seem a very different kind of violence to that of warfare traditionally associated with political geography (and explored in Chapter 11), the distinctions are not clear cut. Pain and Staeheli (2014: 344), for example, push back against the separation of violence as either 'local/everyday or as international/political conflict', and instead think of violence as operating at and across these scales. Pain (2015: 54) argues that 'domestic violence and international warfare' should be considered 'as part of a single complex of violence', working across different but connected scales. Pain (2015: 64) argues that both forms of violence 'share bases of power', and cause 'emotional and psychological' harms as they are 'made and lived' in everyday lives. The home is a key space, though, to explore these complexities, powerfully illustrating the importance of the intersecting scales of violence outlined by Pain (2015). Of course, experiences of domestic violence are also situated in the body – another scale and site that has been foregrounded in feminist geopolitics.

The Body

We are all embodied actors. Our bodies, whatever form they come in, radically shape how we live, experience, and navigate the world around us. Power emanates from, is enforced upon, and courses through the body in various ways. This differs from person to person, sometimes resulting in stark inequalities and violent outworkings. Feminist geopolitical thinking seeks to grapple with these complexities. It foregrounds the body as a key site and space of analysis (Dixon and Marston 2011, Mountz 2018, Smith 2011), but also as a key methodological tool to explore geopolitical worlds (see box below).

In the Field with Olivia Mason: Walking the Jordan Trail

Olivia Mason (2020) explores political geographies of the body through walking. Olivia has undertaken fieldwork at the Jordan Trail, a 650km trail running the length of the country of Jordan.

Why is walking important as a method?

Walking is important as a method in political geography for two reasons. First, to explore embodied accounts of territory and challenge dominant, masculine, and colonial lenses. Second, walking as a method illustrates the uneven politics of mobility. It enables us to question the situated and everyday politics that shape movement, and prompts larger questions about the politics of movement and what walking means in different locations, under different political conditions, and for different individuals.

What did focusing on the body reveal in your fieldwork?

A focus on the body in my fieldwork revealed the experiential and visceral relationships between individuals and political geographies of citizenship, territory, and (post) colonialism. As people walk across territory, their relationship to it is not a calculated or state account but one that is individual, visceral, and in constant relationship with the materiality of ground. Embodied methods in my work therefore challenge fixed ideas of citizenship and territory and illustrate the impacts of (post)colonialism on bodies and cultural spaces.

(Continued)

> **Any top tips for a student interested in in undertaking fieldwork on/in relation to bodies/walking?**
>
> I would encourage undergraduates to use embodied or walking methods in their research, to think creatively and look to other sub-disciplines and disciplines for inspiration. Political geographers have been reluctant to use embodied methods so be excited to challenge that. Consider how you might use drawings, films, photographs, dance, poems, participant diaries, or indeed walking as methods in your research to explore political geography questions.

KEY TERMS: THE BODY

Feminist geopolitics argues that the body is an important geopolitical site. It argues that by 'recentring' attention from 'the state to the fleshy matter of the body', we can explore how bodies differently create and experience the geopolitical, and how different people might experience different vulnerabilities (Clark 2017: 1).

One way of thinking through and with the body is to ask the question: Whose bodies count within geopolitical contexts? Who is made disposable by the power of the state and military? Who is marginalised? How does the body become a site of violence? Jennifer Hyndman's (2001) work on the 'War on Terror' is a powerful example here. Hyndman (2001) explores whose bodies were deemed important in the wars in Iraq and Afghanistan, highlighting the radical difference in the way that the bodies of deceased American soldiers were treated in comparison to those of civilians. Indeed, Hyndman (2001) writes that there was an 'audible silence' around the civilian death tolls in Afghanistan and Iraq, with an American general stating that they (the US military) 'don't do body counts' for civilians. As Figure 3.2 demonstrates, the bodies of American soldiers were memorialised, enrolled in public and patriotic displays of ceremony, and each one was counted, named, and remembered. Yet, the number of Iraqi and Afghani civilians that died as a result of each war remains unknown, each seen as 'collateral damage' in the pursuit of American geopolitical objectives. Their race and ethnicity are key here, the brown 'other' body seen as expendable.

To counter such stark inequalities, Hyndman (2001) calls for more relational ways of engaging with civilian casualties, where the true human cost of war surfaces and people are able to make meaningful connections to those who have lost their lives, and the countless grieving people around those lost, rather than thinking through metrics (or a lack of). Such work challenges us to think in 'more accountable, embodied ways' (Hyndman 2007: 36) and to reflect on how we can more equitably approach, represent, learn from, and make visible people commonly at the margins of geopolitical accounts (see also Koopman 2011).

Figure 3.2 Fallen US Army soldier

Credit: Matthew Woitunski (Creative Commons Attribution 3.0 Unported license) https://commons.wikimedia.org/wiki/File:Fallen_US_Army_Soldier.jpg

Case Study: Abortion Access

Abortion access is another example of how the body might be thought of geopolitically, often in uneven ways. The termination of a pregnancy is a 'routine medical procedure', with 'global abortion statistics suggesting that, on average, a woman will have one abortion in her lifetime' (Calkin and Freeman 2019: 1325). While a prevalent medical procedure, abortion provision and legislation remain varied globally. As a result, abortion remains both 'private', 'highly personal', and 'potentially illegal', with many women experiencing stigma, 'shame, threats and health risks' (Calkin and Freeman 2019: 1330). While it is argued that abortion access is undergoing considerable change following 'advances in technology, medicine, and activism' (Calkin 2019: 22, 2021), there remains a notable silence around abortion that geographers argue is 'reproduced in geographical scholarship' (Calkin and Freeman 2019: 1325).

Sydney Calkin and Cordelia Freeman have explored the political geographies of abortion. Calkin's work reflects on the shifting role of the state in relation to abortion access. Calkin (2019: 22) argues that abortion access is a 'gendered mechanism of state control'. Here, the body is recognised as a 'scale and site upon which politics are performed' (Mountz 2018: 762). The state 'projects' its power onto bodies, Calkin (2019: 22) argues, through its control over access to abortion. Freeman (2020: 899), on the other hand, draws attention to the 'bleeding' that is 'common' after an abortion.

(Continued)

Thinking about a woman's journey to and from an abortion, Freeman (2020: 899) argues that a 'politics of blood' emerges in this travel. For some, journeys are short, and for others they are 'long, expensive, or illegalised' (Freeman 2020: 897). Both geographic and social context matter here too. Experiences are uneven, with 'young women, indigenous women, rural women, women on low incomes, and trans and non-binary people disproportionately affected by obstacles to abortion access' (Freeman 2020: 888). Through the lens of the body, we see how geopolitical structures converge on the body, generating plural and uneven experiences.

Over to You: Whose Bodies Count?

Whose bodies are at the centre of the geopolitical accounts in today's news? Open a news website of your choice. Choose two articles and read these over. Reflect on the three questions below, jotting down your thoughts:

1. Who features in the news stories? Which actors – men, women, political elites, communities, people of particular races, ethnicities or nationalities?
2. How do these actors feature? Who is presented as having power, and who is presented as subject to that power? Are there any forms of resistance?
3. Can you see any links between your news articles and the themes in this chapter (e.g., the geopolitics of everyday life and the body)? How does your thinking about geopolitics change when you reflect on these links?

Violence and the Body

The answer to the question 'whose bodies count?' is inherently violent. It is premised on exclusion, and is often underpinned by gendered and racialised logics. Whilst, as Chapter 12 notes, the body can be a site of resistance and protest (see Fluri 2009), the body is an important site through which wider questions about violence can be raised, addressed, and challenged. Violence, here, is understood as 'a multi-faceted and multi-sited force – interpersonal and institutional, social, economic and political, physical, sexual, emotional and psychological' (Pain and Staeheli 2014: 344). It is something which spans many contexts, experiences, and spaces and does not simply encompass physical violence, as important as this is. Geographical perspectives are important in exploring this further as they engage with the ways that violence is 'raced, sexed and gendered' and at times 'ignored or rendered invisible' (Fluri and Piedalue 2017: 537). Questions of violence are a vital way through which to foreground the body in geopolitical discourse and to shed light on the inequalities associated with safety and security (see Fluri and Piedalue 2017).

> **KEY TERMS: VIOLENCE**
>
> We can understand violence as a practice or process that negatively impacts someone or something's conditions and world, preventing them from living safely, securely, or at all. As such, violence might refer to a particular action (e.g. striking someone), or it may refer to an 'inaction' or failing to act on an issue (Tyner and Rice 2016: 48).

To draw on gender as a starting point, gendered violence is 'intimately interwoven' into geopolitical contexts and relations (Brickell and Maddrell 2016, Pain and Staeheli 2014: 344). Protests across Latin America in November 2022 are a good example of why understanding the intersections between violence and gender is so important. Here, women 'from Buenos Aires to Bogota' took to the streets on the 'International Day for the Elimination of Violence against Women' to call for further 'action from authorities' on the issue of gendered violence (Morland 2022: n.p.). Following both the recognition of the epidemic of violence against women in the region, as well as the statements of the United Nations on the importance of 'redoubling efforts so that the women and girls [therein] can truly exercise their right to live a life free of violence', women took to the streets to resist gendered violence (Morland 2022: n.p.). While recognising that such gender-based violence stems from deep-seated prejudice against women – in other words, it is structural – so too is it important to note that the Latin American women involved were not passive – they responded by gathering and reclaiming public space. In this vein, while recognising how pervasive such forms of violence against women are, feminist geographers also remind us of the importance of practices of resistance and reclaiming by everyday people.

As Mountz (2018) and others have highlighted, violence is also racialised and shaped by wider structural political problems. Again, the Covid-19 pandemic shone a light on this. Whitacre et al. (2021), for example, highlight how 'Black, Native, and Latinx communities' were disproportionately infected and dying in America's largest cities. Wider structural issues of defunded health departments in minority predominant areas were a large contributing factor. On a more individualised level, we see time and again how Blackness is problematically associated with danger and criminality, with profound consequences for Black communities (see for example Bonds 2009, Derickson 2017). These tensions came to the fore in the Black Lives Matter movement, sparked by the killing of the unarmed teenaged Michael Brown in 2014 by a White police office in Ferguson, USA. This instance of police violence against a Black person was 'not an uncommon occurrence' (Derickson 2017: 231). In the face of peaceful protests, 'police patrolled the crowds in heavily armoured cars while wearing bulletproof vests and carrying automatic weapons', a response that many thought resembled an 'occupying military force' rather than 'civil servants seeking to keep the peace' (Coyne and Hall-Blanco 2016: 165). Here we saw Black communities and allied protesters inflicted with different forms of embodied violence, from armoured police vehicles letting out 'high intensity sirens designed to disperse protesters' and acting to damage protesters' hearing (Allen and Jones 2016;

Pasternack 2018), to people coughing and struggling to breathe as tear gas was dispersed into the air. As above, these incidents at once highlight direct violence on Black people, and can be considered in the wider context of the violences of structural racism (see Liebman et al. 2020, McKittrick 2011). Following that to understand racism is to understand power (Gilmore 2002), adopting a structural understanding of violence allows us to understand how racism is 'buried alive', that is 'embedded' into everyday practices and life (Hawthorne 2019: 9).

When considering embodied racialised violence, an intersectional approach is vital. Coined by Kimberlé Crenshaw (1991: 1244), the concept of intersectionality was developed to consider the 'various ways in which race and gender interact' to shape the lives and experiences of Black women. Intersectionality sought to highlight that when we think about lived experiences (for example of violence), we shouldn't see categories such as gender and race as separate or discrete. Rather, Crenshaw (1991) argued that we need to think about such categories together, in order to understand the complex ways that a number of our identity factors (such as 'gender, race, ethnicity, age, health and employment status') often 'work together to compound inequalities and privilege' (Ho and Maddrell 2021: 3). Indeed, feminist work has been critiqued for downplaying race (Daley 2020). As Daley (2020: 2) notes, the experiences of Black women are 'distinct' from those of 'White women' and Blackness is often reduced and 'subsumed' into 'categories of Black masses – immigrant, ethnics, refugees and ghetto residents'. More work is therefore needed to challenge and critique these 'universalising assumptions' and the 'homogenisation' of Black experiences.

███████ KEY TERMS: INTERSECTIONALITY ███████

Intersectionality refers to an approach attentive to the many identity characteristics we have. After all, our identity includes different aspects, such as gender, race, ethnicity, and class. In comparison to thinking, for example, only about gendered violence (violence we experience as a result of our gender) or racialised violence (violence we experience as a result of our race), an intersectional approach (as developed by Kimberlé Crenshaw) encourages us to think about how these different identity characteristics come together to inform different (bodily) experiences.

Emotion

Cutting across much of what has been discussed in this chapter is emotion. Much like the body and home, feminist geopolitics has brought emotions in from the margins. Traditionally and problematically associated with femininity, emotions were seen as trivial or marginal to the geopolitical. However, if we are to understand geopolitics as embodied and situated, then emotions are vital. For Pain and Smith (2008), emotions are one of many things that connect geopolitics to everyday life (see also Williams and Boyce 2013).

Hope, rage, anger, indifference, grief, fear, surprise, disgust – and a whole range of other emotional dispositions – not only shape our everyday engagements with geopolitical events and phenomena, but they shape precisely how those phenomena unfold. They can 'open subjects to others and worlds' but can also shut down such possibilities (Ahmed 2003: 386). Importantly, such conditions are never static. As Ahmed (2003: 386) writes 'emotions stick and slide, they move us in surprising and unexpected ways'.

A wide range of research has taken place to explore these sensibilities further, including a study of children's hopes for peace in the Philippines (Woon 2017); the role of emotion in fieldwork (Woon 2013); anti-immigrant feelings in border areas (Williams and Boyce 2013); humour as a coping mechanism deployed by Central American migrants to generate spaces of collective solidarity (Van Ramshorst 2019); fears of young people as both objects and subjects (Pain et al. 2010); ecological grief as a response to the Climate Emergency (Cunsolo and Ellis 2018); the emotionalisation of the war on terror (Ahmed 2015); and the role of translators at UN Security Council meetings in communicating emotions (Jones 2022: 47). Emotions animate and underpin the geopolitical in so many ways, many of which are yet to be explored. One emotion that has attracted much attention, however, is fear.

Fear

As Pain and Smith (2008: 1) write, 'fear cuts across the personal and societal ... the emotive and rational'. The 'place of fear' they write, 'is as salient as material risk as a driver of political manoeuvring and a constraint on personal well-being'. On an individual scale, we might turn to an event in 2007 whereby Vladmir Putin reportedly tried to scare and intimidate the then German chancellor, Angela Merkel. Merkel, who was widely known to fear dogs, reportedly 'sat frozen' as Putin let his large black Labrador into the room (Fisher 2015). Fear here was mobilised as a direct strategy to intimidate, forming part of Putin's wider politics of machismo where shows of 'strength' and 'masculinity' are designed to present a particular image on the international stage, in opposition to feminine 'weakness' and 'fear'. Individual relationships and fears were a proxy for much wider international geopolitical considerations. More broadly, fear has been an emotion or experience widely explored within political geography. Defined as an 'emotional reaction to a perceived threat', fear always 'has a social meaning' which 'may have a range of positive and negative effects on social and spatial relations' (Pain 2009: 467). In other words, fear does not exist in a social or political vacuum and it has profound spatial consequences.

As Pain (2009: 466) highlights, 9/11 and the subsequent War on Terror 'sparked new interest in the politics and patterns of fear' in political geography. Propagated by the US Government, Western countries and media outlets went as far as to suggest that a 'globalised fear' existed in the post 9/11 world (Pain and Smith 2008). As Ahmed (2003: 390) writes, 'fear is ... named in the very naming of terrorism' with terrorists 'identified as agents of extreme fear', seeking 'to make others afraid (less mobile or less free to move) as well as those who seek to cause death and destruction'. Within this so-called globalised fear, citizens had supposedly become 'paranoid' and 'disproportionately anxious in everyday life' – a state 'encouraged by government actions' (Pain 2009: 466). Such feelings were said to be universally experienced (Pain 2010). As Pain and Smith (2008) write, this fear was materialised in a variety of ways, including announcements on UK trains asking people to be vigilant and on the lookout for 'suspicious' behaviour (see Chapter 10), generating anxiety in everyday spaces. The 'fears' of middle class White people were also used to justify a range of security practices in the US, UK, and elsewhere with isolated events, such as 9/11, used 'as the basis of efforts to regulate demonised bodies' (Ahmed 2015, Williams and Boyce 2013: 900). More broadly, this fear was used to justify the protracted War on Terror and its associated interventionist politics in Afghanistan and Iraq.

In the wake of 9/11, there were very few critiques of this idea of a universal fear, or challenges to the idea that Western countries were 'burning with fear, terror and panic' (Pain 2010: 228). This lack of challenge led to sweeping assertions that did little to shed light on the complex emotional landscape post 9/11. As Pain (2010) writes, fear is never universal or global. Rather it is 'rooted in the existing biographies of places and their social relations'. In other words, fear must be put into context. In the wake of 9/11 for example, fear did not simply emanate from White Western citizens afraid of a violent 'other'. As Williams and Boyce (2013) highlight, the 'demonised bodies' described above, may have feared the spike in highly racialised hate crimes following the attack. Whilst aware of the 'disempowering effects of labelling certain people fearful' (Pain 2010: 231), there was evidence that targeted communities might avoid certain spaces, constrain their appearance in particular ways, or choose to practise their religious beliefs at home rather than in public spaces (Williams and Boyce 2013).

In much stronger terms, for Ahmad (2002: 101), one of the tragedies of a post 9/11 world has been 'an unrelenting, multivalent assault on the bodies, psyches and rights of Arab, Muslim, and South Asian immigrants' in Western countries. The detention of 'Muslim looking' individuals, and an 'epidemic of hate violence' have been key components of this, exposing the 'precariousness of citizenship status for all people of colour' (Ahmad 2002: 101–103). Many incidents went unreported, and others, like 'racial shame', do not get reported, meaning the scale of the problem post 9/11 was never truly quantifiable (Ahmad 2002: 103–104). Fear, here, is far from being universally or evenly experienced. Moreover, we see in Chapter 4 how many Tanzanian citizens feared the reprisals from the United States rather than fearing attacks from Islamic terrorists (Sharp 2011; see also Woon 2013 for nuanced response in the Philippines). There is therefore a need for nuanced understandings of emotions and geopolitical narratives around 'globalised fear'. This nuance can, in part, be achieved by being critical of pronouncements of certain national or global emotional states (see Pain 2010). In the case of fear, whose fear is being discussed? Who gets to name fear, who claims it and who actually feels it? How is it experienced, and what do people do with it? How is it shaped and differentiated by varied lives, communities, and places? What actions are legitimised through this emotion? Such questions are a useful framework through which to interrogate assertions about fear, but also other emotions that animate the geopolitical.

Case Study: Love Under Apartheid

Love Under Apartheid is a project exploring the stories of couples, families, and loving relationships fractured by the Israeli occupation of Palestine – a dimension to the protracted conflict that is often forgotten. The project addresses this, communicating love stories to demonstrate how the occupation does not just exist in news reports and military action but cuts through to the most intimate aspects of Palestinian lives. For Marshall (2014: 350), love is deployed as a counter-geopolitical force in three ways through the Love Under Apartheid project:

1. Love stories directly confront and seek to overcome the division of Palestinians and Israelis. In this sense, love is a geopolitical act and a direct intervention on the wider conflict.
2. The stories create an 'affinity' and a kind of 'intimate knowledge' of Palestinian life among a wide public audience used to seeing Palestinians as 'other'.
3. The experiences of Palestinians make 'intimate the abstract language of universal rights through an appeal to the universal experience of love'. In other words, it draws on an emotion that everyone experiences to humanise Palestinians and to call for their right to love across borders to be enacted.

As Laketa (2016) highlights, emotional geopolitics are here expressed through love, and can be an important way to gain understandings of situations of instability or conflict, with the Israeli occupation of Palestine being a prime example.

Over to You: Exploring Emotions

Find another example that you might explore through the lens of emotional geopolitics. You might want to engage with a paper listed in the second paragraph of the 'emotion' section, or find your own that draws on an emotion – this could be hopeful or otherwise. Think through the following questions as you explore your example:

- What emotions animate your example?
- How does it help you to understand the wider geopolitical context?
- Does it help you to explore it in different ways?
- What would your key conclusion be about the intersections of geopolitics and emotion through your case study?

Conclusion

This chapter has explored the emergence, scope, and goals of a feminist geopolitics – a transformational intervention in critical geopolitics that broadens the actors, sites, scales, and spaces of the geopolitical (Hyndman 2019, Massaro and Williams 2013: 567). It encourages us to reflect carefully and critically on both the people, voices, and experiences that we see represented in the world around us, and on how diverse actors experience and shape political power in different ways. Moreover, feminist geopolitics works to connect the global and elite workings of state and international politics to the more 'micro' scales of the 'mundane' or 'everyday', bringing into the frame considerations that might have otherwise been deemed too 'feminine' to be considered political. This might be, as this chapter has illustrated, through the space of the home, the body, or through emotions. As these examples illustrate, feminist geopolitics is not designed to be page bound – in academic books and journals. Rather, it recognises that politics is enacted and enlivened in the 'streets, home and communities' that 'come together' to create caring, compassionate, and critical ways of being and living (Williams and Massaro 2013: 757). Feminist geopolitics both aims to capture and be 'accountable' to these acts and experiences (Hyndman 2007: 36), and to imaginatively take geopolitics apart and 'put the pieces back together in new ways' (Koopman 2011: 274).

Summary

- Feminist geopolitics has radically transformed understandings of the geopolitical. It strongly critiques early critical geopolitical thought for its focus on elite, White male perspectives.
- In doing so it diversifies the actors and agents of geopolitics by arguing that the geopolitical can be located in everyday people as deeply and profoundly as in political elites.
- It reimagines the sites and scales of geopolitics, understanding the everyday as context in which geopolitics plays out, and the site of the body as one where the geopolitical and everyday converge.
- Feminist geopolitics also broadens our understandings of the spaces of the geopolitical. Often deemed 'feminine' and 'apolitical', attention to the space of the home and practices and experiences of emotion have been central in shifting understanding.
- Grounded in everyday experiences, feminist geopolitics challenges a preoccupation with representation and instead adopts methods that allow everyday contexts, scales, and experiences to emerge.

Follow-on Resources

Makan: an organisation that challenges the 'traditional narrative on Palestine/Israel', instead seeking to amplify the everyday voices of Palestinians working towards 'freedom, justice and equality on grassroots and policy levels'. Their work is grounded in an anti-violent approach, rooted in the 'belief in our shared humanity' and features the Love Under Apartheid Project. See www.makan.org.uk/

The Mass Observation Archive (MOA): a charity that collects material on everyday life in Britain, including written questionnaire data from its panel of volunteer writers who share their perspectives and stories on everything from experiences of Covid-19 and Brexit to views on plastics and protest. See www.massobs.org.uk/

The impact of Covid-19 on women: a United Nations briefing which examines the diverse economic and employment, health, and gender-based violence implications of the global pandemic See www.un.org/sexualviolenceinconflict/wp-content/uploads/2020/06/report/policy-brief-the-impact-of-covid-19-on-women/policy-brief-the-impact-of-covid-19-on-women-en-1.pdf

References

Ahmad, M. (2002). Homeland insecurities: Racial violence the day after September 11. *Social Text, 20*(3), 101–115.

Ahmed, S. (2003). The politics of fear in the making of worlds. *International Journal of Qualitative Studies in Education, 16*(3), 377–398.

Ahmed, S. (2015). The emotionalization of the 'war on terror': Counter-terrorism, fear, risk, insecurity and helplessness. *Criminology & Criminal Justice, 15*(5), 545–560.

Allen, R. and Jones, T. (2016). Alton Sterling protest intensifies as big crowd gathers near Baton Rouge police HQ; officers in riot gear. Available at: www.nola.com/article_6d023048-228e-52c1-81ab-760a02b5b681.html (accessed 5 March 2022).

Blunt, A. and Dowling, R. (2006). *Home*. London and New York: Routledge.

Bonds, A. (2009). Discipline and devolution: Constructions of poverty, race, and criminality in the politics of rural prison development. *Antipode, 41*(3), 416–438.

Brickell, K. (2012a). Geopolitics of home. *Geography Compass, 6*(10), 575–588.

Brickell, K. (2012b). 'Mapping' and 'doing' critical geographies of home. *Progress in Human Geography, 36*(2), 225–244.

Brickell, K. (2020). *Home SOS: Gender, violence and survival in crisis ordinary Cambodia*. Oxford: Wiley.

Brickell, K. and Cuomo, D. (2020). Geographies of violence: Feminist geopolitical approaches. In A. Datta, P. Hopkins, L. Johnston, E. Olson and J. Maria Silva (eds), *Routledge international handbook of gender and feminist geographies* (pp. 297–307). London and New York: Routledge.

Brickell, K. and Maddrell, A. (2016). Gendered violences: The elephant in the room and moving beyond the elephantine. *Dialogues in Human Geography, 6*(2), 206–208.

Calkin, S. (2019). Towards a political geography of abortion. *Political Geography, 69*, 22–29.

Calkin, S. (2021). Transnational abortion pill flows and the political geography of abortion in Ireland. *Territory, Politics, Governance, 9*(2), 163–179.

Calkin, S. and Freeman, C. (2019). Trails and technology: Social and cultural geographies of abortion access. *Social & Cultural Geography, 20*(9), 1325–1332.

Clark, J. H. (2017). Feminist geopolitics and the Middle East: Refuge, belief and peace. *Geography Compass, 11*(2), e12304.

Coyne, C. J. and Hall-Blanco, A. R. (2016). Foreign intervention, police militarization, and minorities. *Peace Review, 28*(2), 165–170.

Crenshaw, K. (1991). Mapping the margins: Intersectionality, identity politics, and violence against women of color. *Stanford Law Review, 43*(6), 1241–1299.

Cunsolo, A. and Ellis, N. R. (2018). Ecological grief as a mental health response to climate change-related loss. *Nature Climate Change, 8*(4), 275–281.

Cuomo, D. (2019). Domestic violence, safe space and vicarious abuse: Inside a Pennsylvania Exchange and Visitation Center. *Gender, Place & Culture, 26*(1), 59–74.

Daley, P. (2020). Lives lived differently: Geography and the study of Black women. *Area, 52*(4): 665–824.

Derickson, K. D. (2017). Urban geography II: Urban geography in the Age of Ferguson. *Progress in Human Geography, 41*(2), 230–244.

Dixon, D. and Marston, S. (2011). Introduction: Feminist engagements with geopolitics. *Gender, Place & Culture, 18*(4), 445–453.

Dixon, D., Faria, C., Sharp, J., Sundberg, J. and Williams, J. (2019). Review forum: *Feminist Geopolitics: Material States* by Deborah P. Dixon. *Political Geography, 73*, 161–167.

Dowler, L. and Sharp, J. P. (2001). A feminist geopolitics? *Space & Polity, 5*, 165–176.

Fisher, M. (2015). This quote about Putin's machismo from Angela Merkel is just devastating. *Vox*, 20 May. Available at: www.vox.com/2014/12/1/7313443/vladimir-putin-merkel (accessed 1 April 2022).

Fluri, J. (2009). Geopolitics of gender and violence 'from below'. *Political Geography, 28*, 259–265.

Fluri, J. L. and Piedalue, A. (2017). Embodying violence: Critical geographies of gender, race, and culture. *Gender, Place & Culture, 24*(4), 534–544.

Freeman, C. (2020). Viapolitics and the emancipatory possibilities of abortion mobilities. *Mobilities, 15*(6), 896–910.

Gilmore, R. W. (2002). Fatal couplings of power and difference: Notes on racism and geography. *The Professional Geographer, 54*(1), 15–24.

Hall, S. M. (2020). Revisiting geographies of social reproduction: Everyday life, the endotic, and the infra-ordinary. *Area, 52*, 812–819.

Hawthorne, C. (2019). Black matters are spatial matters: Black geographies for the twenty-first century. *Geography Compass, 13*, e12468.

Ho, E. and Maddrell, A. (2021). Intolerable intersectional burdens: A COVID-19 research agenda for social and cultural geographies. *Social & Cultural Geography, 22*(1), 1–10.

Hyndman, J. (2001). Towards a feminist geopolitics. *The Canadian Geographer, 2*, 210–222.

Hyndman, J. (2004). Mind the gap: Bridging feminist and political geography through geopolitics. *Political Geography, 23*(3), 307–322.

Hyndman, J. (2007). Feminist geopolitics revisited: Body counts in Iraq. *The Professional Geographer, 59*(1), 35–46.

Hyndman, J. (2019). Unsettling feminist geopolitics: Forging feminist political geographies of violence and displacement. *Gender, Place & Culture, 26*(1), 3–29.

Jones, A. (2022). 'Emotionscapes of geopolitics': Interpreting in the United Nations Security Council. *Transactions of the Institute of British Geographers, 47*(1), 47–62.

Koopman, S. (2011). Alter-geopolitics: Other securities are happening. *Geoforum, 42*, 274–284.

Laketa, S. (2016). Geopolitics of affect and emotions in a post-conflict city. *Geopolitics, 21*(3), 661–685.

Liebman, A., Rhiney, K. and Wallace, R. (2020). To die a thousand deaths: COVID-19, racial capitalism, and anti-Black violence. *Human Geography, 13*(3), 331–335.

Marshall, D. J. (2014). Love stories of the occupation: Storytelling and the counter-geopolitics of intimacy. *Area, 46*(4), 349–351.

Mason, O. (2020). Walking the line: Lines, embodiment and movement on the Jordan Trail. *Cultural Geography, 27*(3), 395–414.

Massaro, V. A. and Williams, J. (2013). Feminist geopolitics. *Geography Compass, 7*(8), 567–577.

McKittrick, K. (2011). On plantations, prisons, and a Black sense of place. *Social & Cultural Geography, 12*(8), 947–963.

Morland, S. (2022). Women across Latin America march against violence in day of protests. *Reuters*, 26 November. Available at: www.reuters.com/world/americas/women-across-latin-america-march-against-violence-day-protests-2022-11-26/ (accessed 3 December 2022).

Mountz, E. (2018). Political geography III: Bodies. *Progress in Human Geography, 42*(5), 759–769.

Naylor, L. (2020). Geopolitics and food sovereignty: Cuban imaginaries. *Geopolitics, 16*(5): 1562–1585.

Pain, R. (2009). Globalized fear? Towards an emotional geopolitics. *Progress in Human Geography, 33*(4), 466–486.

Pain, R. (2010). The new geopolitics of fear. *Geography Compass, 4*(3), 226–240.

Pain, R. (2015). Intimate war. *Political Geography, 44*, 64–73.

Pain, R. and Smith, S. J. (2008). Fear, critical geopolitics and everyday life. In R. Pain and S. J. Smith (eds), *Fear: Critical geopolitics and everyday life* (pp. 1–24). Aldershot: Ashgate.

Pain, R. and Staeheli, L. (2014). Introduction: Intimacy-geopolitics and violence. *Area, 46*(4), 344–360.

Pain, R., Panelli, R., Kindon, S. and Little, J. (2010). Moments in everyday/distant geopolitics: Young people's fears and hopes. *Geoforum, 41*(6), 972–982.

Pasternack, A. (2018). Piercing sound can be excessive police force, federal court rules. *Fast company*, 14 June. Available at: www.fastcompany.com/40585221/piercing-sound-can-be-excessive-police-force-federal-court-rules (accessed 7 April 2022).

Reuschke, D. and Felstead, A. (2020). Changing workplace geographies in the COVID-19 crisis. *Dialogues in Human Geography, 10*(2), 208–212.

Rose-Redwood, R., Kitchin, R., Apostolopoulou, E., Rickards, L., Blackman, T., Crampton, J., Rossi, U. and Buckley, M. (2020). Geographies of the COVID-19 pandemic. *Dialogues in Human Geography*, *10*(2), 97–106.

Sharp, J. (2011). A subaltern critical geopolitics of the war on terror: Postcolonial security in Tanzania. *Geoforum*, *42*(3), 297–305.

Sharp, J. (2020). Materials, forensics and feminist geopolitics. *Progress in Human Geography*, *45*(5).

Smith, S. (2011). She says herself, 'I have no future': Love, fate, and territory in Leh, Jammu and Kashmir, India. *Gender Place and Culture*, *18*(4), 455–476.

Smith, S. (2020). *Political geography: A critical introduction*. London: John Wiley & Sons.

Suliman, S., Farbotko, C., Ransan-Cooper, H., Elizabeth McNamara, K., Thornton, F., McMichael, C. and Kitara, T. (2019). Indigenous (im)mobilities in the Anthropocene. *Mobilities*, *14*(3), 298–318.

Sultana, F. (2014). Gendering climate change: Geographical insights. *The Professional Geographer*, *66*(3), 372–381.

Tyner, J. A. and Rice, S. (2016). To live and let die: Food, famine, and administrative violence in Democratic Kampuchea, 1975–1979. *Political Geography*, *52*, 47–56.

Van Ramshorst, J. P. (2019). Laughing about it: Emotional and affective spaces of humour in the geopolitics of migration. *Geopolitics*, *24*(4), 896–915.

Warrington, M. (2001). 'I must get out': The geographies of domestic violence. *Transactions of the Institute of British Geographers*, *26*, 365–382.

Whitacre, R., Oni-Orisan, A., Gaber, N., Martinez, C., Buchbinder, L., Herd, D. and Holmes, S. M. (2021). COVID-19 and the political geography of racialisation: Ethnographic cases in San Francisco, Los Angeles and Detroit. *Global Public Health*, *16*(8–9), 1396–1410.

Williams, A. J. (2013). Re-orientating vertical geopolitics. *Geopolitics*, *18*(1), 225–246.

Williams, J. and Boyce, G. A. (2013). Fear, loathing and the everyday geopolitics of encounter in the Arizona borderlands. *Geopolitics*, *18*(4), 895–916.

Williams, J. and Massaro, V. (2013). Feminist geopolitics: Unpacking (in)security, animating social change. *Geopolitics*, *18*(4), 751–758.

Woon, C. Y. (2013). Popular geopolitics, audiences and identities: Reading the 'War on Terror' in the Philippines. *Geopolitics*, *19*(3), 656–683.

Woon, C. Y. (2017). Children, critical geopolitics, and peace: Mapping and mobilizing children's hopes for peace in the Philippines. *Annals of the American Association of Geographers*, *107*(1), 200–217.

FOUR
DECOLONISING: DISMANTLING ARCHITECTURES OF PRIVILEGE

Chapter Overview

This chapter engages with calls to decolonise political geography. After setting the scene within broader calls to decolonise geography as a whole, it specifically engages with the 'overwhelming Whiteness' of political geography. It traces how and why calls to decolonise have emerged in political geography, before thinking through how this might take place within the sub-discipline and wider world.

Learning Objectives

1. To understand calls in political geography to 'decolonise'.
2. To think critically about the 'overwhelming Whiteness of political geography' and its colonial past.
3. To think through how 'decolonising' might take place in political geography and the wider world.

Read with: Chapter 2 (Situating Political Geography), Chapter 3 (Feminist Geopolitics)

Geography as a discipline faces significant challenges when thinking about and grappling with its legacies of colonialism and racism. As James Esson (2020) highlights, the history of geography is, in part, a history of empire building, enslavement and colonial endeavours (see also Hawthorne 2019). British geography, he argues, 'was implicated in and benefitted from the promotion of White supremacy as part of these activities' (2020: 709; see also Driver 2000, Hawthorne 2019, Noxolo 2017b). As Noxolo (2017a: 317) notes, geography's history is one of a 'terrible and problematic opening out of the world to colonial and exploitative forces'. Political geography as a sub-discipline of geography is no exception to these violent complexities. As was explored in Chapter 2, political geography has a fraught and incredibly problematic past. Its founding 'father' in Britain was Halford Mackinder, a geographer who promoted Empire, operated through racist belief systems, and championed the place of political geography within colonial projects. Calls to '*de*-colonise', then, refer to the 'radical challenge' of unsettling the practices and knowledges that maintain the legacies of colonialism, and in the process maintain the inequalities that privilege White Western knowledges (see Tuck and Yang 2021: 3). In the words of Noxolo (2017a: 318), a 'decolonial geography' is concerned with how colonial pasts are 'still active in the inequalities of the present'. For Radcliffe (2017: 32, emphasis added), while 'colonial rule may have formally ended', colonial power relations 'permeate *all* forms of knowing about and understanding the world'.

KEY TERMS: DECOLONISATION

Decolonisation entails the removal of ongoing colonial domination, thereby connecting moves to dismantle the racist social classification of the world population under Eurocentric world power to Indigenous-led demands for radical restructuring of land, resources and wealth globally (Esson et al. 2017: 385).

As Noxolo and others have argued, colonial legacies and practices loom large over the contemporary landscape of geography and political geography. Knowledge structures within the discipline are founded upon wider structures of inequality, racism, and architectures of privilege. They are entangled within Western ways of knowing the world that privilege certain (predominantly White) knowledges and practices over those of Black, Brown, and Indigenous communities. While some geographers seek to engage with these complexities, to challenge them, and practise a different way of being, this is by no means a completed task, rather it is an ongoing project. Any textbook of political geography must therefore grapple with the issues this raises, both in terms of how it affects the production of knowledge within political geography and the types of research that are undertaken within the discipline more broadly.

KEY TERMS: POSITIONALITY

... the notion that personal values, views, and location in time and space influence how one understands the world. In this context, gender, race, class, and other aspects of identities are indicators of social and spatial positions and are not fixed, given qualities ... it is essential to take into account personal positions before engaging in research, especially qualitative research. (Warf 2010: 2258)

Before going any further, we must acknowledge that we write this chapter as two White, middle class, British academics who, working within predominantly White institutions, are deeply entangled within violent and problematic colonial politics and power dynamics. We considered asking someone who is better engaged with and in decolonial work to write the chapter, but we also strongly believe, to borrow the words of Jazeel (2017: 334), that decolonial thinking and practice 'should concern us all'. The labour of such work cannot continuously fall into the hands of those who are already subject to the violence of colonialism. Whilst needing to be 'unafraid to fail' (Jazeel 2017: 334) in this endeavour, we write this chapter with the knowledge of our privilege, alongside a hope that in reading the following pages, you would be encouraged to engage with the work of the many Black, Brown, and Indigenous scholars calling for a more just and equitable (political) geography. With this in mind, we will begin by delving more deeply into the wider context of calls to decolonise geography before homing in on political geography. The chapter will end by thinking through what 'decolonising' might mean in practice in the contexts of university lecture halls and classrooms, but also beyond this too.

Geography Has a Problem

As political geographers, we are interested in the intersections between space and power. These intersections may be found in state corridors (see Chapter 7), but they can just as easily be found in our university classrooms too. The power dynamics that emanate from geography's past are, as we've established, very much alive and well, and this shapes how knowledge within the discipline is both produced and consumed. Who writes the papers we read in geography? Who has access to them? Whose voices are heard, cited and published, and conversely, whose are ignored and silenced? Whose papers get read by students?

Understanding race and racism within the discipline is essential in answering these questions. Geography, as Noxolo (2017a: 317) highlights, is persistently and overwhelming White. Desai's work (2017) sheds a searing light on this problem. Described as a 'defining moment for discussions about racism in British higher education geography' (Esson 2020: 709), Desai's intervention powerfully highlights that geography certainly has a problem with race and diversity. The statistics speak for themselves:

- Nationally 21.3% of all UK first-degree undergraduate students are ethnic minorities; for UK geography, this is only 6.3% (Desai 2017: 320).
- Ethnic minority geography students graduate with degree results significantly below those of their White peers. From 2013–2015 11.2% of ethnic minority students attained a first and 69.5% attained an upper second or better as compared with 16.9% and 80.0% for White students, respectively (Desai 2017: 321, Esson 2020: 709).
- Among all UK national staff in the UK, 8.2% are ethnic minorities, which is almost twice the 4.3% of UK national geography staff who are ethnic minorities (Desai 2017: 322).
- 7.3% of UK professors are ethnic minorities. In geography, this falls to 1.4%.

Whilst the statistics are stark, it is important to remember that there are lived experiences behind each of those numbers. As Tolia-Kelly (2017) powerfully illustrates in a diary of her experiences as a Black geographer, Ethnic minority geographers may experience a sense of isolation, marginalisation, and racial discrimination in higher education. This might take the form of being silenced or ignored in meetings, or it could be racialised course feedback where students complain about accents and not being able to understand the lecturer. This may all take place in a context dominated by White students who may be resistant or uncomfortable thinking about explicitly anti-racist agendas (Esson 2020). For Tolia-Kelly (2017: 324), the 'felt violences are part of the fabric of everyday life for our students, researchers, and academic colleagues within institutions'.

These statistics and experiences matter greatly. They shape the very foundations of the discipline, with significant consequences for 'who produces geographical knowledge and how it circulates' (Desai 2017: 322). If we only read the work of White geographers, our understanding of the world can, and always will be White. This is compounded by the fact that the accepted publishing language is nearly always English (see Ferretti 2021). In a world where the majority of people are not White, this is incredibly problematic and results in a discipline that has little openness to difference and diversity and where 'knowledge production is skewed towards the perspectives of Western writers and institutions' (Noxolo 2009: 56). There are a number of initiatives seeking to combat this. 'Why is my curriculum so White?', for example, is a national campaign that seeks to engage with these issues. Prompted by a video from students from University College London (UCL), the campaign highlights a lack of awareness about how many curriculums are comprised of 'White ideas' by 'White authors', thus normalising Whiteness in university life. Whilst impactful, for Esson (2020: 710), it still does not get to the heart of the problem and a more profound question needs asking:

> 'Why is our geography curriculum so White?' could be interpreted as suggesting that there is an acceptable amount of Whiteness a curriculum can reproduce without perpetuating racism. I do not believe such a threshold exists, so perhaps we should start asking 'Why is our geography curriculum White?'

In the Field with Vandana Desai: Decolonising Geography

Vandana Desai is a development geographer with a particular interest in researching on urban India and on the lived experience of the poor.

What does decolonising mean to you?

It means bringing in voices and perspectives from the Global South (GS), challenging othering, critical reflection on the impacts of colonialism on the economies and societies

(Continued)

of countries in the GS, highlighting ongoing disciplinary issues of eurocentrism and explicitly developing antiracist praxis in my teaching, equipping both teaching staff and students to help make the discipline and wider society more equitable and just.

What prompted you to write the (2017) paper and did the results surprise you?

A group of geographers were thinking of starting the Race, Culture and Equality Working Group (RACE) at the Royal Geographical Society (RGS) in 2015. A special issue was proposed for the geography journal *Area*, and as one of the founding members of the group I wanted to draw attention to the staff and student ethnic minority marginalisation in geography. By using national data from HESA and other studies on ethnicity in academia I wrote a short overview article. The findings from my data analysis highlight the predominant 'Whiteness' of the discipline when compared to the number of ethnic minority students and staff, in turn raising troubling equality and diversity issues such as the lack of a pipeline of ethnic minority students from undergraduates to academic staff in geography. The results did not surprise me but presenting evidence in numbers through the article (Desai 2017) proved to be a vital intervention in the discipline.

What advice do you have for students wanting to engage with decolonising agendas and practices?

Acknowledge the experience of the disadvantaged and marginalised, as well as the dominant, both in past and contemporary societies. There is, however, a difference between being diverse and being inclusive. Having students/staff from different diverse backgrounds may make a department/universities more diverse; but it does not automatically make that department/university a welcoming environment for students with diverse heritages or disadvantaged backgrounds. It's important to create safe space and to engage in meaningful, honest, and at times challenging discussions about their experiences, regardless of their background. Develop the capacity and skills to participate in these challenging conversations with more confidence, based on individual experience, and encourage individuals to act for change, support individuals to reflect, understand and create change in their own sphere of influence. In turn, identify ways to tackle inequality and improve the experience of diverse staff and students within the department.

As Esson (2020) and others highlight, the solution cannot simply be adding Black, Brown, and Indigenous perspectives into the mix as this does not fundamentally change the underlying problems. Such solutions might be what Tuck and Yang (2021) refer to as 'moves to innocence' whereby those in positions of privilege aim to relieve feelings of guilt or complicity by seeking to incorporate Brown, Black, and Indigenous thinking without changing their position of privilege. Decolonisation is thus a much more radical endeavour. Rather than simply adding in the work of those that have been excluded, decolonisation 'seeks to topple the coloniality of power and its constitutive matrix' (Esson et al. 2017: 385) and fundamentally rethink and reimagine the world from and with spaces and knowledges that have otherwise been marginalised. This involves confronting White supremacy and racism (Esson et al. 2017) and beginning conversations from and with the work of marginalised scholarship. This includes knowledges outside of the Western canon (Radcliffe 2017), and beginning conversations with Critical Black scholarship, Indigenous theory, and feminist and queer theory (Jazeel 2017). In short Black, Brown, and Indigenous practice, voice, and thought must be a starting point. To do otherwise, writes Esson et al. (2017: 386), is to run the 'risk of speaking not for but instead of those not only willing and able, but eager and equipped, to speak for themselves'.

This is not to say that White scholars are exempt from engaging with this work or that the burden of such work should fall to those who are already disenfranchised by colonial politics. Craggs and Neate (2020: 899), for example, seek to take up the call to decolonise geography. They ask the question, 'What if, rather than starting from the United States or the United Kingdom in histories or geography, we start from Nigeria?'. Drawing on archival evidence and new oral history interviews, Craggs and Neate explore the histories of Nigerian geographers working in Nigeria's first university from 1948–1990. Their work highlights the intellectual contributions of Nigerian geographers, particularly with regards to quantitative research, urban geography, and national and regional development. Craggs and Neate (2020: 899) argue that the 'view from Nigeria' offers significant new perspectives on the discipline, contributing to the urgent task of decolonising geography's history and demonstrating that Nigeria's absence is a result of the continued coloniality of intellectual and political relationships after decolonisation.

As a result, they shed light on how the Anglo–American hegemony of geography has shut down opportunities for those that do not conform to this system. Acknowledging and engaging with the dynamics of positionality is key here. It is important to remember that even when such work is seeking to tackle geography's violent colonial politics, Craggs and Neate, and all Western geographers, are still publishing and conducting research within the context of predominantly White, funded institutions. Without institutional access to papers like Craggs and Neate's, journal articles can be very expensive to access, and remain out of the reach of some scholars in Nigeria and other contexts that form the subject of Western decolonial analysis. Any effort to dismantle and uproot colonial legacies should be welcomed, but it is worth noting that it is very difficult to escape colonial dynamics within the Western university system. As Jazeel (2017: 335) notes, 'we are operating from within a privileged context'. Decolonial practice and process are far from simple and can be fraught – yet it remains vital work (Naylor et al. 2018: 205).

Over to You: Self-Reflection

'Universities are White spaces, in which Whiteness – and White privilege – dominates' (Tolia-Kelly 2017: 327).

Set aside half an hour to respond to the following five questions:

1. How does your own positionality affect your practice as a geography student? Think carefully about race, gender, sexuality, and how these identities intersect.
2. How might your positionality grant you privilege or opportunity, or how do you feel it might raise challenges for you as you undertake your degree?
3. When writing feedback for your courses, do you reflect on any conscious, or unconscious, biases you might have? How might these inform or impact the feedback you give?
4. Do some research on your reading list for political geography – is it overwhelmingly White?
5. How diverse and inclusive is your department? How do you think this affects your learning?

Beyond the discipline, geographers are also paying attention to how decolonisation plays out in streets, everyday spaces, cities, and workplaces. As Tuck and Yang (2021) assert, decolonisation is not a metaphor, rather it is associated with action and everyday struggle. It is something that people confront every day, whether that be Indigenous communities fighting for land rights (see Daigle 2019), or the Black Lives Matter movement confronting ongoing racist violence. The dismantling of privilege manifests in a number of ways, including a literal dismantling of structures and material remnants of colonial power. The 'Rhodes Must Fall' campaign is a prime example of this literal dismantling. Originating at the University of Cape Town (UCT) in 2015, the campaign originally sought to force the removal of a statue of Cecil Rhodes, a nineteenth-century British colonialist, in South Africa. Sparked by student Chumani Maxwele throwing a bucket of human waste over the statue, the campaign resulted in the removal of the statue (see Figure 4.1), and led to widespread protests on the campus – and around the world – about institutional racism, White supremacy, and the celebration of colonialists via statues and monuments.

Black Geographies

Engaging specifically with the challenges outlined above, Black geographies is a body of thought that critiques 'the erasure of Blackness within the Whiteness and coloniality of geographical thought' while shining a light on 'Black spatial thought and agency' (Noxolo 2022: 1). As Hawthorne (2019: 4) highlights, Black geographic thought has existed for many years in university spaces, in political structures and in 'everyday

Figure 4.1 Rhodes falls (9 April 2015)

Credit: Desmond Bowles (CC BY-SA 2.0) https://en.wikipedia.org/wiki/Rhodes_Must_Fall#/media/File:-RMF_Statue_Removal_04_Desmond_Bowles.jpg

practices of Black space-making' – it has, however, not always been recognised within the discipline of geography (see also Bledsoe and Wright 2019 on the many expressions of Black geography). For Noxolo (2022: 1), Black geographies speaks about the spatial experiences of Black people, but also speaks *from* 'the voices of Black geography', drawing heavily upon modes of thinking 'developed within the field of Black/African diaspora studies' (Hawthorne 2019: 5). Importantly, as Hawthorne (2019: 8) highlights, this is not a case of adding a few Black authors to a syllabus – 'to add diversity and stir'. On the contrary it is a call to foreground the 'subjects, voices, and experiences that have been systematically excluded from the mainstream spaces' of geography. To put it another way:

> Black Geographies asks how the analytical tools of critical human geography can be used to engage with the spatial politics and practices of Blackness, and how an engagement with questions of Blackness can in turn complicate foundational geographical categories such as capital, scale, nation, and empire. (Hawthorne 2019: 8–9)

A key tenet of this process is shifting the lens of analysis away from the Black body. All too often, Black bodies are reduced to the unit of analysis through the vectors of racism, violence, and death. For Hawthorne (2019), Noxolo (2022), and others, de-centring the Black body opens up a 'new avenue for the study of racism and Black resistance' (Hawthorne 2019: 5). In light of pressing contemporary challenges that disproportionately affect Black people (such as climate change, surveillance and policing, nationalism, the rise of the far right, and racism, to name a few), sustained and careful thought and attention is needed. This shift also offers ways to re-imagine key concepts within political geography.

As Hawthorne (2019: 5) highlights, due to the upheaval of the trans-Atlantic slave trade, Black people have been imagined as 'lacking geography' or as 'victims of geography'.

Black geographies instead seeks to 'find Black Geographies wherever they might be' (Noxolo 2022: 1235). In moving *with* Black geographies, places and spaces in this way, the conventional geographical boundaries that form the foundation of political geography (e.g., 'the state', borders, understandings of what makes a 'nation') are uprooted. In the words of Noxolo (2022: 1235), 'they very often overflow conventional geographical boundaries' and require a thinking beyond constructs like the nation-state. Instead, the task 'is to seek and find Black Geographies wherever they might be, without geopolitical limits' (Noxolo 2022: 1235). This might be exploring the geographies of Black migrants, refugees, Black queer communities, the everyday effects of racialised surveillance and racial control, or the geographies of the everyday spaces that White subjects have traditionally occupied within geographical thought. This might also involve re-imagining Black narratives from a spatial perspective. Sowande Mustakeem (2016) offers a powerful example of this. As she articulates, narratives of the slave trade often neglect the lived experiences of Black people in the Middle Passage. It is seen as a transit zone and often stripped of its geography as lived *place*. Drawing on extensive archival research, Mustakeem (2016) reimagines the Middle Passage as a place of intense lived experience. She situates the geographies of slavery firmly aboard ship spaces and, in doing so, offers harrowing accounts of the brutality of slavery as they affected not just men, but women, disabled and pregnant Black people, while also recounting how the ship functioned as a space of resistance, rebellion, and challenge to White supremacy. The ship and the Middle Passage are fundamentally re-imagined through Black geographies and the effects are profound. Such work demonstrates the importance of Black perspectives and unsettling interventions on events and time periods that have 'settled' historical records and narratives. The challenge for Black Geographies going forward as Noxolo (2022), and also Desai (2017), demonstrate, is ensuring there are enough Black Geographers employed at universities to continue this vital work.

Case Study: Dreading the Map and Unsettling Spaces of Privilege

The 'Creative Approaches to Race and (In)security in the Caribbean and the UK' (CARICUK) is a project led by Dr Pat Noxolo which aims to 'transform discussions about race and anti-racism in UK higher education institutions' through collaborations with artists.

One element of the project is an artistic intervention by Sonia E. Barrett entitled 'Dreading the Map' (March 2021; see Figure 4.2). Situated within the Map Room at the Royal Geographical Society (a space deeply embedded within geography's colonial histories), the sculpture draws on surplus maps of the Caribbean and East Africa from the RGS collections and uses Black hair techniques, including dreading, to 'remake and reclaim' what the maps represent.

(Continued)

> Culturally, spaces of Black hair styling are predominantly female, and are 'filled with discussions around self- and community-care' (CARICUK 2021). This stands in stark contrast with the 'grand' setting of the Map Room, which is filled with images of the White, male, explorer. In the process, the space was subverted, filled with 'Black women's language, perspectives and practices, a reimagining of what the space can and should mean'.
>
> We can think of 'Dreading the Map' as 'an explicitly anti-colonial work installed in the heart of one aspect of British colonialism' (CARICUK 2021).

Decolonising Political Geography

Clearly, everything mentioned above is intensely geopolitical. These discussions are premised on injustice, inequality, racism, power and how these dynamics and intersections manifest spatially. Yet political geography as a sub-discipline, dominated as it is by White Western academics, has been relatively slow to engage with these discussions and practices. As Dowler and Sharp highlighted in 2001, while 'marginal voices have made great impacts on geography and related disciplines', 'their impact on political geography has been much slighter' (2001: 165). Sharp (2011) offered an important intervention seeking to address this imbalance in her analysis of the response to 11 September 2001 (9/11) in Tanzanian newspapers. Drawing on a 'subaltern' approach, Sharp argues that Tanzania's newspapers offer an alternative scripting of global geopolitics that was hard to find in the wave of American patriotism following 9/11.

Figure 4.2 'Dreading the Map', an installation by Sonia Barrett, in the Map Room of the Royal Geographical Society. Photography by Damian Griffiths, reproduced with permission

> **KEY TERMS: SUBALTERN**
>
> A term with its origins in the military to define an officer of the British Army below the rank of a captain. Within geopolitics, it refers to analyses of countries, contexts, actors, movements, and communities that are often in positions of marginality. It denotes the need to find space for 'other voices' in the international (Sharp 2011).

Far from being swept up in this wave, newspapers in Tanzania were critical of the 'War on Terror'. While in the US discourses of global fear abounded, in Tanzania, feelings of fear were directed at the US and possible reprisals, and newspapers critiqued the role of the US in global peace, arguing that it's 'smug arrogant isolationism' had begotten the disaster of 9/11 (see Sharp 2011: 301). Tanzanian perspectives are often silenced in geopolitical discourses. Sharp argues that by addressing this, geopolitics is reorientated to the 'margins', demonstrating in the process that there is another way to 'do' and imagine geopolitics.

However, Dowler and Sharp also noted in 2001 that the experiences of the marginalised are all too often used as the 'raw materials' for research and geopolitical thinking. Within this, there is a lack of openness and concerted engagement with the 'process of theorising to the knowledges and wisdom' of Black, Brown, and Indigenous communities. Where this work is undertaken, it is often in predominantly White, Western institutions and in the English language (Dowler and Sharp 2001: 170–171). Twelve years later in 2013, Sharp (2013: 20) noted that 'critical geopolitics remains a particularly western way of knowing' where Western understandings and knowledge systems are privileged. Five years on again and Naylor et al. (2018) noted that non-Western ontologies and ways of thinking and being in the world are often neglected, and that engagements within political geography are premised on discourses that rely on a world divided into 'Global North' and 'Global South'. In this world, the North is more often than not privileged. As Daigle (in Naylor et al. 2018: 10) argues, 'political geography ... has and continues to be shaped by a large number of academics from the "north" who examine colonialism in the "south"'. As a result, Naylor et al. (2018: 200) argue that political geography often perpetuates an 'asymmetrical geopolitics of knowledge' whereby knowledge is produced *about* Black, Brown, and Indigenous communities rather than *with* them.

A powerful example countering this comes from Michelle Daigle. While not claiming to speak *for* Indigenous communities in colonial Canada, Daigle (2019) draws on her own experiences as a member of the Cree nation and Constance Lake First Nation. The Cree nation have kinship relationships with neighbouring Indigenous Territories. These relationships informed Daigle's understandings of her own research process, which importantly centres 'the voiced and legal traditions of Indigenous peoples' (Daigle 2019: 299). In this context, the research community is a far cry from being the 'raw material' of a research project. Rather, this research explores geopolitical complexities in a research process that is underpinned by 'long-term, reflexive, and reciprocal relationship building' (Daigle 2019: 299).

Such relationships and positionalities are crucial in Daigle's (2019) research into food sovereignty practices of Anishinaabe people in and beyond the Treaty 3 territory in Ontario, Canada. This Treaty agreement, signed by the Anishinaabe nation and the Government of Canada in 1873, comprises '55,000 28 First Nation reserves, and a population of 25,000 members with half living on-reserve and half living off-reserve' (Daigle 2019: 298). Within this context, the Canada–US border has colonised Anishinaabe territory, and food harvesting grounds are not neatly contained within these boundaries. On the contrary food harvesting grounds cross this border. As Daigle (2019: 297) and as Chapter 7 explore, sovereignty is constructed by a range of practices and processes, it is 'shaped across space according to specific histories and identities, and local socio-ecological realties and dynamics'. Food is one such practice and dynamic and Daigle (2019: 297) explores how Indigenous 'food harvesting and sharing practices shapes movements for decolonisation and Indigenous self-determination', whilst also resisting and complicating Euro-centric notions of sovereignty and colonial logics of state power.

Drawing on 30 interviews, Daigle's (2019) findings powerfully illustrate how settler colonial logics loom large over food sovereignty. To begin with, the discourses of the Canadian state do not engage with Indigenous ways of knowing and being where relationships with non-human kin such as the land, water, animals, and plants 'complicate Euro-centric notions of sovereignty' that are premised on capitalist logics of ownership, control, and exploitation (Daigle 2019: 300). As one research participant highlighted, 'We don't see food as an object that you consume. You have to pay your respects' (Daigle 2019: 303). Exerting food sovereignty is thus a fight conducted on multiple fronts. This has taken the form of a road block by the Grassy Narrows First Nation in 2002 to prevent destructive practices by a British pulp and paper company. This was, as Daigle (2019: 305) asserts, a 'necessary act of resistance against extractive industry so that local hunters, trappers, fishers and foragers can continue harvesting food'. In another example, Steve and Iris Jourdain speak of the issues related to the US and Canadian border. Community members harvesting fish on local waterways 'find themselves subject to the colonial jurisdictions of both Canada and the United States' (Daigle 2019: 307). As Steve stated, 'we're exempt from the law in Canada but not in the United States'. This is particularly challenging given that the lake falls under both jurisdictions, an invisible line in the water dividing the two, and of course fish do not respect this line. This has led to violent confrontations with US authorities. As the Jourdains highlight:

> They fly drones over here now. There are 250 of us here. And, they are going to send patrol boats over here just for us? They're just some guys playing cowboys and Indians. But the guys here fought back and we refused to go to court when we were charged. This is our home territory. We didn't recognize the boundary. At different seasons we would go out on the lake ... To be a good provider you have to go where the fish are. (Daigle 2019: 307–308)

To enact food harvesting in this context is to resist settler colonialism and challenge the spatial logics of White supremacy. For Daigle (2019: 312) these everyday acts of 'resistance and resurgence' in Anishinaabe territory shed light on the way that Indigenous food practices and harvesting cultures 'refuse colonial territorial boundaries'. Daigle's (2019) work is an important intervention, one which takes up Naylor et al.'s (2018: 200) challenge to both think deeply about where the privilege of knowledge production sits and to carefully co-produce knowledge from *within* sites of alterity, rather than outside of them. We can also see such impulses in the 'In the field' box below, where we explore research on ancestral spirits.

In the Field with Cynthia Nkiruka Anyadi: Thinking with Ancestral Spirits

Cynthia Nkiruka Anyadi is a PhD student at Royal Holloway, University of London. Her research explores how connections to ancestral spirits and lands within Igbo Nigerian culture are being challenged through migration.

Why are you interested in ancestral spirits and lands?

I'm interested in emotional connections to an other-worldly or ancestral spiritual plane because, despite how prevalent such connections are across almost all cultures, within geography they are paid very little attention.

How have you explored ancestral spirits and lands?

I approach these ideas using a mixture of qualitative methods. As my research focusses on the objects which people use to connect to lost loved ones or places, these objects are at the centre of my methodology. This begins with object elicitation exercises, where the discussion with my interlocutors revolves around the object, its meanings and value, and what position it holds in their life. This feeds into an oral history that explores in more depth the journeys, experiences, and beliefs of my interlocutor. Since returning knowledge to the community I'm working with is an essential part of my research, 3D modelling emerged as a way for me to recreate and share the objects in question with a broader audience in a way that was engaging and interactive.

Do you have any top tips for undergraduate geographers interested in Indigenous experiences and understanding more-than-human worlds?

I think the most important tip is to interrogate why you're doing the research, how you're doing it, and how it will contribute to or benefit the communities which you are working with. Learn as much as you can, not only from the work of other academics, but even more importantly from people who are established within the community and have worked within it for a long time. You should always be open to adjusting (or completely overhauling ...) your research in response to what you learn throughout your fieldwork.

This is not to discount the research of White, Western academics (Daigle in Naylor et al. 2018: 201) who are working critically in this field. Theriault's (2017) work offers a case in point here (see Case study below). To reiterate Jazeel's (2017: 334) call at the beginning of this chapter, geography's 'decolonial imperative should concern us all'. What it does do, however, is provide an opportunity to confront the Whiteness of political geography, and to 'examine, discuss, and contend' with the impacts of colonialism. Moreover, it prompts all political geographers to consider how our own bodies 'speak' in our writing (Noxolo 2009):

- How does your positionality impact your engagement with the world?
- How does it shape the kinds of research you might consider doing or not doing in your degree?
- How might you be reproducing colonial logics in your thinking and writing in essays and assessments?
- What are our responsibilities as postcolonial political geographers?

Case Study: 'What do Dreams and the Beings Who Visit Them Have to do with State Power?' (Theriault 2017: 114)

Theriault (2017) argues that the 'supernatural' has remained outside of the remit of political geography, despite its profound effects on geopolitical phenomenon (see Chapter 5). Drawing on 18 months of ethnographic fieldwork on Palawan Island in the Philippines (see Figure 4.3), Theriault explores the complexities of forest governance at sites of particular importance to Indigenous communities.

Theriault engages directly with Indigenous philosophies to explore the significance of dreams, invisible tree people ('taw na diki megkebiri') and other metaphysical agencies in the politics of the landscape. Spaces, for example, that Western ways of thinking may designate as 'wilderness' are believed to be inhabited by these beings. This has significant implications for how the forests and lands are used, governed and managed. Indigenous ontologies and Western ways of understanding are brought into conversation, and sometimes conflict, in this process. For Theriault (2017: 114), this process demonstrates that the supernatural has agency, and such forces are 'no less significant in the (de)constitution of state power than many of the more directly observable agencies whose interactions we are accustomed to tracing'.

The challenge posed by Theriault is to engage more directly with ideas, beliefs, and beings outside of Western ways of knowing the world and to break down binaries that frame Western ontologies as 'modern' and in opposition with traditional Indigenous knowledges. The challenge for political geographers is to engage more comprehensively with multifaceted understandings of the world that complicate and perhaps uproot and unsettle Western ways of thinking.

Figure 4.3 USAID Measuring Impact Conservation Enterprise Retrospective (Philippines; Nagkakaisang Tribu ng Palawan)

Credit: USAID Biodiversity & Forestry (This work is in the public domain) https://commons.wikimedia.org/wiki/File:USAID_Measuring_Impact_Conservation_Enterprise_Retrospective_(Philippines;_Nagkakaisang_Tribu_ng_Palawan)_(39581745244).jpg

Conclusion: In the Classroom and Beyond

Political geography has a long way to go in the process and practice of decolonising. As Desai (2017) highlights, part of this challenge is addressing the relative lack of Black, Brown, and Indigenous scholars working in the field. Another part of this challenge lies in expanding the remit of the decolonial. For Naylor et al. (2018: 200) decolonial scholarship tends to operate through a heteronormative gaze and more must be done to address intersectional issues along the lines of 'gender, sexual identity, or economic difference' (explored further in Chapter 11). Deepening and strengthening engagement with decolonial scholarship is key across all fields of geography, and political geography is far from being an exception to this. Importantly, as Noxolo et al. (2017: 385) argue, this process must go beyond treating decolonisation as a 'theme' or buzzword. It must be premised on practical action, both methodological and theoretical. It must, in the words of Jazeel (2017: 334), be 'collective, cautious, confrontational'.

As a student of political geography this task might seem quite daunting, and that is because tackling 'overwhelming Whiteness' is by its very nature overwhelming (Noxolo 2017a: 317). Yet there are a number of steps within university settings that can be taken at both collective and individual levels. The first is to think about the politics of citation. As Ahmed (2017; see also Sharp et al. 2019) notes, citation is intensely geopolitical. Who we cite in our work speaks to whose work we value and whose ideas and

56 | POLITICAL GEOGRAPHY

knowledge systems we deem to be 'worth' citing. It is all too easy, particularly in political geography – dominated as it is by White men – to cite the 'big' names that appear in paper after paper. This is not to say that this work is not valuable, but that we must also look beyond this canon if we are to take seriously the call to diversify the discipline. This might take time, additional effort and care, but as highlighted in this chapter, such work is invaluable.

Thinking more broadly and collectively, Byron (2020) highlights the need to think through the politics of university Geography Societies. Does your GeogSoc reproduce the colonial politics and Whiteness discussed in this chapter? As Byron (2020: 696) writes, the:

> … identity of a society is performed through its membership, its practices, the activities it organises, the membership of its committees, its openness, and its responsiveness to critical challenges to those practices from the entire spectrum of the student body.

It cannot be assumed, therefore, that GeogSocs are by their very nature attuned to decolonising discourses and anti-racist practices. As with calls to diversify geography higher education staff (Desai 2017), university societies also need to be engaged in the wider spirit of equality, diversity, and inclusion. This might include thinking carefully about 'ball' culture (summer balls, Christmas balls, etc.) that many students may not be able to afford, and, for example, providing events where alcohol consumption is not an (implicit or explicit) pre-requisite (Byron 2020).

Of course, the challenge of decolonising is bigger than any individual effort or GeogSoc restructure. It goes without saying that this chapter can only ever scratch the surface of the practices and ideas associated with decolonising political geography. These 6000 or so words should be treated as a snapshot, and an invitation to delve deeper into Black, Brown, and Indigenous literatures that underpin the preceding pages. It should also not be considered in isolation from the other chapters in this book. The imperative to decolonise stretches to every corner of political geography and it is our aim to centre work that responds to these calls throughout the pages the follow.

Summary

- This chapter has explored the need to decolonise geography and political geography.
- Both the history of geography and political geography (see Chapter 2) are violent, premised on exploitation and deeply uneven power dynamics.
- Calls to decolonise seek to address these power imbalances, to recognise these problematic histories, and to directly engage with the ever-present legacies of these histories in the present day.

- Within this framework, decolonising is not simply a concept. It is an ongoing practice, process, and call for proactive change. This can manifest in many ways, from thinking carefully about where we source our knowledges, to challenging prevailing Whiteness in our universities and everyday lives.

Follow-on Resources

Black Geographers: a community 'working to tackle the erasure of Black people in geography'. See www.blackgeographers.com/ (@blackgeogorg on Twitter)

CARICUK (Creative Approaches to Race and In/security in the Caribbean and UK): a collaborative project between artists and geographers that 'aimed to transform discussions about race in UK higher education institutions' by 'redefining race as an insecurity'. See https://caricuk.co.uk/

Why is my curriculum White? A short film produced by students and staff at UCL that explores Whiteness in university curriculums. See www.youtube.com/watch?v=Dscx4h2l-Pk&t=299s

References

Ahmed, S. (2017). *Living a feminist life*. Durham, NC: Duke University Press.

Bledsoe, A. and Wright, W. J. (2019). The pluralities of Black geographies. *Antipode, 51*(2), 419–437.

Byron, M. (2020). Acknowledging, confronting, and transforming extra-curricular spaces in geography. *Area, 52*(4), 695–700.

CARICUK (2021). Dreading the Map. Available at: www.rgs.org/geography/news/reflecting-on-caricuk/ (accessed 5 August 2023).

Craggs, R. and Neate, H. (2020). What happens if we start from Nigeria? Diversifying histories of geography. *Annals of the American Association of Geographers, 110*(3), 899–916.

Daigle, M. (2019). Tracing the terrain of Indigenous food sovereignties. *The Journal of Peasant Studies, 46*(2), 297–315.

Desai, V. (2017). Black and Minority Ethnic (BME) student and staff in contemporary British Geography, *Area,* 49, 320–323.

Dowler, L. and Sharp, J. (2001). A feminist geopolitics? *Space and Polity, 5*(3), 165–176.

Driver, F. (2000). *Geography militant: Cultures of exploration and empire*. London: Wiley.

Esson, J. (2020). 'The why and the White': Racism and curriculum reform in British geography. *Area, 52*(4), 708–715.

Esson, J., Noxolo, P., Baxter, R., Daley, P. and Byron, M. (2017). The 2017 RGS-IBG chair's theme: Decolonising geographical knowledges, or reproducing coloniality? *Area, 49*(3), 384–388.

Ferretti, F. (2021). Geopolitics of decolonisation: The subaltern diplomacies of Lusophone Africa (1961–1974). *Political Geography, 85,* 102326.

Hawthorne, C. (2019). Black matters are spatial matters: Black geographies for the twenty-first century. *Geography Compass, 13*(11), e12468.

Jazeel, T. (2017). Mainstreaming geography's decolonial imperative. *Transactions of the Institute of British Geographers, 42,* 334–337.

Mustakeem, S. M. (2016). *Slavery at sea: Terror, sex, and sickness in the Middle Passage.* Chicago, IL: University of Illinois Press.

Naylor, L., Daigle, M., Zaragocin, S., Ramírez, M. M. and Gilmartin, M. (2018). Interventions: Bringing the decolonial to political geography. *Political Geography, 66,* 199–209.

Noxolo, P. (2009). 'My paper, my paper': Reflections on the embodied production of postcolonial geographical responsibility in academic writing. *Geoforum, 40*(1), 55–65.

Noxolo, P. (2017a). Introduction: Decolonising geographical knowledge in a colonised and re-colonising postcolonial world. *Area, 49*(3), 317–319.

Noxolo, P. (2017b). Decolonial theory in a time of the re-colonisation of UK research. *Transactions of the Institute of British Geographers, 42*(3), 342–344.

Noxolo, P. (2022). Geographies of race and ethnicity 1: Black geographies. *Progress in Human Geography, 46*(5), 1232–1240.

Radcliffe, S.A. (2017). Decolonising geographical knowledges. *Transactions of the Institute of British Geographers, 42*(3), 329–333.

Sharp, J. (2011). A subaltern critical geopolitics of the war on terror: Postcolonial security in Tanzania. *Geoforum, 42*(3), 297–305.

Sharp, J. P. (2013). Geopolitics at the margins? Reconsidering genealogies of critical geopolitics. *Political Geography, 37,* 20–29.

Sharp, J., Sundberg, J., Williams, J., Faria, C. and Dixon, D. (2019). Review forum: *Feminist geopolitics: Material states* by Deborah P. Dixon. *Political Geography, 73,* 161–167.

Theriault, N. (2017). A forest of dreams: Ontological multiplicity and the fantasies of environmental government in the Philippines. *Political Geography, 58,* 114–127.

Tolia-Kelly, D. P. (2017). A day in the life of a geographer: 'Lone', Black, female. *Area, 49*(3), 324–328.

Tuck, E. and Yang, K. W. (2021). Decolonization is not a metaphor. *Tabula Rasa, 38,* 61–111.

Warf, B. (2010). Positionality. In *Encyclopedia of geography* (Vol. 1, p. 2258). London: Sage. Available at: https://dx.doi.org/10.4135/9781412939591.n913 (accessed 17 May 2023).

FIVE

NON-HUMAN WORLDS: FROM OBJECTS TO ANIMALS

Chapter Overview

Following the 'material turn' in cultural geography, political geographers are increasingly turning to objects and the 'more than human' to interrogate and understand the geopolitical world. This chapter begins with a conceptual overview of this body of work, highlighting key scholars, definitions, and theoretical lenses. It then draws on four examples (objects, elements, animals, and invisible beings) to bring these ideas to life. In doing so, it explores the diverse and multifaceted ways in which political geographers engage with non-human worlds.

Key Learning Objectives

1. To understand why it is important to look beyond human actors in political geography.
2. To gain a critical insight into non-human actors that act at multiple scales, and the impact this has on the geopolitical world.
3. To provide a new lens through which to critically engage with and analyse geopolitical phenomena.

Read with: Chapter 2 (Situating Political Geography), Chapter 12 (Peace and Resistance), Chapter 13 (Surveillance)

More than ever, it is becoming apparent that the geopolitical world extends well beyond the human. Indeed, it is now widely recognised that humans form part of a complex web of agencies in which non-humans (such as objects, elements, non-human animals, spirits, and other material forces) come together to produce the world around us. In other words, human beings alone do not determine how geopolitical events come into being, and nor should they form the sole focus of our analysis of geopolitical worlds.

We only need to look at the global Covid-19 pandemic to see that this is the case. In a matter of months humans were held hostage to a virus circulating across the world. Over the course of the global crisis, passports – objects often associated with mobility (see Chapter 10) – became defunct as borders closed, quarantine hotels opened, and homes were locked down. Humans, in this case, were on the back foot against agencies that were invisible to the naked eye. Non-human agents and agencies thus have the capacity to radically uproot political, social, and cultural landscapes.

The purpose of this chapter is to explore some of the complex political geographies that surface as the human and non-human collide, interact, and transform one another. It will tease out why these interactions matter across multiple fronts, including the significance of objects, elements, animals, and spirits. Before delving into these particular examples, it first sets the conceptual scene, exploring how and why political geography has engaged with actors and agencies that both exist alongside and exceed the human.

Beyond Environmental Determinism

As explored in Chapter 2, political geography has a troubled history when it comes to the material, particularly in relation to the environment. Haunted by the spectres of environmental determinism, geopolitics as a field has arguably been slower than others to grapple with the topic of materiality (Dittmer 2014, Squire 2016). Whilst the material and the non-human have become central to political geography in recent years, the adoption of the 'material imagination' (Anderson and Wylie 2009: 318) can be found much earlier in other sub-disciplines within geography.

Cultural geographers have been a driving force behind this agenda, navigating the material in different ways, often foregrounding the connections between earth and life (Whatmore 2006). Known as the 'material turn', this work has dismantled the idea that the human is the sole and most important actor within political, social, and cultural worlds. On the contrary, work by key thinkers, including Jane Bennett (2010), pushes back against the idea that non-human entities and life are just 'passive stuff'. Bennett (2010: vii) argues that Western thought has a habit of dividing the world into 'dull matter (objects, things) and vibrant life (us beings)'. In other words, Western thought has treated objects and matter as inert, background 'things' rather than entities possessing lively geographical agency.

================= KEY TERMS: NON-HUMAN AGENCY =================

The capacity of 'things' and non-humans (this could be anything from edibles to weather conditions, or everyday objects) to demonstrate independence or 'aliveness' beyond or outside of human experience. In other words, such 'actants' have agency and influence of their own. (Bennett 2010: xvi)

To rectify this, Bennett (2010) calls for the need to engage proactively with the lively role that non-humans such as objects, elements, and resources play in public life. For example, Bennett (2010: viii) asks what difference it would make to energy policy if electricity was understood to be an 'actant' with agency rather than simply a commodity. Here, she seeks to give voice to the power of 'things'. As a result, humans emerge not as distinct, isolated entities but rather as beings that are entangled within the material world – whether that be objects, resources, elements, animals, organic or inorganic matter. In opening our eyes to the vibrancy and vitality of matter in all its forms, we can understand the world with greater nuance and depth. Moreover, it opens up the possibilities for more ethical ways of engaging with the world that are attentive to the lives, liveliness and complexities of non-humans.

The 'material turn' then, is concerned with making a place within geography for the things, beings, and matter of the world that extends beyond the human. This might also be termed a 'post-human' approach whereby the human is decentred (although importantly not disregarded) as the prime actor in geographical thought. Suddenly that which was once deemed to be 'out there' is brought into the very heart of academic discourse and understandings of what it means to be human (Whatmore 2006). In doing so, both humans and non-humans emerge as co-creators and collaborators.

KEY TERMS: POST-HUMAN

The idea that the human is not the privileged or only actor of consequence in the geographical (and geopolitical) world and that humans are not autonomous or separate from the world of nature, matter, and animals (see Sundberg 2014).

Beyond simply stating that 'matter' matters, political geographers, and others interested in post-human approaches, have used two key frameworks to help think through and grapple with the non-human world. These approaches provide both conceptual, and at times methodological, foundations for this work and are often cited in research across many different themes in political geography.

Actor Network Theory (ANT)

ANT has been a key conceptual and methodological lens through which geographers have engaged with the material and non-human world. Pioneered by sociologists Bruno Latour, Michael Callon, and John Law, ANT emerged as an approach in the 1980s and has since become a departure point and inspiration for those looking to understand how humans and non-humans share agency and work together to co-produce the world (Müller 2015). The key argument of ANT is that understandings of the social and political world will always be incomplete and insufficient if the whole range of actors participating in any given context or situation are not first considered. This may include human actors but, crucially, it also includes non-human actors – from germs, to tables, to animals, to coffee cups. These actors come together to form nodes which, as a whole, comprise a network that produces the world around us. For example, if we were to examine a speech delivered by the president of the United States from the Oval Office, the president would be one actor, but so too would the flags that stand either side of them, the papers on their desk, the tele-prompt giving them the words to say, the camera filming them, and any other object or entity that has been positioned within the frame to produce that particular geopolitical moment.

Importantly, within ANT, all of these entities stand on an equal footing. In other words, each entity is understood as equally important, and it is the associations that emerge between each actor that generate power or determine a particular situation (see Müller 2015). Fundamentally, ANT is concerned with tracing these associations to better understand how networks of humans and non-humans work together to produce the world. For political geographers this approach offers an opportunity to explore how power dynamics emerge in the relationships between different actors, and how these dynamics might unravel as agency is distributed throughout the network. As a result, ANT has become a popular means of breaking down the divisions between human and non-human, people and nature, actors and objects. Importantly, it also provides a framework to explore how particular orders, power dynamics, or geopolitical phenomena emerge (Müller 2015: 30).

Whilst ANT has been very important in thinking about the material turn in geography, this approach does have limitations. The primary critique of ANT is that it neglects how different actors within the network have varying capacities to shape that network. Remember ANT places each actor on an equal footing but, in doing so, it discounts pre-existing power dynamics and asymmetries that might shape that network (see Routledge 2008). Humans, for example, are capable of intention and of having an agenda. Similarly, race, class, gender, sexuality, ethnicity and other intersectional issues are not taken into account when thinking through the construction of a network and how power is distributed across it.

Assemblage

Assemblage can be thought of as a conceptual sibling to ANT (Müller 2015). Indeed, the approaches share many similarities. As Müller (2015: 27) highlights, both are concerned with why orders 'emerge in particular ways, how they hold together, how they reach across or mould space and how they fall apart'. Both are also interested in disrupting the idea that the human is the be-all-and-end-all of geopolitics by distributing agency across human and post-human worlds. French philosophers Gilles Deleuze and Félix Guattari first discussed the idea of assemblage in the 1980s to denote arrangements of different beings, entities, and actors that link together to form a whole. Crucially (unlike ANT) exterior factors are taken into consideration so assemblage is better placed to account for factors like race, class, sexuality, intentions, and agendas in the formation of power structures. This means that whilst associations between humans and other agents and actors are important, other external factors are also crucial to understand the assemblage as a whole (Dittmer 2016, Müller 2015: 28).

Case Study: The Arctic

As a constantly shifting environment, the Arctic is a useful context to explore assemblage further (Depledge 2013, 2015). Interests in the Arctic are widespread and varied – from oil and gas interests, to shipping lanes, to Indigenous rights, to environmental and conservation concerns. The Arctic, in the words of Bruun and Medby (2014: 915), 'is many different things at once: a homeland, a highway, a stage, a (science) laboratory', a pool of resources, a habitat, a space of unknown potential.

Melting sea ice thus prompts a range of different 'assemblage' responses. Governments, Indigenous communities, activists, shipping companies, and the oil and gas industry, for example, will each assemble the Arctic in different ways. For one, it is a home, for another, a commercial opportunity, for another, a space of potential transit. For animals, it is a habitat. In this sense, there is no 'single discreet, geographically knowable Arctic' (Depledge 2013: 126) but, rather, multiple Arctics. As the ice melts, these assemblages shift and change, responding to the ice, which is itself an actor provoking different responses.

Figure 5.1 Iceberg in the Arctic with its underside exposed

Credit: AWeith (Creative Commons Attribution-Share Alike 4.0 International license) https://commons.wikimedia.org/wiki/File:Iceberg_in_the_Arctic_with_its_underside_exposed.jpg

In assemblage theory, the world is always being configured and re-configured. In the words of Depledge (2015: 91), 'the geopolitical stage is far from a permanent reality waiting to be discovered or contested'. On the contrary, the elements within any given assemblage can be arranged and re-arranged as relationships are formed between each entity both within and outside of the assemblage. In this sense they produce the geopolitical world – but this world is not fixed, but rather contingent, as things and people assemble and re-assemble. Assemblage thinking thus insists that the world does not have to be a particular way just because it is a particular way, 'opening up avenues for alternative orderings and thus for political action' (Müller 2015: 32–33). This potential and the capacity of assemblage to help explore questions of agency and power has made it a popular analytical tool within political geography, used to understand a range of themes, including the Arctic (Depledge 2015), practices of diplomacy (Dittmer 2015), drone warfare (Williams 2011), and social movements (Davies 2012).

Over to You: Assembling an Assemblage

Choose an image from this chapter. Spend some time reflecting on the image.

1. What does the image show and what is the context? (Some additional research might be needed here.)
2. How might you deconstruct the image into different parts?
3. How do these parts come together to form an assemblage?
4. How might different actors assemble and re-assemble the image in different ways? (For example, how might the views of a protester and state actor differ?)

Political Geography and the Non-human

So why do these approaches matter to political geography? A number of political geographers deconstruct the world through non-human approaches. Here we can look to work on the geopolitics of disease (Ingram 2009), ice (Bruun 2020), military recruitment paraphernalia (Rech 2020), biomimetics (Johnson 2015), sturgeon and caviar (Dickinson 2022), bank notes (Mwangi 2002), archaeology and the presence of the state (Miller et al. 2020), and CDs and music (Hughes and Forman 2017), to name but a few of the diverse interventions turning the attention of political geographers to the non-human world. For Squire (2015: 148), this has brought much to the sub-discipline, including an emphasis on the 'generative powers of "matter"' and the complex ways that non-humans and social worlds intertwine and intersect. Such approaches challenge political geography's early focus on representation, instead understanding power as something that is constituted by the messy relationships between social and non-human forces. Below are four key areas in which this has unfolded.

Objects

The study of objects has been a key component of the 'material turn' within geopolitics. Often this has been in relation to unpacking the manifestations of state power in everyday life. The work of Meehan et al. (2013) is a useful starting point here. Drawing on the

HBO television series *The Wire*, the authors draw out the centrality of objects in shaping the series and the lives of those in it, making important linkages to the 'real' world along the way. Set in Baltimore, USA, the TV show dramatises a range of issues, from the drug trade to the struggles of the public school system. Within this context, Meehan et al. (2013: 4) argue that the series is ripe with objects that are protagonists within the storylines, 'breaking the human-centred narrative structure of conventional television'. Two key objects that emerge in the series are the wiretap and CCTV cameras, which extend the reach of the state into private and domestic spaces. For Meehan et al. (2013: 4) the CCTV camera 'unleashed a new geography of state power', shaping how and when crimes occur, 'how power is exercised, how proof is assembled, how "reality" is conceptualized and understood' (Meehan et al. 2013: 5). CCTV cameras exert agency, altering people's mobility, behaviour, and sense of safety or fear. Objects, in this case study, work to 'enable, disable, and transform state power', producing and policing the conditions of the state in the process (Meehan et al. 2013: 2).

Whilst the CCTV camera may represent a more overt expression of state power (see Figure 5.2), we can also think of more banal, mundane objects within this nexus too. For Raento (2006) the postage stamp offers a prime example. They are, after all, official state documents that circulate within countries and across borders without much thought. And yet each stamp bears particular imagery, iconography, and celebrations of national achievements, whilst simultaneously erasing and silencing controversial periods of history from the collective memory. For Mwangi (2002), Kenyan bank notes from the 1920s

Figure 5.2 The harbour by the Pilica river in Tomaszów Mazowiecki, Poland. Closed-circuit television (CCTV)

Credit: Warszawska róg Szerokiej w Tomaszowie Mazowieckim, w województwie łódzkim, PL (This work has been released into the public domain by its author) https://commons.wikimedia.org/wiki/File:The_harbor_by_the_Pilica_river_in_Tomasz%C3%B3w_Mazowiecki,_Poland.Closed-circuit_television_(CCTV).jpg

to the 1960s function in a similar way, working to chart a key period in Kenyan history as it moved from British colonial rule to becoming an independent nation in 1963. Mwangi found that the design of the currency was heavily influenced by the geopolitical context in which it was produced and that it reflected the self-imagination of the dominant classes. Throughout the period, currency design 'evolved from insisting on White dominance, to an ambiguous suggestion of multi-racialism, to a doomed attempt at federalism and finally, to African independence' (Mwangi 2002: 31).

We might think of the poppy within this framework too. In the UK, the poppy is an object that circulates widely each year to mark and remember those who have lost their lives as a result of war. Thousands of people wear the poppy during this time and it can be seen emblazoned on objects from pizzas in supermarkets to items of clothing. For Basham (2016: 883) 'communities of feeling' emerge around the poppy through which people find their 'place' in the national story – a process that is both gendered and racialised. Basham (2016: 883) argues that both the Poppy Appeal and the poppy itself are objects inviting people to 'remember military sacrifice, whilst forgetting the violence and bloodiness of actual warfare'. In this sense the poppy is much more than the sum of its paper and plastic parts. It embodies and, importantly, projects certain ideals and atmospheres into the world around it (see also Rech 2020).

Disobedient Objects

Whilst the above examples have usefully outlined how objects might bring the state into everyday lives, there are also powerful examples of objects working to disrupt, unsettle, and resist state practices. Catherine Flood and Gavin Grindon's (2014) work on disobedient objects provides compelling examples of objects used to subvert established power structures.

KEY TERMS: DISOBEDIENT OBJECTS

This refers both to an exhibition at London's Victoria and Albert (V&A) museum, curated by Catherine Flood and Gavin Grindon, and to objects that are created by 'ordinary people' (whether individuals or social movements) to resist and subvert state power. As Flood and Grindon highlight, object-making has long been a part of social movement cultures. They describe such objects as providing 'ingenious and sometimes beautiful solutions to complex problems, often produced with limited resources under duress' (Flood and Grindon 2014).

The 'Disobedient Objects' exhibition at the Victoria and Albert (V&A) museum sought to highlight the powerful role that objects play in movements for social change and to showcase the ingenuity and creativity that has emerged across the world as individuals and communities resist expressions of state power. The objects were described

Figure 5.3 Hong Kong Umbrella Revolution.

Credit: Pasu Au Yeung (Creative Commons Attribution 2.0 Generic license) https://commons.wikimedia.org/wiki/File:Hong_Kong_Umbrella_Revolution_-umbrellarevolution_-UmbrellaMovement_(15292823874).jpg

as acts of rebellion and included defaced currency, makeshift drones, a slingshot made from the tongue and laces of a shoe used by a Palestinian against an Israeli tank, and a gas mask made from a re-purposed plastic bottle. The mask was originally used to mitigate the effects of tear gas being used by the Turkish government in record amounts to disperse protesters in Istanbul in 2013. It has since been used in protests all over the world, including in the Black Lives Matter protests in Ferguson, USA. We can also think of the umbrella within this framework of disobedience. Mobilised in Hong Kong in pro-democracy protests, the umbrella has become an iconic symbol of a movement seeking universal suffrage (see Chan 2014, Yuen 2015). The umbrella was used in 2014 as a shield by protesters against pepper spray and tear gas. It came to define the movement (Chan 2014), and later, to shield protesters from the gaze of CCTV surveillance systems (see Figure 5.3). It is a mundane object that represents and embodies privacy, self-defence, and defiance, collectively and creativity, in the face of the Chinese government.

As Flood and Grindon highlight (2014), by making the objects protagonists in stories of resistance, new histories of geopolitical events and struggles emerge. These are histories 'from below', capturing the everyday interventions of individuals and collective movements from the ground. Through disobedient objects, we see people re-writing geopolitical scripts to usher in new ways of engaging with the world. They are objects that generate 'affective energetics of hope and rage', embodying a rawness that emerges as they come into conflict with state power (Flood and Grindon 2014).

> ## Over to You: Geopolitical Objects
>
> Find an object in the room around you that you think might speak to any of the geopolitical themes and ideas found in this book. Using a piece of paper, brainstorm the following:
>
> 1. Why do you think this object might be geopolitical?
> 2. What associations and relationships emerge through the object?
> 3. Does it have agency in its own right?
> 4. How might it relate to the theoretical approaches outlined at the beginning of the chapter?

Elements

Elements are another area that have attracted attention in the material turn within geopolitics (Benwell 2020, Squire 2016). This could be in the form of water, air, fire, earth, or as Nassar (2018) highlights, dust. These substances have previously been understood as a backdrop or stage on which geopolitical events unfold, rather than as substances with agency (Dalby 2007, Lehman 2013). Geographers including Adey (2015) and Dalby (2007) have called for the 'geo' in geopolitics to be taken seriously. Andrew Barry (2013: 13), for example, demonstrates the value of 're-materialising our understandings of (geo)politics' in his analysis of disputes along an oil pipeline. His research highlights the 'critical part that materials play in political life' and argues that we can no longer 'think of material artefacts and physical systems such as ... water and earth as passive and stable foundations' (Barry 2013: 1). On the contrary, these substances interact intricately with the political and 'other material and immaterial entities' to form parts of assemblages but also prove agential in their own right as they enter into relationships with the social and political (Barry 2013: 34).

Jessica Lehman's (2013) work provides a useful example of this. Drawing on Latour's ideas of ANT and tracing associations, Lehman explores how the ocean can be 'enlivened' as an actor in Batticaloa, Sri Lanka, in the wake of the 2004 tsunami. Through its relationships with those who live on the coast, she locates the ocean as a site of 'anxiety, security, disaster, (im)mobility and risk' (Lehman 2013: 497). The ocean is instrumental to the political, economic, and cultural geographies of Sri Lanka but Lehman seeks to explore its agency in a less instrumental way. She found, for example, that the sea is pivotal in defining the rhythms of the daily life of fisherfolk who are able to read the weather, currents, and presence of fish by looking at the colour of the water and sky, the temperature of the ocean, and the angle at which fish are swimming (Lehman 2013: 492). The tsunami is perhaps the most obvious example of the ocean's agency. Nearly all of Lehman's participants had lost a loved one. Overall, almost 3,000 people died, with around 60,000 displaced. Participants noticed the sea behaving strangely in the lead up to the event, with jellyfish and snakes found in unusual places. Suddenly, the sea did not behave as people expected, with radical and devastating consequences. The agency of the elemental is underscored.

Animals

Beyond the 'stuff' and matter of geopolitics, animals have been the subject of a wide range of scholarship seeking to account for the diverse and multifaceted ways that non-humans shape geopolitical worlds. Drawing on the rich subfield of animal geographies (see Buller 2014, 2016; Wolch and Emel 1998), political geographers are increasingly refuting the idea that animals exist simply as passive beings or backgrounds to human life. Work by scholars such as Hobson (2007) and Srinivasan (2016) have foregrounded animal life, bringing it into conversation with the geopolitical. For Hobson (2007: 351), animals are not incidental to geopolitics – rather they are inherently part of it. In exploring this, Hobson argues that we gain a broader understanding of how the geopolitical is constituted. The world is, after all, 'always already inhabited' (Whatmore 2002: 3). Animals are part of the heterogeneous networks that constitute political life, and they co-create the histories and geopolitical subjectivities that might otherwise be taken for granted (Hobson 2007: 263). In light of this, a significant body of literature is emerging that critically engages with animals in a wide range of ways, both on land and at sea (see Dickinson 2022).

This scholarship includes work on the intersections of animals and warfare. Isla Forsyth (2017), for example, draws on the case study of Wojtek the bear (see Figure 5.4) to acknowledge the role and lived experiences of animals who have been co-opted into the military (see also Squire 2020). In the Second World War, Wojtek became a 'mascot, pet, and officially enlisted soldier of the Polish army', helping soldiers unload ammunition (Forsyth 2017: 495). He subsequently became a popular figure with his story published, serialised in magazines, and later memorialised in exhibitions. Forsyth foregrounds Wojtek as a protagonist, exploring the ethical questions that emerged in his relationship with the military, arguing that the lived experiences of animals matter in our understanding of geopolitical events.

Within the military–animal nexus, Johnson (2015) and Johnson and Goldstein's (2015) work highlights the enmeshing of biological life into the military through the practice of biomimetics, a process that aims to mimic features or characteristics of the natural world for strategic gain. As Johnson (2015) highlights, a wide range of animals, including lobsters, have been studied, experimented on, and robotically replicated by the US militaries in order to achieve certain military objectives (see also Jackman 2021).

Beyond the vectors of warfare, other studies have explored the relationship between nationalism and animals (Raento 2016), empire building (Kosek 2010), the role of animals in confounding territorial ambitions (Squire 2020), human–shark encounters (Gibbs 2021), the fleshy geopolitics of sturgeon and caviar (Dickinson 2022), and the ways in

Figure 5.4 Wojtek the bear

Credit: Imperial War Museum (This work created by the United Kingdom Government is in the public domain. This is because it is one of the following: It is a photograph taken prior to 1 June 1957; or It was published prior to 1973; or It is an artistic work other than a photograph or engraving (e.g. a painting) which was created prior to 1973. HMSO has declared that the expiry of Crown Copyrights applies worldwide) https://commons.wikimedia.org/wiki/File:Wojtek_the_bear.jpg

which fish complicate regulatory practices (Bear and Eden 2008). Transcending land and sea spaces, this research collectively attunes the geopolitical to the diverse range of animals that co-create the world, accounting for the moments that animals and non-human life are co-opted, manipulated, and managed, but also importantly where they 'speak back', confound, shape, and drive change (Dickinson 2022, Squire 2020).

Case Study: Cats at the Border (Sundberg 2011)

In the Rio Grande Valley at the US–Mexico border, it is not just humans determining how the area is monitored and policed. As Sundberg (2011) highlights, wild cats (including ocelots and jaguarundis) disrupt and inflect daily border enforcement practices. Sundberg explores the implications of a 1990s initiative to install approximately 50 miles of stadium-style lights along the riverbank of the border. Officials believed it would help them to see more effectively and remove the advantage of darkness from 'criminals'.

(Continued)

After campaigns from conservation groups, it was, however, decided that the use of lights at the border would disturb the behaviours of endangered ocelot and jaguarundi cats.

The cats came to matter 'tremendously to the politics of boundary enforcement', eventually forming part of a network that compelled Border Patrol to change its operational plans (Sundberg 2011: 331). Not only are these actors 'whose properties energies, and potentialities matter tremendously to political outcomes' (Sundberg 2011: 318), but they are actors who can facilitate the emergence of a 'more collaborative and therefore accountable ecological politics' (Sundberg 2011: 333). This is important in accounting for the ways in which animals 'push back, challenge, and rewrite' (Massaro and Williams 2013: 567) geopolitical phenomena that may otherwise be deemed the preserve of the 'human'.

In the Field with Hannah Dickinson: Sturgeon Encounters

Hannah Dickinson is a political–environmental geographer who follows the global circulation and trade of marine species and their derivatives. Drawing on more-than-human approaches, Hannah's research highlights the overlooked significance of marine species and oceanic ecologies in shaping geopolitics in the Anthropocene.

How did you come to research sturgeon?

My research on sturgeon began with an interest in the geopolitical and security implications of illegal wildlife trade in the European Union. This led me to researching illicit trafficking in sturgeon caviar, as I wanted to draw more attention to the prevalence of the illegal caviar trade in Europe. In studying the illegal caviar trade I also spent a lot of time thinking about sturgeon, who are now the most critically endangered group of species on the planet (in part due to an unsustainable caviar trade and poaching). My research has developed to consider how these extraordinary 'living fossils' have become unexpectedly embroiled in geopolitical–ecological issues including sovereignty disputes, green energy in Europe, biodiversity conservation, and securitisation of EU borders.

What research methods did you use?

In both my research on sturgeon and caviar, and current research on marine biomaterials, I am interested in circulation and following the movement of animals, commodities, materials, and ideas. I therefore take a lot of inspiration from 'Follow-the-Thing' methodologies, and also 'Follow-the-Policy' approaches that have developed from 'thing-following'. I work in a multi-sited way and follow the international movement of animals and their derivatives through different regulatory, scientific, geopolitical, and

(Continued)

economic spaces. I am interested in developing the following methods to account for breakages, stoppages, and gaps in the routes you follow; and along the way I interview key actors, conduct participant observation at meetings and conferences, and analyse policy documents to try to make sense of the politics embedded in following methodologies.

Why do you think it's important that political geographers engage with animals?

For a long time political geography has side-lined non-human animals. However, it is exciting to see more and more political geographers engaging with animals as actors that co-produce (geo)political space through their movement, behaviours, and physiologies. It is imperative that we engage with animals in our accounts of political geography because our political world has *always* been more-than-human, and animals intersect with virtually all aspects of political geography: they cross borders; they appear on flags and currency; they are mobilised in warfare; they reside in our homes and spaces of intimate geopolitics. Thinking with animals provides opportunities to rethink, disrupt, and enliven our conventional understandings of political geography. Nevertheless, there is a tendency to focus on the political geographies of charismatic and terrestrial megafauna. I try to challenge these imbalances in my own work by foregrounding the political geographies of marine species such as sturgeon, shrimp, and eels.

Spiritual Beings

Within wider moves to foreground the post-human, there is one area that has largely been neglected – that of the spiritual and the 'supernatural' or 'metaphysical' (Theriault 2017: 597). Ver Beek (2000) and Beban and Work (2014: 597) argue that such knowledges and experiences have been excluded, rationalised, suppressed, and 'systematically avoided' within political geography. This is largely due to the primacy of Western ways of thinking within the discipline that shape how knowledge is produced and what kinds of non-human actors are deemed to be significant. A growing body of work is seeking to address this and to proactively engage with knowledge systems and practices where spirits are important geopolitical actors. Theriault's (2017) work is a case in point. In his work, Theriault explores how invisible forest people on the Palawan Island of the Philippines shape relationships between Indigenous communities, the environment, and state-led conservation efforts. The forest people in Theriault's (2017: 121) research are the 'occupants and cultivators of the *talun* which includes old growth forests and other spaces many westerners would consider to be "wilderness"'. The Palawan believe that the forest people can use powerful magic to attack them if they act in a way that is not consistent with their wishes, such as clearing a forest area without consent. Such non-human agencies can complicate state-led initiatives and are often not considered in their planning. Such work helps to decentre both 'capitalist understandings of land as resource' and understandings whereby humans are the only actors with agency (Beban and Work 2014: 594, see also de la Cadena 2010: 358).

Spirituality is a pertinent issue beyond land too. As Childs (2019: n.p.) describes, for communities of the Duke of York Islands, Papua New Guinea, which lies 30km from the world's first commercial deep sea mine site (known as Solwara 1), mining the seabed has significant spiritual and cultural implications. Indeed, the clan chief of the Islands powerfully asserted that 'when they start mining the seabed, they'll start mining part of me' (in Childs 2019: n.p.). While it has been assumed, argues Childs (2019: n.p.), that 'there is limited human impact from mining in the deep sea ... such thinking is a fallacy' because, for the people of the Islands, 'deep sea mining disturbs a sense of who they are', including the spirits that inhabit their culture and beliefs. Indeed, central to this belief system is that certain spirits – masalai – are understood as guardians of the seabed and its resources. 'The digging up of the seabed', argues Childs (2019: n.p.), therefore 'cuts through the very fabric of their spiritual world and its sacred links to the sea and land'.

Theriault (2017: 114) suggests that within these contexts, invisible beings are 'no less significant in the (de)constitution of state power than many of the more directly observable agencies whose interactions we are accustomed to tracing'. In other words, whether one 'believes' in their existence or not, the relationships that emerge through these beings have agency and impact. There are many ways of knowing and understanding the world and no single way of doing so is 'right' or 'accurate'. Rather, it is more productive to think through distributions of agency between humans and non-humans in understanding how the world is brought into being. In doing so, space is made to challenge hegemonic assumptions and geopolitical practices and raise important questions about the ways that Western thought processes can be violently imposed on people who engage with the world very differently (Sundberg 2014: 34). It is worth noting here that undertaking this work in political geography requires great care. Selectively invoking Indigenous perspectives and belief systems can reproduce the power dynamics that mean such systems get excluded in the first place (Cameron et al. 2014, see Chapter 4). This is particularly important given that such selective invocations have been used to frame various Indigenous practices and belief systems as superstitious, primitive, magic, and naive (Cameron et al. 2014: 21).

Conclusions

This chapter has foregrounded the non-human as a key way of thinking about geopolitics. In a world where our interactions with the material and non-human seem increasingly profound and intense, such approaches are extremely important in making sense of a constantly changing world that is inhabited and shaped by a range of actors. Attending to the non-human diversifies the subjects of political geography, expands and stretches understandings of geopolitical events and phenomena and, importantly, enables ethical questions about the relationships between the human and non-human to come to the fore.

As has been illustrated, this might include analysing objects, elements, animals, and invisible beings. These categories are a starting point to explore the ways in which we might think about the non-human, and to challenge established modes of thinking about the world that centre upon the human. In doing so, we see how the non-human acts in a diverse range of contexts, from CCTV cameras to tsunamis, from disobedient objects to forest beings. Each exerts agency, shaping and co-producing the world around us. There are, however, many other examples. In the wake of the pandemic, disease is a clear vector for further interrogation, and we can think of technologies as non-human actors too (see Chapter 13). The list could be endless, but whatever the context, it is clear that non-human agency matters; it is vibrant and worthy of our sustained attention in grappling with geopolitical phenomena, from the everyday to the global.

Summary

- Post-human approaches aim to foreground non-human actors and agencies within political geography.
- This involves thinking through the complex web of agencies, both human and non-human, that work together to create geopolitical worlds.
- Actor Network Theory and Assemblage are two frameworks used by political geographers to undertake this work.
- Four examples of powerful non-human geopolitical actors are objects, elements, animals and spiritual beings, but we can think broadly here about disease, technologies, and other agencies that move with and beyond the human to deconstruct and understand the politics of our world.

Follow-on Resources

Beastly Business: This project explores the illegal wildlife trade, with a particular focus on songbirds, eels, and bears in Europe. It raises a number of important questions around cross-border mobilities and politics of this illicit and harmful trade. See https://beastly-business.org/

Objects from the Borderlands: For ten years, Susan Harbage has documented and collected objects from the US–Mexico border, creating an 'Anti-Archive' 'that challenges who is worthy of documentation, attention, and remembrance'. See http://susanharbag epage.blogspot.com/p/objects-from-borderlands.html

Into the Abyss: This is a short video by John Childs (see Childs 2019), exploring the politics of deep sea mining in Papua New Guinea, including Indigenous perspectives. See www.youtube.com/watch?v=ymXG8BMFoBs

References

Adey, P. (2015). Air's affinities: Geopolitics, chemical affect and the force of the elemental. *Dialogues in Human Geography, 5*(1), 54–75.

Anderson, B. and Wylie, J. (2009). On geography and materiality. *Environment and Planning A, 41*(2), 318–335.

Barry, A. (2013). *Material politics: Disputes along the pipeline.* London: John Wiley & Sons.

Basham, V. (2016). Gender, race, militarism and remembrance: The everyday geopolitics of the poppy. *Gender, Place & Culture, 23*(6), 883–896.

Bear, C. and Eden, S. (2008). Making space for fish: The regional, network and fluid spaces of fisheries certification. *Social & Cultural Geography, 9*(5), 487–504.

Beban, A. and Work, C. (2014). The spirits are crying: Dispossessing land and possessing bodies in rural Cambodia. *Antipode, 46*(3), 593–610.

Bennett, J. (2010). *Vibrant matter.* Durham, NC: Duke University Press.

Benwell, M. C. (2020). Going underground: Banal nationalism and subterranean elements in Argentina's Falklands/Malvinas claim. *Geopolitics, 25*(1), 88–108.

Bruun, J. M. (2020). Invading the Whiteness: Science, (sub) terrain, and US militarisation of the Greenland ice sheet. *Geopolitics, 25*(1), 167–188.

Bruun, J. M. and Medby, I. A. (2014). Theorising the thaw: Geopolitics in a changing Arctic. *Geography Compass, 8*(12), 915–929.

Buller, H. (2014). Animal geographies I. *Progress in Human Geography, 38*(2), 308–318.

Buller, H. (2016). Animal geographies III: Ethics. *Progress in Human Geography, 40*(3), 422–430.

Cameron, E., de Leeuw, S. and Desbiens, C. (2014). Indigeneity and ontology. *Cultural Geographies, 21*(1), 19–26.

Chan, J. (2014). Hong Kong's umbrella movement. *The Round Table, 103*(6), 571–580.

Childs, J. (2019). Deep sea mining threatens indigenous culture in Papua New Guinea, *The Conversation*, 19 February. Available at: https://theconversation.com/deep-sea-mining-threatens-indigenous-culture-in-papua-new-guinea-112012 (accessed 19 February 2019).

Dalby, S. (2007). Anthropocene geopolitics: Globalisation, empire, environment and critique. *Geography Compass, 1*(1), 103–118.

Davies, A. D. (2012). Assemblage and social movements: Tibet Support Groups and the spatialities of political organisation. *Transactions of the Institute of British Geographers, 37*(2), 273–286.

De la Cadena, M. (2010). Indigenous cosmopolitics in the Andes: Conceptual reflections beyond 'politics'. *Cultural Anthropology, 25*(2), 334–370.

Depledge, D. (2013). Assembling a (British) Arctic. *The Polar Journal, 3*(1), 163–177.

Depledge, D. (2015). Geopolitical material: Assemblages of geopower and the constitution of the geopolitical stage. *Political Geography, 45*, 91–92.

Dickinson, H. (2022). Caviar matter(s): The material politics of the European caviar grey market. *Political Geography, 99*, 102737.

Dittmer, J. (2014). Geopolitical assemblages and complexity. *Progress in Human Geography, 38*(3), 385–401.

Dittmer, J. (2015). Everyday diplomacy: UK/USA intelligence cooperation and geopolitical assemblages. *Annals of the Association of American Geographers, 105*(3), 604–619.

Dittmer, J. (2016). Theorizing a more-than-human diplomacy: Assembling the British Foreign Office, 1839–1874. *The Hague Journal of Diplomacy, 11*(1), 78–104.

Flood, C. and Grindon, G. (2014). *Disobedient objects.* London: Harry N Abrams.

Forsyth, I. (2017). A bear's biography: Hybrid warfare and the more-than-human battlespace. *Environment and Planning D: Society and Space, 35*(3), 495–512.

Gibbs, L. (2021). Agency in human–shark encounter. *Environment and Planning E: Nature and Space, 4*(2), 645–666.

Hobson, K. (2007). Political animals? On animals as subjects in an enlarged political geography. *Political Geography, 26*(3), 250–267.

Hughes, S. M. and Forman, P. (2017). A material politics of citizenship: The potential of circulating materials from UK Immigration Removal Centres. *Citizenship Studies, 21*(6), 675–692.

Ingram, A. (2009). The geopolitics of disease. *Geography Compass, 3*(6), 2084–2097.

Jackman, A. (2021). Visualizations of the small military drone: Normalization through 'naturalization'. *Critical Military Studies, 8*(4), 339–364.

Johnson, E. R. (2015). Of lobsters, laboratories, and war: Animal studies and the temporality of more-than-human encounters. *Environment and Planning D: Society and Space, 33*(2), 296–313.

Johnson, E. R. and Goldstein, J. (2015). Biomimetic futures: Life, death, and the enclosure of a more-than-human intellect. *Annals of the Association of American Geographers, 105*(2), 387–396.

Kosek, J. (2010). Ecologies of empire: On the new uses of the honeybee. *Cultural Anthropology, 25*(4), 650–678.

Lehman, J. S. (2013). Relating to the sea: Enlivening the ocean as an actor in Eastern Sri Lanka. *Environment and Planning D: Society and Space, 31*(3), 485–501.

Massaro, V. A. and Williams, J. (2013). Feminist geopolitics. *Geography Compass, 7*(8), 567–577.

Meehan, K., Shaw, I. G. R. and Marston, S. A. (2013). Political geographies of the object. *Political Geography, 33*, 1–10.

Miller, J. C., Prieto, M. and Vila, X. M. A. (2021). The geopolitics of presence and absence at the ruins of Fort Henry. *Environment and Planning D: Society and Space, 39*(1), 139–157.

Müller, M. (2015). Assemblages and actor-networks: Rethinking socio-material power, politics and space. *Geography Compass, 9*(1), 27–41.

Mwangi, W. (2002). The lion, the native and the coffee plant: Political imagery and the ambiguous art of currency design in colonial Kenya. *Geopolitics, 7*(1), 31–62.

Nassar, A. (2018). Where the dust settles: Fieldwork, subjectivity and materiality in Cairo. *Contemporary Social Science, 13*(3–4), 412–428.

Raento, P. (2006). Communicating geopolitics through postage stamps: The case of Finland. *Geopolitics, 11*(4), 601–629.

Raento, P. (2016). A geopolitics of the horse in Finland. *Geopolitics, 21*(4), 945–968.

Rech, M. (2020). Ephemera(l) geopolitics: The material cultures of British military recruitment. *Geopolitics, 25*(5), 1075–1098.

Routledge, P. (2008). Acting in the network: ANT and the politics of generating associations. *Environment and Planning D: Society and Space, 26*(2), 199–217.

Squire, V. (2015). Reshaping critical geopolitics? The materialist challenge. *Review of International Studies, 41*(1), 139–159.

Squire, R. (2016). Rock, water, air and fire: Foregrounding the elements in the Gibraltar–Spain dispute. *Environment and Planning D: Society and Space, 34*(3), 545–563.

Squire, R. (2020). Companions, zappers, and invaders: The animal geopolitics of Sealab I, II, and III (1964–1969). *Political Geography, 82*, 102224.

Srinivasan, K. (2016). Towards a political animal geography? *Political Geography, 50*, 76–78.

Sundberg, J. (2011). Diabolic Caminos in the desert and cat fights on the Rio: A posthumanist political ecology of boundary enforcement in the United States–Mexico borderlands. *Annals of the Association of American Geographers, 101*(2), 318–336.

Sundberg, J. (2014). Decolonizing posthumanist geographies. *Cultural Geographies, 21*(1), 33–47.

Theriault, N. (2017). A forest of dreams: Ontological multiplicity and the fantasies of environmental government in the Philippines. *Political Geography, 58*, 114–127.

Ver Beek, K. A. (2000). Spirituality: A development taboo. *Development in Practice, 10*(1), 31–43.

Whatmore, S. (2002). *Hybrid geographies: Natures cultures spaces.* London: Sage.

Whatmore, S. (2006). Materialist returns: Practising cultural geography in and for a more-than-human world. *Cultural Geographies, 13*(4), 600–609.

Williams, A. J. (2011). Enabling persistent presence? Performing the embodied geopolitics of the unmanned aerial vehicle assemblage. *Political Geography, 30*(7), 381–390.

Wolch, J. R. and Emel, J. (eds) (1998). *Animal geographies: Place, politics, and identity in the nature-culture borderlands.* London: Verso.

Yuen, S. (2015). Hong Kong after the Umbrella Movement. An uncertain future for 'One Country Two Systems'. *China Perspectives, 1*, 49–53.

SIX

POPULAR GEOPOLITICS: SHAPING GEOPOLITICAL IMAGINATIONS

Chapter Overview

We are constantly bombarded by geopolitical themes, ideas, and concepts through popular culture. Films, games, toys, music and other sources of entertainment are vital in shaping our understandings of the world around us and are formative in the construction of geopolitical imaginations both at an everyday and elite level. Drawing on diverse examples, this chapter explores the significance of play, films, music and other forms of popular culture in political geography, before charting future directions for popular geopolitics.

Learning Objectives

1. To explore what popular geopolitics is and why it matters.
2. To understand how different popular outputs shape geopolitical events and understandings of them.
3. To understand the role of mediums including film, games, play, and music in challenging dominant geopolitical narratives.

Read with: Chapter 2 (Situating Political Geography), Chapter 3 (Feminist Geopolitics), Chapter 13 (Surveillance)

Whether we are conscious of it or not, popular culture makes and shapes us. It is woven into the fabric of everyday life, providing a backdrop to evenings in front of the television at home, and taking centre stage as new releases hit cinemas and games consoles alike. Streaming services like Netflix and Amazon Prime have only intensified this relationship, whilst smartphones connect their owners to worlds of popular culture like never before. The films and TV we watch, the music we listen to, the games we play, the toys we play(ed) with are all important geopolitical artefacts. They matter because they are representations and lively objects that actively shape the world around us and, crucially, our perceptions of that world. They might, for example, work to cement ideas of things like 'good' and 'evil', 'friend' and 'enemy', move people to action after seeing visions of a world devasted by climate change, or inspire someone to enlist in the military. For Dittmer and Bos (2019: 25), it is 'through popular culture (at least in part) that we decide who we are, who we want to be, and how we want people to understand us'. The study of popular culture is thus extremely important and inextricably linked to geopolitics and the formation of the geopolitical imagination. This chapter unpacks this relationship. It charts how contemporary popular geopolitics was established, provides examples of how we can engage critically with the 'popular' world around us, and thinks through future directions of this important subfield.

KEY TERMS: GEOPOLITICAL IMAGINATION

Geopolitical imaginations are the results of people's attempts to make sense of the world (Dodds 2008a: 447). It refers to how people form their understandings of the geopolitical and how this then shapes their interactions with the world. Popular culture is key in the formation of the geopolitical imagination.

What is Popular Geopolitics?

As explored in Chapter 2, critical geopolitics was a key turning point in the discipline in the 1990s. It paved the way for political geographers to critically examine and engage with geopolitical texts produced by geopolitical elites and statesmen. Jo Sharp (1993), however, highlighted that this approach could only ever provide a partial understanding of geopolitical worlds. Geopolitics, as Sharp writes (1993: 493), does not simply 'trickle down' from elite contexts into everyday lives. Whilst providing important insights, interpreting elite texts cannot account for the interpretations of everyday people. A president, prime-minister, or world leader might, for example, deliver a speech responding to a key global event. Political geographers can critically engage with that speech, but this analysis will not tell us much about how it impacts people's opinions, behaviours, and perspectives. Sharp argued that political geographers should be more attentive to how elite texts are experienced in the 'real' world, and that more attention should be paid to popular sources of geopolitical information – such as educational sources and the popular media. Whilst such sources might have been deemed trivial in early geopolitical thought, Sharp argued that they remain central to the construction of the geopolitical imagination.

Sharp's (1993) foundational study of the magazine *Reader's Digest* is a useful starting point here. Sharp's analysis explores the Cold War period from 1980–1990 when the

USA and the Soviet Union were locked in ideological competition. Within this context, Sharp found that the articles in the magazine were not geopolitically innocent. On the contrary, they were 'written in such a way that they perpetuate a particular discourse of "America"' (Sharp 1993: 496). For example, the magazine created binary discourses about the USA and the USSR. The USSR was framed as being totalitarian, degenerative, and overly aggressive. The USA was framed as the progressive, rational, forward-thinking opposite, seeking liberty, freedom, and democracy. The USA became the 'good' to the 'evil' Soviet other, premised on democracy and freedom. The USSR, writes Sharp (1993: 496), became a 'negative space in which the *Reader's Digest* projects all those values which are antithetical to its own ("American") values'. Within this system of understanding, the US is framed as 'right' and the USSR, by implication, as 'wrong' – they are polar opposites and one cannot sympathise with the values of the USSR whilst maintaining 'American' ideals. Designed as a magazine for mass consumption disseminating knowledge of the world, the *Digest* makes and shapes perceptions of America and the USSR in the popular imagination. For Sharp (1993: 491), this alone makes popular sources, such as the *Digest* and media more broadly, worthy of interrogation for political geographers.

KEY TERMS: POPULAR GEOPOLITICS

This approach explores how geopolitical discourses 'saturate' popular cultures and the 'everyday'. It is concerned with how these cultures shape how we see the world, other people, and how we contextualise ourselves in the world around us (Dittmer and Bos 2019, Dittmer and Dodds 2008).

Following Sharp's (1993) work on the *Reader's Digest*, there has been significant effort to address the lack of understanding about how geopolitical discourses 'saturate popular culture' (Dittmer and Dodds 2008: 441). Indeed 'popular geopolitics' is now a substantial sub-field of political geography and formed an 'essential element' of the move toward critical geopolitics outlined in Chapter 2 (Dodds 2008a: 440). As Dodds (2008a: 443) notes, popular geopolitics became 'increasingly widespread' in the 1990s and continues to be an important component of the sub-discipline today.

Key thinkers including Klaus Dodds and Jason Dittmer were pivotal in this develop-ment, making connections between popular culture and questions of power, and how geopolitical phenomena like war, diplomacy, and nationalism are consumed in 'our liv-ing rooms, shopping malls, movie theatres, and on the internet' (Dittmer and Bos 2019: 191–192). This has subsequently expanded to include everything from comic books, to sporting activities, novels, memorial statues, museums, and toys.

Popular geopolitics has undoubtedly been an important means through which to interrogate the effect of popular culture on everyday life. For Dittmer and Bos (2019: xix), it is 'doubly' important because it not only explores how popular culture conveys information about places and geopolitical phenomena, but it is also consumed in various other contexts and sites. In other words, it can 'convey ideas about places from one place to another', and to people far removed from the sites being represented. As a result, audiences assign 'values to places' that they see, hear, or experience through popular culture, constructing 'hierarchies of people and places that matter and those that do not' in the process (Dittmer and Bos 2019: xix). Studying both the subject matters of popular culture and how they are experienced by audiences and viewers thus forms two of the central pillars of undertaking research in popular geopolitics.

Case Study: Travel Blogs (Henry 2021)

As Jacob Henry (2021) highlights, online environments warrant further attention in popular geopolitics. Indeed, platforms like social media, blogs, and forums are increasingly important in shaping how people understand space and place (see Chapter 13).

Henry explores this in more detail through the medium of the travel blog. While an under-analysed site of popular geopolitics, Henry argues that bloggers are key actors in representing and reshaping geopolitical narratives. After all, all travel narratives differentiate 'here from there' and are thus inherently geopolitical.

Drawing on the method of 'netography', Henry analyses the travel blogs of international volunteer teachers to explore experiences of the border in Namibia. He found that the blog provided insights into the everyday perspective on the geopolitics of mobility and borders. For example, the bloggers depicted a world 'in which borders yield to Whiteness allowing the travellers to experience unfettered movement, even as they present the wrong currencies and paperwork' (Henry 2021: 833). The privilege of the White Western traveller is revealed through the blogs, alongside the role of the blogger as a writer of geopolitical narratives through the details of their 'on the ground' experiences.

Films and Television

Films and television have been key mediums through which geographers have explored how geopolitics saturates everyday lives. For Power and Crampton (2005: 195), screened experiences work to 'reflect, reify, explain, author, support, undermine, and challenge hegemonic geopolitical discourse'. In other words, they can make the geopolitical intelligible to popular audiences, thus making them extremely important in the construction of the geopolitical imagination, identity, and understandings of 'place' in the world. As Carter and McCormack (2006: 236) note, part of the power of film comes in its ability to make us feel something. It affects us, prompting emotional and subconscious responses to the spaces, places, and power dynamics being screened in front of us. The relationship between the 'reel' and the 'real' is extremely powerful and worthy of deconstruction.

Within political geography, a range of interventions have sought to grapple with these complexities. Hollywood and Western productions have often been the subject of this intrigue. The geopolitics of James Bond (Dodds 2005), the feminist geopolitics of *Hunger Games* protagonist Katniss Everdeen (Kirby 2015), and the role of satire in the long-running television show *South Park* (Thorogood 2016) are just a few examples of how political geographers have engaged with a range of geopolitical ideas and themes through the mediums of films and television. Perhaps one of the most studied areas, however, has been the relationship between Hollywood and the War on Terror.

Film and the War on Terror

When two planes flew into the twin towers in 2001, millions tuned in to the news to watch in horror and confusion as the scenes unfolded on the streets of New York, USA. Whilst atrocities and acts of terror involving mass loss of life are all too common around the world, this was a first on American soil. As President George W. Bush cried 'War', publics in America and elsewhere struggled to make sense of what had taken place and the images they were seeing on the screen. Many analysts, commentators, and everyday people turned to Hollywood to provide a frame of reference, comparing their experiences to a variety of Hollywood films. As Power and Crampton (2005: 193) write, movies provided 'a language and imagery that commentators drew upon in making sense of the attacks and their geopolitical implications'. Disaster films proved a particularly powerful vector for this, displaying, as they do, scenes of peril and struggles for survival in the face of existential threat (see Carter and McCormack 2006).

In the wake of 9/11 and the War on Terror, however, Hollywood did much more than provide a frame of reference. As Dodds (2008a: 477) highlights, Hollywood has a long history of rallying 'around the flag in times of crises'. 9/11 was no exception to this. Shortly after the attacks on New York and Washington, the office of President Bush convened a series of meetings with Hollywood executives, screenwriters, and specialists in disaster movies to solicit the help of Hollywood in the War against Terror and to imagine responses to future disastrous scenarios (Power and Crampton 2005: 193). At this meeting, known as the Beverly Hills summit, leading Hollywood figures 'pledged their support and reaffirmed the significance' of the relationship between the media and the military. As Der Derian (2000) and others have noted, this relationship – often known as the Military–Industrial–Media–Entertainment complex or network (Der Derian 2000) – was not new. On the contrary there had been a longstanding relationship between Hollywood, government, and the military, particularly during the Cold War, and the connections 'between film, identity, geopolitics, and foreign policy' were already 'complex and varied' (Power and Crampton 2005: 198). Since the Second World War, 'Hollywood has had a long and profitable relationship with various government bodies' including the Central Intelligence Agency (CIA) and Department of Defense (Dodds 2008b: 232). Indeed, as Dodds (2008b: 232) asserts, classic films such as *Top Gun* (1986) and *Independence Day* (1996) would not have been made without the support of the US military, who approve scripts in exchange for equipment, expertise, and resources.

The catastrophic events of 9/11 prompted a reaffirmation of this relationship, stimulated new Hollywood productions, and generated an upswell of films riding the waves of US patriotism and interventionist policies. Key to these narratives were the ways in which films shored up the lines of 'them' and 'us', 'good' and 'evil', 'civilised' and 'barbaric' within society. For Power and Crampton (2005: 198) 'film represents a unique way' of arranging dramas and actors, providing visualisations and spatialisations of national boundaries, dangers to the 'homeland' and iterations of American identity. There are many examples of this emerging in the wake of 9/11 and the protracted War on Terror. Some, as might be expected, dealt explicitly with the events of that day (see *World Trade Centre* 2006, *United 95* 2005), others formed part of a new generation of 'warrior politics' engaging in US military exploits via courageous and virtuous protagonists (*Tears of the Sun* 2003), whilst a new generation of superhero films (e.g., *Iron Man* 2008) presented grand narratives of good triumphing over evil. The American hero, in many examples, is set in opposition to an 'evil' other, often taking the form of an Arab terrorist devoid of empathy and morality, and conflating Islam with Islamic fundamentalism (Dodds 2008b, Khatib 2006).

Case Study: *Black Hawk Down* (2001)

Ridley Scott's (2001) film *Black Hawk Down* is often cited as an important example when thinking about the intersections of film and geopolitics. The film engages with America's UN-backed intervention in Somalia in 1993. Whilst the intervention itself was widely seen as disastrous, the film constructs a narrative that, for many, rejuvenated 'American values of freedom and democracy that had been so badly damaged after 9/11', whilst also justifying American imperialism and the securing of American interests and ambitions overseas (Lisle and Pepper 2005: 166).

It was made prior to 9/11 and the Pentagon and Department of Defence were heavily involved in its production. Film makers used military hardware including planes, Black Hawk helicopters, and military personnel, which were key to both the filming itself and in advising producers on making it realistic. It sought to rehabilitate the intervention as 'success in the popular imagination' (Lisle and Pepper 2005: 171–172) and the timing of its release was crucial to this. It was brought forward from March 2002 to December 2001 to an audience still raw from the events three months earlier. It capitalised on 'renewed American patriotism' (Lisle and Pepper 2005: 172) with the themes of comradeship and brotherhood crucial in shaping how the film resonated with audiences in a post 9/11 world (Carter and McCormack 2006: 220). In contrast to a well-meaning and disciplined US military, local Somalis are framed as 'gun-toting', 'marauding savages' (Lisle and Pepper 2005: 174). Given the mood of the time, the reaction to the film was unsurprisingly positive.

This is not to say that there were not critical voices. In the years following 9/11, and as the effects of the War on Terror became increasingly apparent, productions emerged that engaged with the behaviour of the US on the international stage. Gavin Hood's *Rendition* (2007), for example, grappled with the practice of extraordinary rendition, where terrorism suspects are, quite literally at times, taken off the streets to be held in detention centres outside of the US without trial or legal representation. *Lions for Lambs* (Robert Redford, 2007) also sought to provide a critical narrative of events that had unfolded. Very few Hollywood films, however engaged with the perspectives of the victims of the War on Terror and the experiences of Iraqi and Afghan people. As Sharp (2011) and Falah et al. (2006) have argued, there remains a need within Western political geography to diversify the accounts of geopolitical events conveyed within popular culture and to undertake research on films, cinema, and other mediums that are created in the Middle East and Global South (see also Power and Crampton 2005).

Over to You: Building a Case Study

Choose a film or television programme. This could be something you're watching at the moment or something you've watched in the past. Aim to deconstruct it with a critical, geopolitical eye by responding to the questions below.

- Representational logics: What and who is being represented? Who are these representations aimed at? Who is framed as the 'other'?
- Structures of feeling: How does it make you feel? How does it want/ask you to feel?
- Intertextuality: How can this be read alongside other popular outputs and geopolitical contexts?
- Audiences: How and in what ways has the film or television programme been consumed? Forums and the IMDB database might be useful here. Has it received a critical reception anywhere?
- How else might we critically deconstruct such examples?
- How might this process change the way you engage with films and other media moving forward?

Music

Broadly speaking, political geographers have been slower to engage with music in a sustained and critical way (Dell'Agnese 2015: 171, Kirby 2019). As Dell'Agnese (2015: 172) highlights, this is incongruent with the centrality of music in geopolitics at multiple scales. We might, for example, think of the ways that national anthems, hymns, or even a musical instrument become associated with national identity and state building. On the other hand, popular music can be a vehicle for dissent, protest, and an entry point for publics to engage with geopolitical moods, events, and phenomena. We could turn to any number of examples here. Kirby (2019), for example, draws on instrumental film music to explore how it enforces or challenges geopolitical ideals. Romantic scores, for example, reinforce gender norms whilst more bombastic scoring is often used to celebrate Western national identities (Kirby 2019: 1). We could, as Dell'Agnese (2015: 172) writes, explore how hip hop works as a 'vehicle for a social geography of discomfort' and as a practice of resistance, or as Garvis (2020: 3) highlights, how music gave 'people hope and confidence in their collective struggle' during the 2011 Egyptian revolution. In popular culture we could also turn to overtly geopolitical examples such as Childish Gambino's 'This is America'. The lyrics, combined with the music, make powerful statements about being Black in America, with dominant themes of race, guns, and violence punctuating the accompanying video. For Johnson (2018), 'This is America' is about the terror, violence and injustice that the Black 'body gets exposed to'. The song and video are examples of how marginalised peoples use every available platform 'to punch at America's conscience' (Johnson 2018).

Whilst geopolitics has traditionally been anchored 'in the visual', music 'remains one of the central popular activities of everyday life' (Garvis 2020: 1–2). It has a key role to play in the 'making of place and identity' and should, as Dell'Agnese (2017: 172) argues, be considered a 'powerful vehicle of geopolitical discourse'. It has also been more successful than other branches of popular geopolitics in diversifying the subject matters of geopolitics. Whilst Hollywood has dominated the popular geopolitics of film, work within music accounts for a much more heterogenous range of voices, experiences, and narratives. The following sections engage with this in a number of ways, beginning with resistance.

Resistance

Whilst geopolitics may have been slower to engage with music, early work by Gibson (1998) demonstrates how powerful it is as a medium in challenging the status quo. In his work, Gibson (1998: 164–165) explores the role of Aboriginal music in Australia in providing a 'platform for the expression of localised voices' that would otherwise remain marginal. Whilst an atmosphere of 'tension and struggle pervades' Indigenous affairs at the national political level, popular music provides an important medium through which to voice key political issues and spotlight the marginalisation and discrimination experienced by Aboriginal people. For Gibson (1998: 165) music is key in promoting acceptance for 'strategies for self-determination' and an 'amplifier of localised indigenous narratives'. In a highly discriminatory environment music becomes 'a crucial public sphere of geopolitical change' (Gibson 1998: 165). Beyond the content of the music itself, Indigenous musicians have acted as mediators and ambassadors for Aboriginal communities, whilst 'new spaces of self-determination' are forged through the networks of events, venues, recording complexes, and a range of other sites and spaces involved in the production and consumption of the music. The Barunga Festival (see Figure 6.1) is a prime example of this. The Festival has become a permanent fixture on the Australian music calendar and is held at the 'Aboriginal community of Barunga' in the Northern Territory (Gibson 1998: 171). For Gibson (1998: 172), the Barunga community have 'rewritten some of its colonial history through popular music', creating spaces of empowerment, resistance, and revitalisation.

Figure 6.1 Barunga Festival

Credit: Peter Hall42 (Creative Commons Attribution-Share Alike 4.0 International license)
https://commons.wikimedia.org/wiki/File:Barunga_Festival.jpg

In a very different spatial and geopolitical context, Dell'Agnese (2015) explores the geopolitics of the US–Mexico border through a Mexican form of song known as the 'corrido' – a 'kind of ballad' with a poetic form that is known for being political in nature. As Dell'Agnese (2015) highlights, they have a long history of exploring 'defiance and oppression at the border' with the theme of conflict between the US and Mexico looming large. Whilst we might often think of contemporary struggles and violence at this border, Dell'Agnese (2015: 178) demonstrates how corridos have 'long played an important role in the making of migrant memory and identity'. At the end of the nineteenth century, for example, they were already being performed by immigrants who had crossed from Mexico to the USA with meanings that conveyed a sense of rebellion against US laws, alongside exploring themes of belonging. For Dell'Agnese (2015: 178) they became 'one of the most important music genres for the expression of interethnic conflict and resistance'. They are so powerful that in 2009, the US border patrol sought to co-opt the corrido in an anti-immigration campaign, 'No más cruces en la frontera' ('No more crosses on the border'). Songs encouraging migrants to stay at home were produced with themes of 'desperation and death' punctuating airwaves. Indeed, they were aired on local radio stations without a disclaimer that they had been paid for by the Homeland Security Agency (Dell'Agnese 2015: 184). In many ways, corridos emerge as a form of 'boundary music' (Dell'Agnese 2015: 179) that engages with contestation, identity, movement, and belonging at the border. The border is in many ways produced through sound here, creating a '(music)-scape ... that stands for all the walls, barbed wire, and undocumented immigrants of the world' (Dell'Agnese 2015: 185).

In another example, we can draw on Cordelia Freeman's (2020) work to think through the significance of the music video in diversification and challenging hegemonic norms. As she highlights, music videos have often been a highly problematic arena where hegemonic gender and sexuality tropes are propagated. This often involves the sexualisation of women's bodies and the representation of heterosexual relationships as the 'norm'. However, as Freeman (2020: 1007) explores, music videos have been an important medium through which to normalise LGBTQ+ desires. The increasing number of 'out LGBTQ musicians and music video directors' has been a key driver of this and instrumental in shifting 'who is in control of the music video gaze'. The US-based Japanese–American musician Hayley Kiyoko is one example of an LGBTQ performer and director who generated a 'queer gaze' through her music videos. She is a champion of the LGBTQ+ community and also seeks to increase the visibility of women of colour in the industry. Such work is particularly important in an industry where lesbian sexuality has 'often been used to pander to the heterosexual male spectator' (Freeman 2020: 1008). The medium of the online video is key to this, providing a much needed platform and space of production and consumption for more diverse representations in an otherwise 'overly White mainstream LGBTQ music culture' (Freeman 2020: 1009). The online environment demonstrates how new geopolitical imaginations can be forged in digital space and highlights the need for further research into the geopolitics of the 'digital worlds in which many of us now live' (Woods 2021: 475, see Chapter 13).

Case Study: Music Materialities (Hughes and Foreman 2017)

While digital platforms have undoubtedly transformed the geopolitical agency of music, it is important not to disregard the materiality of music too. Hughes and Foreman (2017) explore the significance of materiality in the context of the charity Music in Detention (now known as Hear Me Out). As they explore, there are extremely strict rules governing what is allowed in and out of immigration detention centres in the UK. This might be to prevent news of 'human rights abuses from circulating beyond' detention centre walls or to prevent the release of information that might show detainees are too comfortable or having 'too good a time', thus enabling sensationalist headlines about how taxpayers' money is being 'inappropriately spent'. It is thus very difficult to know the space of the detention centre, as it is designed to be obscured. However, there is also a rule that states that 'All detained persons shall be provided with an opportunity to participate in activities to meet, as far as possible, their recreational and intellectual needs and the relief of boredom'.

Music is a key part of this and Hear Me Out seeks to empower and enable detainees to share their experiences via the medium of music. The instruments themselves (including drums, guitars, and keyboards) alongside production technology are key to this process as they can transcend the borders of the detention centre. At the same time, these material objects enable the experiences of those inside to escape confinement via online recordings or CDs distributed by the charity.

Playing the Political: Toys and Video Games

Practices of play and ludic geopolitics have become increasingly important to understandings of popular geopolitics. This might be in the form of boardgames, or the way that both children and adults interact with everything from Lego to action figures. Carter and Woodyer (2020) have been at the forefront of work calling for play to be understood as a form of popular geopolitics, arguing that the 'pallet of objects and interactions we might associate with popular culture' needs to be expanded to capture the multifaceted and nuanced ways that the popular and the geopolitical intersect in everyday contexts. For Carter and Woodyer (2020), play is a key means through which the geopolitical is domesticated and a medium through which people form their understandings of geopolitical worlds (see also Ambrosio and Ross 2021 on boardgames). The dynamic and often messy process of playing with toys and games within the home has been overlooked within popular geopolitics – something that is important to address if we are to better understand moments and networks of encounter between objects, bodies, embodied practices, and geopolitics.

KEY TERMS: LUDIC GEOPOLITICS

A form of popular geopolitics that explores the circulation of geopolitical power through play, toys, and the agency of children (and adults) as consumers and users.

Where we locate the 'popular' in popular geopolitics is a key question here and one which Woodyer and Carter (2020) engage with in their work exploring the Her Majesty's Armed Forces (HMAF) toy range. Launched in 2009 amidst the wars in Iraq and Afghanistan, the toys were a collaborative endeavour by the toy producer Character Options and the UK Ministry of Defence who directly licensed the products. They feature military-themed action figures, costumes, and weapon accessories, with details modelled on the uniforms and equipment used by serving British troops. For Woodyer and Carter (2020: 1051) the toys could be seen as an attempt to tie into a national mood of 're-enchantment with the Armed Forces', and a medium through which the wars in Afghanistan and Iraq were brought into everyday domestic play spaces in UK homes. We might also think of the ongoing gendering of toys as a prime example of how play is inherently geopolitical.

Video Games

One of the biggest areas of research into play and popular geopolitics is that of video games. Bringing geopolitical themes, concepts and ideas into living rooms all over the world, video games are an important medium through which to understand how everyday people form their geopolitical imaginations and understandings of the world. War games have proved to be of particular interest to political geographers, representing as they do military interventions, far-away places, and the workings of war. At times, these links between the military and the popular are particularly overt. The game America's Army, for example, is developed, designed, produced and circulated by the US Army for the purposes of military training and recruitment (Bos 2018: 56). It's available freely online as a first-player shooter game. In addition to the gameplay itself, real soldiers and players 'discuss tactical and technical issues' in a large online community that only cements the 'realism' of the game (Salter 2011: 368). For Salter (2011: 368), other games like Call of Duty provide a critical entry point for exploring how geopolitical 'identities, scripts, and narratives are constructed'. This could be through the valorisation of militaristic interventions that 'elide historical contexts and ethical dilemmas', or the sanitisation and gamification of warfare environments (Salter, 2011: 368). Here, the gameplay represents a very particular geopolitical context – one premised on a Western, masculine frame of violence that dehumanises and 'others' the enemy. Within this context, Western bodies simply respawn when killed, whilst 'target' bodies disappear. Fictional landscapes in the Middle East and Central Asia often provide the backdrop to these interventions with the enemy presented as fearful, violent, and barbaric. As Salter (2011: 371) writes, the 'moral cartography of these games is entirely ego-centric' in that the self, often represented by the West, is in the right while the 'other' enemy is always 'worthy of extermination'. For these reasons, and many more, military-themed video games have become an 'important everyday cultural artefact that shape popular understandings of geopolitics' and which are 'reflective of contemporary cultures of militarism' (Bos 2018: 54).

Beyond Western military narratives, there are examples of games and work seeking to offer more accountable perspectives on war. This War of Mine (TWoM) is a single player war survival game. Released by 11 bit Studios in 2014, the game is played from a civilian perspective. Rather than a first-person shooter, TWoM makes 'survivors' of war the protagonists in their narrative. The player must keep a mixed group of survivors alive amidst civil war by scavenging resources, ensuring safety, and maintaining physical and mental health (de Smale et al. 2017: 388). This becomes increasingly difficult as the game progresses – resources become more scarce, children must be cared for, altruism costs player time and resources; conflicting moral choices emerge, and, unlike many other games, there are no instructions to follow. The player must muddle through with no guide, the aim being to represent the disorientation of wartime for civilians as closely as possible. This includes both permanent death (no respawn) to simulate the precariousness of life in war and the profound challenges of famine, sickness, and suffering, alongside the boredom that can also characterise civilian experience. The game is designed to introduce moral questions to war contexts and to counter the narratives presented in games like Call of Duty (see Figure 6.2) which de-humanise war and 'selectively filter the reality of conflict' (de Smale et al. 2017: 388).

In the examples above, video games are read as texts – as artefacts and representations to be critically examined. Moving beyond this, Bos (2021: 97) calls for further work on how video games exceed representation. This might be through events like launch nights that see cities re-imagined in the launching of games like Call of Duty with green, militaristic lighting and men dressed as soldiers patrolling venues (Bos 2021). We might

Figure 6.2 Call of Duty XP 2011 – Modern Warfare 3 Gauntlet

Credit: Creative Commons Attribution 2.0 Generic license (The Conmunity - Pop Culture Geek) https://commons.wikimedia.org/wiki/File:Call_of_Duty_XP_2011_-_Modern_Warfare_3_Gauntlet_(6113477795).jpg

also research the embodied encounters (see Chapter 3) that emerge in gaming contexts whether in the home or at big events, through competitions where players play against one another, through the increasingly large audiences who watch others play on mediums like Twitch, or through adverts we pass by in spaces like underground train stations.

There is also a need to explore games that are not centred on the state and military. As Mukherjee (2018: 504) states, the postcolonial and decolonial have 'remained on the margins of game studies' and there is a significant lack of engagement within popular geopolitics on games produced and consumed in the Global South. Moreover, non-war games like Animal Crossings: New Horizons, whilst not dealing with warfare and violence, can certainly be read through a geopolitical lens. Within the context of the global Covid-19 pandemic, Animal Crossing surged in popularity. It was seen to provide a 'dreamland' to escape to amidst 'cruel reality' (Zhu 2021), and to construct new, better, worlds and realties. The online cooperative element of the game enabled players from all over the world to connect, crossing borders and circumventing the isolation and physical distance brought about by the pandemic (Lewis et al. 2021). Indeed, the game was removed from some websites in China after Hong Kong activists used their online world to 'create politically sensitive images and slogans' which they then screenshotted and shared on social media (Davidson 2020). Games that cross social barriers, borders, and divides both feed into and offer great potential in understanding how people come to understand the world around them and formulate their geopolitical imagination.

In the Field with Dan Bos: Video Games

Dr Daniel Bos is a senior lecturer in human geography at the University of Chester. His research explores the relationship between geopolitics and popular culture.

What drew you to research video games?

Unsurprisingly my interest in video games stemmed from playing military-themed video games. Despite not being very good at them, I became particularly interested in the shift in storylines, from more historical to contemporary conflicts, and how this shift was reflective of current geopolitical events, namely the 'War on Terror'. At this time, and during my Geography undergraduate degree, I was introduced to military geography (Professor Rachel Woodward) and critical and popular geopolitics (Professor Nick Megoran). Both were hugely influential, especially when discussing the role of the media and popular culture in shaping public perceptions of geopolitics and militarism. However, this scholarship was very much in its early stages. Noticeably there had been limited interest in military-themed video games, despite their mass popularity. Furthermore, such research often overlooked how audiences consumed and made sense of popular geopolitical texts and objects.

What are the key challenges in your research?

Where to begin! Videogames are complex media forms to analyse. The nature of video games requires multiple play-throughs and calls into question the researcher's positionality as their interaction with the video game worlds ultimately shapes the popular geopolitical analysis being made. One of the key challenges I faced with this research was exploring the experiential aspects of play. A 'more-than-representational' geopolitical analysis pushed me to think creatively and innovatively, especially when attempting to capture and understand the geopolitical implications of the affective encounters of playing virtual war. I spent a lot of time experimenting with different techniques and technologies, eventually using video ethnography to document play *in situ*. This presented rich insights into the embodied nature of play and allowed me to consider the role of the domestic setting in which popular geopolitical consumption regularly occurs. Researching popular geopolitics can be messy, intensive, and unpredictable, but thinking through some of these challenges is part of the fun!

Are there areas of popular geopolitics you think need further research?

Various popular cultural texts, representations, objects, and performances await popular geopolitical analysis. In particular, social media offers an interesting case study, especially concerning its participatory and interactive nature and its continuing influence on emerging geopolitical events and issues. This area certainly poses interesting theoretical and methodological questions that can enrich the field.

(Continued)

There is also a need to expand the geographical focus of popular geopolitics and move beyond Anglo-American case studies to understand better the varied cultural contexts in which popular geopolitical consumption happens. Finally, whilst there is undoubtedly further scope for more audience and reception-based studies, there is also a need for insights into the processes and practices that go into the production of popular geopolitical texts. What is clear is that there are many possible avenues to take the study of popular geopolitics forward, making it a fascinating area of political geography to research and study!

Over to You: Decentring the State and Military

Literature within popular geopolitics on video games tends to focus on the state, violence, and war. As outlined above, there are other ways to read and play geopolitics through this medium. Using climate change as a case study, do some research about the types of video game experiences that engage with this issue in a playful or everyday way:

1. How does your example use play to engage with climate change?
2. Is it overtly political, or more subtle? What are the effects of this?
3. How does it further your understanding about popular culture and its intersections with geopolitics?

Conclusions: Future Directions

This chapter provided a small snapshot into some of the ways we can begin to understand popular geopolitics – whether that be through films and television, music, or play and video games. This is only really the beginning. The remit of the 'popular' is as broad as the mediums people engage with. It might also include news outlets, comic books, novels, virtual reality, social media, memes – the list is endless but similar logics course through each. Each helps us to understand how we place ourselves in the world, how we form understandings of the 'other' and create distinctions between safety and danger. It provides a lens through which to understand the geopolitical imagination and to critically deconstruct manifestations of the geopolitical in the everyday that otherwise might go by unnoticed, assumed to be a passive backdrop or soundtrack to our lives. Popular geopolitics is lively, expansive, and vitally important in understanding how the popular influences the political and vice versa.

And yet despite the wealth of literature that has emerged in this field, there are a number of areas in need of further research. Firstly, there is a clear need to diversify the subjects of popular geopolitics. As Dittmer and Dodds highlight (2008: 54), the sources of popular geopolitics have been concentrated on those 'produced and consumed in Europe and

North America'. Whilst this is changing with an increasing focus on contexts beyond the West, there is still much work to be done in decolonising popular geopolitics. Moreover, whilst there has been some work exploring queer popular geopolitics, there is certainly scope for more on the popular geopolitics of LGBTQ+ communities. Even less research has been undertaken on the intersectional issues cross-cutting these two underdeveloped areas. Popular geopolitics thus remains an area ripe for further research and exploration.

Summary

- We all engage with popular culture in one way or another. This chapter explored *why* this matters geopolitically, arguing that popular sources actively shape our geopolitical imaginations.
- Popular geopolitics is a way of analysing the intersections between the popular and political. A key pillar of critical geopolitics, it has continued to flourish as a field within political geography.
- Key focuses of this work have included film and television, music, play, and video games.
- There is work to do in diversifying these accounts and in recognising the variety of outputs and mediums that might be considered under the umbrella of popular geopolitics.

Follow-on Resources

Hear Me Out music: This charity 'takes music-making into UK immigration detention centres' to enable people to tell their stories, and for people to hear them. They are committed to changing attitudes to migrants. See https://hearmeoutmusic.org.uk/

Ludic geopolitics: Led by Tara Woodyer, this blog contains a range of excellent blog posts exploring the intersections between toys, play, and war. See https://ludicgeopolitics. wordpress.com

The Karrabing Film Collective: This is a grass roots Indigenous organisation that uses filmmaking as a 'means of self-organisation and social analysis'. Part of their work is engaging audiences in different forms of 'collective Indigenous agency'. See https:// karrabing.info/karrabing-film-collective

References

Ambrosio, T. and Ross, J. (2021). Performing the Cold War through the 'best board game on the planet': The ludic geopolitics of Twilight Struggle. *Geopolitics*, *28*(2), 846–878.

Bos, D. (2018). Answering the Call of Duty: Everyday encounters with the popular geopolitics of military-themed videogames, *Political Geography*, *63*, 54–64.

Bos, D. (2021). Popular geopolitics 'beyond the screen': Bringing Modern Warfare to the city. *Environment and Planning C: Politics and Space, 39*(1), 94–113.

Carter, S. and McCormack, D. P. (2006). Film, geopolitics and the affective logics of intervention. *Political Geography, 25*(2), 228–245.

Carter, S. and Woodyer, T. (2020). Introduction: Domesticating geopolitics, *Geopolitics, 25*(5), 1045–1049.

Davidson, H. (2020). Animal Crossing game removed from sale in China over Hong Kong democracy message. *The Guardian*, 14 December. Available at: www.theguardian.com/world/2020/apr/14/animal-crossing-game-removed-from-sale-in-china-over-hong-kong-democracy-messages (accessed 18 May 2023).

De Smale, S., Kors, M. J. and Sandovar, A. M. (2017). The case of This War of Mine: A production studies perspective on moral game design. *Games and Culture, 14*(4), 387–409.

Dell'Agnese, E. (2015). 'Welcome to Tijuana': Popular music on the US–Mexico border. *Geopolitics, 20*(1), 171–192.

Der Derian, J. (2000). Virtuous war/virtual theory. *International Affairs, 76*(4), 771–788.

Dittmer, J. and Bos, D. (2019). *Popular culture, geopolitics, and identity*. London: Rowman & Littlefield.

Dittmer, J. and Dodds, K. (2008). Popular geopolitics past and future: Fandom, identities and audiences. *Geopolitics, 13*(3), 437–457.

Dodds, K. (2005). Screening geopolitics: James Bond and the early Cold War films (1962–1967). *Geopolitics, 10*(2), 266–289.

Dodds, K. (2008a). 'Have you seen any good films lately?' Geopolitics, film and international relations. *Geography Compass, 2(2)*, 476–494.

Dodds, K. (2008b). Screening terror: Hollywood, the United States and the construction of danger. *Critical Studies on Terrorism, 1*(2), 227–243.

Falah, G. W., Flint, C. and Mamadouh, V. (2006). Just war and extraterritoriality: The popular geopolitics of the United States' war on Iraq as reflected in newspapers of the Arab world. *Annals of the Association of American Geographers, 96*(1), 142–164.

Freeman, C. (2020). Filming female desire: Queering the gaze of pop music videos. *Cultural Studies, 34*(6), 1007–1032.

Garviş, A. (2020). Geopolitical music to the students' minds. *Journal of Geography in Higher Education, 46*(2), 204–221.

Gibson, C. (1998). 'We sing our home, We dance our land': Indigenous self-determination and contemporary geopolitics in Australian Popular Music. *Environment and Planning D: Society and Space, 16*(2), 163–184.

Henry, J. (2021). The geopolitics of travel blogging. *Geopolitics, 26*(3), 817–837.

Hughes, S. M. and Forman, P. (2017). A material politics of citizenship: The potential of circulating materials from UK Immigration Removal Centres. *Citizenship Studies, 21*(6), 675–692.

Johnson, T. (2018). Donald Glover's 'This is America' is a nightmare we can't afford to look away from. *Rolling Stone*, 8 May. Available at: www.rollingstone.com/music/music-news/donald-glovers-this-is-america-is-a-nightmare-we-cant-afford-to-look-away-from-630177/ (accessed 18 May 2023).

Khatib, L. (2006). *Filming the modern Middle East*. London: I. B. Tauris.

Kirby, P. (2015). The girl on fire: The Hunger Games, feminist geopolitics and the contemporary female action hero. *Geopolitics, 20*(2), 460–478.

Kirby, P. (2019). Sound and fury? Film score and the geopolitics of instrumental music. *Political Geography, 75*, 102054.

Lewis, J. E., Trojovsky, M. and Jameson, M. M. (2021). New social horizons: Anxiety, isolation, and Animal Crossing during the COVID-19 pandemic. *Frontiers in Virtual Reality, 2*, 14.

Lisle, D. and Pepper, A. (2005). The new face of global Hollywood: Black Hawk Down and the politics of meta-sovereignty. *Geopolitics, 20*(2), 460–478.

Mukherjee, S. (2018). Playing subaltern: Video games and postcolonialism. *Games and Culture, 13*(5), 504–520.

Power, M. and Crampton, A. (2005). Reel geopolitics: Cinemato-graphing political space. *Geopolitics, 10*(2), 193–203.

Salter, M. B. (2011). The geographical imaginations of video games: Diplomacy, civilization, America's Army and Grand Theft Auto IV. *Geopolitics, 16*(2), 359–388.

Sharp, J. P. (1993). Publishing American identity: Popular geopolitics, myth and The Reader's Digest. *Political Geography, 12*(6), 491–503.

Sharp, J. (2011). A subaltern critical geopolitics of the war on terror: Postcolonial security in Tanzania. *Geoforum, 42*(3), 297–305.

Thorogood, J. (2016). Satire and geopolitics: Vulgarity, ambiguity and the body grotesque in South Park. *Geopolitics, 21*(1), 215–235.

Woods, O. (2021). Clashing cyphers, contagious content: The digital geopolitics of grime. *Transactions of the Institute of British Geographers, 46*(2), 464–477.

Woodyer, T. and Carter, S. (2020). Domesticating the geopolitical: Rethinking popular geopolitics through play. *Geopolitics, 25*(5), 1050–1074.

Zhu, L. (2021). The psychology behind video games during COVID-19 pandemic: A case study of Animal Crossing: New Horizons. *Human Behavior and Emerging Technologies, 3*(1), 157–159.

SEVEN

STATES AND TERRITORY: HEIGHTS, DEPTHS, THINKING 'VOLUME'

Chapter Overview

The 'state' and 'territory' are two key concepts within political geography and are widely seen as the building blocks of the geopolitical world. This chapter takes each concept in turn, beginning with the state. From spectacular expressions of state power to the 'countless mundane social and material practices' through which the state is actualised (see Painter 2006), it explores the state as an evolving, lively construct rather than a static institution. It then turns to the concept of territory, tracing understandings of this phenomenon through to notions of 'volume'. Territory, like the state, is understood as an evolving and dynamic concept. The chapter concludes by thinking about future challenges to these constructs in relation to the Climate Emergency.

Learning Objectives

1. To understand the state as an evolving concept without a fixed definition.
2. To understand how thinking on territory has evolved from 'area' to 'volume'.
3. To think critically about scenarios that might challenge our understandings of both the state and territory.

Read with: Chapter 9 (Nationalism), Chapter 12 (Peace and Resistance), Chapter 8 (Borders)

The 'State'

The state is often taken for granted. Indeed, it's difficult to imagine the world map without states. Whilst many predicted the demise of the nation state in the wake of globalisation (see Ohmae 1995), the state has only become more important. Despite goods, commodities, technologies and (some) peoples crossing borders at a pace and scale never seen before, the 'death' of the nation state was declared 'prematurely' (Moisio and Paasi 2013: 257–258). As Painter and Jeffrey (2009: 21) assert, 'states remain the preeminent forms of political authority in the modern world.' Stricter and more violent border policies see the state asserting itself more powerfully than ever before, while the spread of Covid-19 and the ensuing global pandemic only saw the reassertion of state power over both borders and our everyday lives. No agencies, write Painter and Jeffrey (2009: 21), 'assert their power over us quite so insistently as the states in which we live'.

KEY TERMS: SOVEREIGNTY

This refers to the idea that states have sole authority to govern and that this authority will be recognised in the international state system. Sovereignty can be breached, with the invasion of Ukraine by Russia in 2022, and Iraq by the US in 2001 as prime examples. For McConnell (2016: 109), sovereignty is a 'principle invoked to defend national interests, justify violence and claim independence'.

Far from disappearing in the wake of globalisation, 'states across the world appear to have lost none of their appetite for enforcing their will over their own citizens, territories, and resources, and on occasion, over those of other states too' (Painter 2006: 752). Whilst writing in 2006, Painter's assertion remains as relevant as ever. As he goes on to write, 'spectacular expressions of state power are everywhere'. Beyond these overt and violent expressions, the power of the state over our lives is profound. Indeed, to imagine any other international system or regime would require a radical and revolutionary upheaval of the world as we know it. From an early age we're presented with maps like the image in Figure 7.1, that depict a colourful set of shapes that slot together to form a world of states. These representations offer a very neat view of the state, defined by clearly demarcated lines separating it from neighboring territories. Traditionally within political geography, these lines and neat boundaries have been important in defining the 'state'. The state, for many, was seen as a bounded entity and power container, whereby political authority, territory and population are collapsed into a 'single unproblematic actor: the sovereign state' (Biersteker and Weber 1996 in McConnell 2009a: 1907). It was also taken for granted within this framework that the 'power container' would have precisely demarcated boundaries, recognised internationally by other state actors and supranational organisations such as the United Nations, and that the state would spread its control to every corner of the territory and to every part of civil society (Moisio and Paasi 2013: 256). In other words, sovereignty would be absolute. As this section of the chapter will explore, the realities are much messier and more difficult to pin down.

Defining the State?

Recent scholarship within political geography has pushed far beyond ideas of the state as a neatly bounded power container in ways that make defining the state challenging.

STATES AND TERRITORY | 99

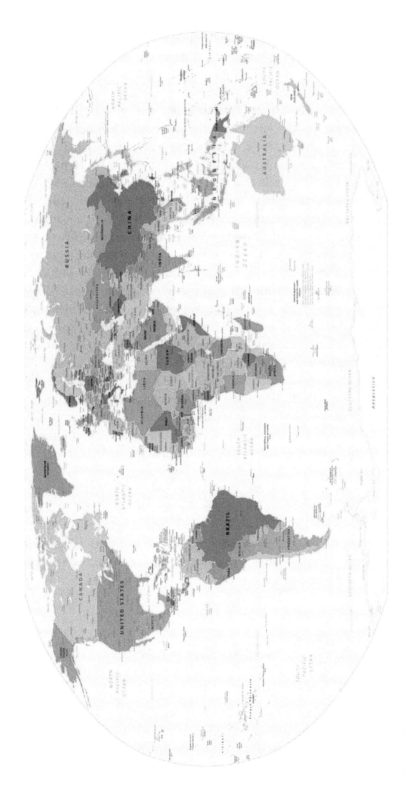

Figure 7.1 A simple political map of the world

Source: https://en.wikipedia.org/wiki/World_map#/media/File:World_Map_(political).svg

As Painter (2006: 755) argues, the concept of the state is 'notoriously slippery'. This does not mean that the state is an illusion or an abstract entity, but it can be helpful to think of the state as an amalgamation or assemblage of different components (see Chapter 5). For Desbiens et al. (2004: 242), 'the state is not a unitary object but is, rather, a set of practices enacted through relationships between people, places, and institutions'. In other words, it can be found at the intersection of a range of actors, practices, and networks that work together to form what we might recognise as the state. In this sense, the state does not have a 'universal essence' (Moisio and Paasi 2013: 255). Its meaning can morph and change depending on context as it is enacted across multiple scales. Thinking of the characteristics and practices of the state can be a productive way to grapple with these complexities. As an example, states gather, record, and store information on their citizens. This might include data gathering processes of the census, for example. It is worth noting here that 'state' and 'statistics' share the same linguistic root (Painter and Jeffrey 2009). For Björkdahl (2018: 37) thinking through the state as a set of characteristics and practices enables the attribution of agency to the actors we might traditionally associate with the state (e.g., political elites, government departments, state militaries), but also to material objects like maps and flags, to constructs like the border, to bus timetabling and the highway code that dictate how drivers behave on the road, to the language that is spoken within a given space, or the national curriculum in schools. 'Stateness' is thus performed by political elites 'as well as through mundane everyday practices' by those inhabiting that state (Björkdahl 2018: 37). It will also always have material geographies that keep the state in circulation among the public, whether that be coins and money, stamps marked with the state sovereign, or the presence of flags in buildings and at national events. All of these work to create a sense of inside/outside, demarcating the state within its boundaries as well as beyond.

Within this framework, the state is not all seeing and powerful (see Mountz 2003). On the contrary, control will never be total and this control is 'always and everywhere challenged' in different ways (Moisio and Pasaai 2013: 256, see Chapter 12). This might be through relatively banal acts like speeding, challenging the safety limits set by the law of the government, through the movement of both people and objects across borders that a government does not deem legal, or via mass protests on the streets. In understanding the state as a series of practices and performance, we can deconstruct it and think through what makes and unmakes the state (see Gallagher 2022).

Over to You

What makes a state?

Take a moment to consider the following questions. Repeat this at the end of the chapter and see if your answers have changed.

(Continued)

1. What makes a state? If you were the leader of an organisation seeking to become a state, what would you need? Think carefully here about the different things that 'make' the state you live in.
2. How has the state affected your day so far? Think carefully about your day up until this point. Make a list of all the ways the state has impacted your day. Again, think broadly and creatively. What does this list tell you about the role of the state in your life?

Everyday States

As was explored in Chapter 3, geopolitics is not just something that occurs at state or international levels. It is an everyday phenomenon, with the mundane, sometimes banal trappings of life being of geopolitical significance. The workings of the state are no exception. As Jones et al. (2004: 20) write, 'rather like the air we breathe, states are organisations that surround us as individuals, influencing, and in many ways, offering sustenance to the lives we lead'. The mundane and everyday, life sustaining contexts of the state are just as important as grand military expressions of power in understanding the making and remaking of the state in the world around us (Painter 2006). This is particularly important when recognising that the state is not something that exists outside of society. On the contrary 'everyday life is permeated by stateness in various guises' (Painter 2006: 753).

As McKinnon (2016: 285) powerfully highlights, this begins at birth. In the UK, more often than not, the birthing process is managed and facilitated by the National Health Service (NHS), a state-funded organisation. In the UK, once born, we are gendered and named, we are assigned a state identity, citizenship, and thus our wider place in the geopolitical world. Moreover, birth itself is not universally experienced. As a report by MBBRACE-UK (2021) highlighted, Black women in the UK are four times more likely, and Asian women twice as likely, to die in childbirth than White women. A range of factors contribute to this, such as the pain of Black women not being taken seriously. After a child is born, data will be collected as they work their way through life, from health to education participation. At school, the national curriculum is set by the Department of Education (see Benwell 2014 for an example from the Falklands Islands). It is in these contexts where we learn a curated and limited version of national history – of national victories and shared traumas. From major life events to minor illness, to the banal rhythms of everyday life, we are brought into contact with the state 'in ways that are so taken for granted they are barely noticeable' (Painter 2006: 753). Painter (2006: 753) illustrates this perfectly in his analysis of how the state impacts a drink at the pub:

the state decides when and where the pub can open, the possible sizes of our serving of beer, how much of its price goes in tax, whether our children can come to the pub with us, whether we can listen to live music while we drink and how our drinks are labelled.

It also sets the amount of alcohol someone can drink before they are no longer able to drive, dictating the journey away from the pub too. In abiding by these laws and regulations, we enact the state (see Mountz 2003), bringing it into being in everyday contexts. For Painter (2006: 755) such examples highlight just how imbricated the state is in our everyday lives. It also challenges the idea that the state is an abstract entity existing outside of society. On the contrary, it is carefully constructed and deconstructed in the world around us on multiple scales. In this sense, it is always in a state of process and becoming.

Complicating Ideas of the State

There are also phenomena and practices that stretch our understanding of the state even further. Ideas of what the state is, and importantly, what it *could* be are further complicated when we consider entities and people that seem to exist outside of the state system. These 'anomalous' phenomena offer an opportunity to re-think understandings of the state, and what statehood means to individual people and citizens.

The Tibetan Government-in-Exile (TGiE) is a case in point (see McConnell 2009a, 2009b, 2012). After China's People's Liberation Army (PLA) forcibly overran Tibet in 1950–1951, 80,000 Tibetans, including the Dalai Lama, sought refuge in India, Nepal, and Bhutan. In 1960, the Dalai Lama re-established the Tibetan Government in India where today the majority of exiled Tibetans reside (McConnell 2009b). The primary remit of this initiative was to restore freedom in Tibet and to help Tibetan refugees. Over the following years, this exiled community became increasingly organised and institutionalised, with the TGiE 'widely regarded as one of the most established' exiled structures 'in the world' (McConnell 2009b: 343). The TGiE employ a number of strategies to embody statehood without formal recognition. They are organised around democratic principles, with a legislature, executive, and seven government departments (McConnell 2012: 79). While Tibetan settlements distributed throughout India operate on Indian land under Indian law, the TGiE has authority within these areas, 'overseeing local government structures, and administering health and education institutions' (McConnell 2012: 79). As we have explored, the state is something that is practised and enacted and the TGiE do this in a number of other ways, including (see McConnell 2009b: 343):

- holding of democratic elections
- gathering census data and statistical analysis
- 'national' archives and buildings (see Figure 7.2)
- the provision of healthcare services
- a voluntary taxation system
- the issuing of Tibetan passport-like documents
- the establishment of quasi 'embassies' in a number of states

These are examples of the practice of stateness that are enacted by the TGiE. In other words, if the TGiE were ever to be internationally recognised as a state, it would have established processes, practices and materialities that would help it to function, and gain legitimacy.

Figure 7.2 Tibetan Parliament in Exile - Gangchen Kyishong - Himachal Pradesh - India

Credit: Adam Jones (Creative Commons Attribution-Share Alike 2.0 Generic license) https://commons.wikimedia.org/wiki/File:Tibetan_Parliament_in_Exile_-_Gangchen_Kyishong_-_Himachal_Pradesh_-_India_(26171749793).jpg

As McConnell (2009a) highlights, the TGiE is an important example of a version of statehood outside of the traditional system. They hold, for example, no jurisdiction over a given territory, operating instead from within a 'foreign' territory of other sovereign states, such as India (McConnell 2009a: 1906). They are not recognised on the international stage and yet command 'significant political authority' (McConnell 2009a: 1907). They function almost as a state-in-waiting, a 'population-in-training to govern in the homeland; and a population-as-cultural-repository, preserving Tibetan identity outside the home territory' (McConnell 2009b: 346). They thus fit very awkwardly into the system of states we are used to seeing represented on a world map, but in doing so, they offer a moment through which to consider how the state system might be different, how it might be imagined beyond the lines on a map, and how an organised population can lay claim to 'statehood' in different ways, even without a given territory. As McConnell (2009a: 1913) states, 'the continued existence of geopolitical anomalies' and the ambiguous status of both people and collective populations demonstrates how there is a need for a more open and diverse international 'state' system, and how the 'state' we so often take for granted is socially constructed through certain practices, imaginations, and technologies.

Territory

Hand-in-hand with the concept of the state is the concept and practice of territory. In traditional geopolitical thinking, territory is defined as the bounded, inert, area of land 'under the control of a group of people, usually a state' (Elden 2013: 322, see also Peters et al. 2018). The state claims sovereignty over territory and this forms the area over which power can be exerted. In this static definition, territory is concerned with ideas around power and space – both how space is controlled, contested, and claimed, and how it is mobilised as a practice connected with cartography and map making. As Elden (2010: 809) writes, historically cartography has not just been used to represent territory, 'but is actively complicit in its production'. States were key advocates of this approach, keen to bound, extend, and draw lines around the areas they sought to control. In Chapter 2 (Situating Political Geography), we saw the sheer power and violence of such thinking in the evolution of political geography, whereby colonial territories were imposed on Indigenous and Afro-descendant peoples (Halvorsen 2019: 796). Meanwhile in Figure 7.1 we see a modern day example of the power of cartography, the states and territories they control neatly coloured and naturalised in our geopolitical imaginations.

Recent scholarship, however, has challenged these ideas. Much like the evolution of thinking around the state, thinking on territory has also expanded. Far from being an inert, flat space as depicted in many maps, territory is now understood as a 'vibrant entity' and 'political technology' (Elden 2018: 810). In other words, it is fluid, enacted, and produced (Elden 2010: 812). For Huang (2022: 2), rather than seeing territory as a naturalised spatial category that we take for granted, territory might better be understood as 'the effects of an ensemble of heterogenous performances, practices, and technologies'. In other words, like the state, territory is something that is actively performed and enacted and does not naturally occur. In Huang's (2022: 2) words, 'making and maintaining a territory ... usually requires considerable, continuous, and repetitive inputs of labour, expertise, and resources'. This might be in the form of policing borders, developing narratives around territory in the national imaginary, and 'building legitimacy internationally' (Huang 2022: 2). In this sense, territory is always in process and is constituted at multiple scales – from the international to everyday.

Acknowledging that territory is always in process and that it is the result of dynamic processes and practices is important. As Elden (2013) and Halvorsen (2019) have highlighted, territory is a concept rooted in Western political thought and this has implications for how it is thought about and practised. Traditional thinking on territory ties it to ideas of top-down 'control and regulation of space by dominant forms related to the modern, colonial state' as understood in Western, and particularly, Anglophone contexts (Halvorsen 2019: 794). It is thus predicated on a knowledge system with its origins in colonial practice and thinking (see also Jackman et al. 2020). In understanding territory as a dynamic system that is enacted and performed, there are opportunities to deconstruct these logics and open 'territory' out to a wider range of actors, scales, contexts, and knowledge systems.

> **KEY TERMS: TERRITORY**
>
> Territory can be understood as 'the appropriation of space in pursuit of political projects' (Halvorsen 2019: 794).

This works on a number of levels. Firstly, in relation to the state, it sheds light on the many ways that the state might act to create territory. This is not necessarily always through 'hard power' tactics, such as a military invasion or border control measures. It might be through 'softer' strategies such as through tourism (see the Case study box below), or even through mundane and everyday representations that reinforce a state's territory. In the UK, weather reports on the television would be a prime example, with England, Wales, Scotland and Northern Ireland highlighted while Ireland is erased as it is not part of the UK territory. Such banal manifestations reinforce the idea (albeit perhaps subconsciously) of a bounded and defined space that 'makes' the UK.

Beyond this, however, Halvorsen's (2019: 794) definition also enables us to remove the spotlight on the state as the chief appropriator of space. In doing so, it leaves open the possibility to explore how territorial practices are resisted, protested, redefined and reimagined by a range of actors, including those involved in grassroots, 'bottom-up' struggles, and localised organisations and individuals seeking different ways of being and relating to space. The state might be the protagonist of territory but it is not the *only* actor seeking to establish, defend, or resist it. Moreover, in shedding the Westernised preoccupation with the state, we can begin to engage with the multifaceted expressions of territory construction and deconstruction beyond Western contexts. As Halvorsen (2019: 790) highlights, political geography has been slow to engage with territory-making practices beyond Western, Eurocentric contexts. There is a pressing need (Halvorsen 2019: 794, see also Haesbaert and Mason-Deese 2020, Jackman et al. 2020) to decolonise understandings of territory and to move toward a more open reading of the construct that allows for 'overlapping and entangled appropriations of space'. This might involve thinking through how 'ancestral and present memories' redefine under-standings and imaginaries of territory, or the foregrounding of embodied accounts of ter-ritory (Satizábal and Zurita 2022: 6). As Satizábal and Zurita (2022) highlight, 'territories are political and lived spaces, enacted via everyday practices and human–non human interactions'. Working in the context of Mexico, they bring visibility to the work of the Brigada Feminista (Feminist Brigade) who created alternative, 'counter hegemonic' terri-tories in the aftermath of an earthquake in 2017 (Satizábal and Zurita 2022: 1). The earth-quake disproportionately affected Mexico's female population. More women died than men, more were injured, and more were lost under the rubble. Beyond the earthquake, the Mexican state relied on practices that dehumanised and alienated women's bodies from their territories, creating spaces under state control where women are marginalised and vulnerable to violence (Satizábal and Zurita 2022: 13). In the aftermath of the earth-quake, the brigade demanded the rescue of trapped women, created safe spaces and ter-ritories for women affected, and opened a space to make migrant women workers visible

(Satizábal and Zurita 2022: 12). For Satizábal and Zurita (2022: 3), 'they metaphorically and physically held – and continue to hold – the bodies of women to emancipate the territories of violence produced by the state'. In this process of holding bodies, space is held too, and safer territories for women are enacted.

Case Study: Tourism, Territory, and the South China Sea (Huang 2022)

The South China Sea (SCS) is a hotly contested maritime territory. A number of states lay claim to space within the SCS, including China, who asserts sovereignty over a large U-shaped area known as the nine-dash line. This line was originally published on a map by China in 1947. China assert their territorial claim through various practices including cartography, island building within the sea, and the presence of military vessels and personnel. However, as Huang (2022) highlights, claims to territory also involve 'softer' initiatives such as tourism to the Xisha Islands – a disputed archipelago in the SCS.

Tours began in 2013 with cruises to three non-military islands. As Huang (2022) writes, they are highly exclusive, open only to Chinese citizens without criminal records. The tours are underpinned by patriotic discourses, stating factually that the SCS has been China's territory since 'ancient times'. Huang's (2022) research demonstrates that territory is not only constituted at the state level. In this case study, 'citizenry understandings' are also extremely important. Tourism provides a practice through which Chinese citizens 'learn national-territorial mindsets and internalise ideologies of the state' whilst also feeling involved in the territory-making process (Huang 2022: 3).

The complexities of territory can be seen more broadly in the context of the 'territorial turn' in Latin America (Haesbaert and Mason-Deese 2020: 265). The 'turn' describes a shift in the 1990s within Latin America whereby states in Latin America now recognise 'Indigenous and Afro-descendant tenure rights to around 200 million hectares of land' (Bryan 2012: 215). Such was the case with the 'Kue Tuvy Aché community in the Paraguay–Brazil borderlands' who, after a struggle lasting over a decade, secured the land rights to a 4,600-hectare parcel of land (known as Finca 470) in 2012 (Correia 2019: 11). For many, this might be construed as loss of national sovereignty over a bounded territory, yet in understanding territory as a process, we can challenge these Westernised logics of territorial control. Instead, we can see how territory is continually produced, challenged, and how historical dispossession and racial politics come to matter in its construction. For Bryan (2012: 215, emphasis added), this challenge is key as it 'shifts attention away from an emphasis on control *over* territory and towards a consideration of how power works *through* territory'. This is also a multi-layered and far from straightforward phenomenon. As Correia (2019: 13) highlights, whilst the Aché community may have won the rights, they must now 'defend their territory from loggers, marijuana producers' and reconcile with neighbouring Indigenous Guaraní communities who 'also claim the land as their traditional territory'. Territory in this example is constantly being asserted, contested, made and remade. The 'work needed to assemble territory', Correia (2019: 13) adds, 'is never finished'.

In the Field with Paula Satizábal: Grappling with Territory

Paula Satizábal is a critical political ecologist working on the multiplicity of human and non-human interactions shaping understandings of territory, place, and power in fluid and marine geographies.

What drew you to engaging with questions around territory?

My research has rarely drawn on territory as a starting point of inquiry, however, often ended up thinking *with* and *about* territory in making sense of the struggles of ocean peoples, feminist and senior activists, and farmers. In doing this, I position dominant governance interventions as territorial projects that work to subordinate existing and customary territorial configurations, thus, mediating human–non-human relations with profound and also violent manifestations. My engagement with territory is centred on studying these relations, challenging the separation between territories and the experiences of living and being in complex and dynamic spaces.

How do you understand territory in your work?

I understand territory as historical, lived, and political projects shaped by material and power relations, emerging as complex, situated, and embodied. This understanding of territory has been informed by lived experiences in coastal and marine spaces and disaster contexts, drawing inspiration from Indigenous ontologies, communitarian feminists, and decolonial academics and activists in Abya Yala, who emphasise the relationality of territory, bodies, and the Earth. Importantly, plural understandings of territory create emancipatory possibilities opening space to imagine and learn from relational territorial configurations that unsettle colonial territorial interventions.

What research methods have you used to explore territory in practice?

I have approached territory using a political ecology lens, working in collaboration with academics' and activists' commitment to listening to difficult stories and lived experiences of territorial struggles. Together we have drawn on in-depth and semi-structured interviews, participant observations, focus groups, and critical discourse analysis. Recently, this work has been shaped by our own feminist reflexivity, recognising that 'we' also make territories and have a role to play in subverting the meanings and practices that separate our own research and bodies from the places where we work and do research and the complexities of the Earth.

From Area to Volume

Beyond exploring its constructed and lively nature, political geographers have also begun to think through the *dimensions* of territory. For Graham (2016: 1), studies of territory and sovereignty had 'long been flattened by a reliance on flat maps – and, more recently, aerial and satellite images' offering a 'disembodied … God's eye view from high above' (Graham 2016: 1). As Elden (2013: 35) argues, 'we all-too-often think of the spaces of geography as areas not volumes'. In other words, we tend to think about political spaces in two dimensional terms. Challenging this assumption, Elden (2013: 35) asks us to consider what it would mean to understand territory as 'volume' rather than area, thinking with heights and depths rather than *across* a two dimensional flat surface. In doing so, spaces and contexts that would otherwise go unaccounted for are brought into the frame. We might for example think about territory and the power of the state through the sea, tunnels, airspace, underground infrastructures, underwater spaces, the subterranean, and high-rise buildings. There are also many more examples, such as Libassi's (2022) work on gold mining in the Pongkor region of West Java Indonesia. Worldwide, 'subsurface resources are typically the domain of the state' (Libassi 2022: 1). In other words state sovereignty extends downwards as well as across a given territory. Like processes of territory above ground, Libassi (2022) highlights how state control of the underground is always partial and contested. In Indonesia, unlicensed small-scale miners challenge the sovereignty of state, occupying and extracting resources from state-owned space, leading to direct confrontation both above and below ground.

The work of Eyal Weizman (2002, 2012) was formative in this shift, bringing volume to territory through an exploration of the territorial dispute between Israel and Palestine on the West Bank. This protracted, highly volatile territorial contest could not simply be mapped in atlases and cartographic surveys. On the contrary, airy and subterranean spaces are central to the dispute, with Weizman's analysis moving from the hills and valleys of the West Bank to the politics of water and sewage, to subterranean infrastructure and archaeology beneath the ground, to the control over airspace. In this 'politics of verticality' (Weizman 2002) voluminous spaces like the air are domains of conflict and control. Airspaces are, as Weizman (2002) writes, mostly absent from political maps, yet they are extremely important. Article 1 of the 1944 Chicago Convention states that states have control of their airspace, meaning that sovereignty extends vertically and through the volume of air. In the context of the West Bank, Israel holds control over the airspace, using 'its domination … to drop a net of surveillance and pinpoint executions over the territory' (Weizman 2002). Controlling the airspace forms part of a regime of fear wielded by Israel over Palestinians.

Beyond this top-down approach (see Williams 2013), we can think of air in geopolitical terms 'on the ground' too. This might be in the use of tear gas against populations by the state during protests (see Figure 7.3), where the air becomes weaponised, causing tearing, burning, blurred vision and a range of other symptoms on those whom the gas touches (Feigenbaum and Kanngieser 2015: 81). This takes place the world over, from protests against the Chinese State in Hong Kong, to police brutality against fans at the

2022 Champions League final in France. Or, we might think of the politics in accessing clean air to breathe in the first place. As Nieuwenhuis (2016: 478) highlights, air pollution is the fourth highest risk factor for death. The problem, they add, is that 'clean air has for a long time been thought of as mere "nothing"' (Nieuwenhuis 2016: 478), yet it is inherently political, speaking to questions about the dispersal of state power through territory, with decisions on who is believed to be expendable, while wealthy (often White) individuals breathe more freely. Access to breath, and to air, are geopolitical phenomena, often rooted in structural racism (Apata 2020).

Beyond state interventions, brutality, and neglect, heights and depths can also be spaces of 'imagination, inspiration, reflection, power and resistance' (Nieuwenhuis 2016: 478). As we explored earlier in the chapter, states do not exercise their power over and through territory evenly, and there are always spaces where territorial claims are challenged, reimagined, and resisted. To return to the context of the Israel–Palestine dispute, Palestinians have developed makeshift strategies to take power in the air against an overwhelming Israeli military. Kites 'trailing burning rags and booby-trapped balloons' have been floated across the Gaza strip, wreaking havoc in some areas of Israel (Salah and Tarnopolsky 2018). Indeed the *LA Times* reported in 2018 that at least 7,410 acres of farmland and national parkland have been incinerated as a result of these objects (Salah and Tarnopolsky 2018). Inflated condoms and party balloons bearing celebratory texts have also been used as they are 'sturdier – not to mention snarkier' than conventional balloons. Indeed, in 2018, 'a southern Israeli highway was blocked for an hour as sappers

Figure 7.3 Protesters use tennis rackets to bat away tear gas

Credit: Studio Incendo (Creative Commons Attribution 2.0 Generic license) https://commons.wikimedia.org/wiki/File:Protesters_use_tennis_rackets_to_bat_away_tear_gas._(50267655062).jpg

defused a booby-trapped balloon bearing the message I ♡ YOU' (Salah and Tarnopolsky 2018). Height, air, and wind become subversive here, mobilised by everyday people using everyday objects. In a very different context, underwater spaces have also been used as sites of protests. In 2021, for example, climate scientist and activist Shaama Sandooyea, scuba dived on the 'Saya de Malha Bank, a climate-critical site owing to its vast seagrass meadows, 735km off the coast of Seychelles' (Greenpeace 2021). Whilst underwater, Shaama displayed a placard bearing the messages 'Youth Strike for Climate' and 'Nou Reklam Lazistis Klimatik', Mauritian creole for 'We Demand Climate Justice'. Occupying an underwater site at risk of being destroyed was key, giving a worldwide audience access to a space that would otherwise be out of sight and out of mind.

Over to You: Contesting Territory Through Volume

As you have read, heights and depths are drawn into processes whereby dominant territorial practices are resisted and contested. Find your own example of a protest. This might be taken from elsewhere in the book (see Chapter 12), or from your own research:

1. How do heights and depths matter in that protest?
2. How is territory contested and reconfigured through these spaces?
3. What role does the body play in this?

Conclusions and Future Challenges

Despite optimism in the 1990s that globalisation would see the end of the state and obsessions with territory, they remain two key concepts in our understanding of the ordering of the world. States maintain their enthusiasm for exercising sovereignty over territory and this seems unlikely to change. Recent thinking within political geography is helpful in deconstructing and getting to grips with the implications of this, notably in reimagining both 'the state' and 'territory' as socially constructed and as enacted through various practices, imaginaries, materialities, and processes. In other words, neither states nor territory simply exist or just naturally occur. This is not to limit the power of these constructs. Far from being abstract, the ways that they are enacted powerfully shape the world around us in uneven, and often violent ways. Moreover, these are not constructs that are simply accepted. As we have demonstrated, territory is not the sole preserve of the state and state power can be resisted, challenged, and reimagined on multiple scales and across multiple contexts. The need to engage with these complexities will only become more pressing in the coming years. Global challenges like the Climate Emergency present new difficulties as well as opportunities for thinking on both the state and territory. What, for example, happens to notions of statehood and sovereignty if a low-lying island state disappears due to sea level rise? For example Yamamoto and Esteban (2010) assert, what the status of an island State would be if its entire territory were to be submerged is unclear. This is a very real concern for states like Tuvalu, an island state where the majority of the land mass sites are barely three metres above sea level (Yamamoto and Esteban 2010). A number of locals report fears of their home being 'swallowed' by the rising water (Ainge Roy 2019). This is further complicated by the fact that many communities on low-lying states do not want to move and would rather find adaptation measures (Jamero et al. 2017). As we explored in Chapter 3 (Feminist Geopolitics), ideas of belonging are very much entangled with ideas of territory and 'home'. Such complexities remain (at the time of writing) to be addressed, but as the Climate Emergency intensifies, notions of the state and territory will only be further complicated.

Summary

- Understandings of the state have evolved in political geography. Far from being a static power container, it is now understood as a lively construct, and a set of practices that are enacted and performed.
- The state operates at multiple and intersecting scales. It powerfully shapes and courses through everyday life whilst shaping wider international and global questions.
- There is scope to complicate the state and imagine a differently ordered world. The TGiE provides a key example of this.
- Like the state, the chapter also complicated understandings of territory. Rather than seeing it as inert space, territory is dynamic, contested, and always in process.
- It is important to understand how power works through heights and depths (i.e., territory as volume) in the making and unmaking of territory.
- Understandings of the state and territory will only get more complex as climate change intensifies.

Follow-on Resources

Central Tibetan Administration: On this website, you can find out more about the Tibetan Administration – explore government departments, key issues, and learn more about the TGIE. See https://tibet.net/

1984: This is a novel by George Orwell written in 1949. It is a dystopian 'social science fiction' novel set in London whereby the protagonist navigates life under a tyrannical regime. It raises important questions about the power of the state.

Babushkas of Chernobyl: This project and film follows a community of babushkas (older women or grandmothers) as they refuse to leave a contaminated and potentially lethal landscape around the Chernobyl nuclear power plant. Determined to stay in their homes, the film offers insights into alternative territory making from the ground up, with the state largely absent in their lives. See https://thebabushkasofchernobyl.com/

References

Ainge Roy, E. (2019). 'One day we'll disappear': Tuvalu's sinking islands. *The Guardian*, 16 May. Available at: www.theguardian.com/global-development/2019/may/16/one-day-disappear-tuvalu-sinking-islands-rising-seas-climate-change (accessed 19 May 2023).

Apata, G. O. (2020). 'I can't breathe': The suffocating nature of racism. *Theory, Culture & Society*, *37*(7–8), 241–254.

Benwell, M. C. (2014). From the banal to the blatant: Expressions of nationalism in secondary schools in Argentina and the Falkland Islands. *Geoforum*, *52*, 51–60.

Björkdahl, A. (2018). Republika Srpska: Imaginary, performance and spatialization. *Political Geography*, *66*, 34–43.

Bryan, J. (2012). Rethinking territory: Social justice and neoliberalism in Latin America's territorial turn. *Geography Compass*, *6*(4), 215–226.

Correia, J. E. (2019). Unsettling territory: Indigenous mobilizations, the territorial turn, and the limits of land rights in the Paraguay–Brazil borderlands. *Journal of Latin American Geography*, *18*(1), 11–37.

Desbiens, C., Mountz, A. and Walton-Roberts, M. (2004). Guest editorial. Introduction: Reconceptualizing the state from the margins of political geography. *Political Geography*, *23*, 241–243.

Elden, S. (2010). Land, terrain, territory. *Progress in Human Geography*, *34*(6), 799–817.

Elden, S. (2013). Secure the volume: Vertical geopolitics and the depth of power. *Political Geography*, *34*, 35–51.

Elden, S. (2018). Dynamic territories, ICELAW project. Available at: https://icelawproject.org/reflections-2/dynamic-territories/ (accessed 19 May 2023).

Feigenbaum, A. and Kanngieser, A. (2015). For a politics of atmospheric governance. *Dialogues in Human Geography*, *5*(1), 80–84.

Gallagher, J. (2022). Making sense of the state: Citizens and state buildings in South Africa. *Political Geography*, *98*, 102674.

Graham, S. (2016). *Vertical: The city from satellites to bunkers*. London: Verso Books.

Greenpeace (2021). World's first underwater climate strike calls for ocean protection. Available at: www.greenpeace.org/international/press-release/46920/worlds-first-underwater-climate-strike-calls-for-ocean-protection/ (accessed 19 May 2023).

Haesbaert, R. and Mason-Deese, L. (2020). Territory/ies from a Latin American perspective. *Journal of Latin American Geography*, *19*(1), 258–268.

Halvorsen, S. (2019). Decolonising territory: Dialogues with Latin American knowledges and grassroots strategies. *Progress in Human Geography*, *43*(5), 790–814.

Huang, Y. (2022). Consuming geopolitics and feeling maritime territoriality: The case of China's patriotic tourism in the South China Sea. *Political Geography*, *98*, 102669.

Jackman, A., Squire, R., Bruun, J. and Thornton, P. (2020). Unearthing feminist territories and terrains. *Political Geography*, *80*, 102180.

Jamero, L., Onuki, M., Esteban, M., Billones-Sensano, X. K., Tan, N., Nellas, A., Takagi, H., Danh Thao, N. and Valenzuela, V. P. (2017). Small-island communities in the Philippines prefer local measures to relocation in response to sea-level rise. *Nature Climate Change*, *7*(8), 581–586.

Jones, M., Jones, R. and Wood, M. (2004). *An introduction to political geography*. London: Routledge.

Libassi, M. (2022). Contested subterranean territory: Gold mining and competing claims to Indonesia's underground. *Political Geography*, *98*, 102675.

McConnell, F. (2009a). Governments-in-exile: Statehood, statelessness and the reconfiguration of territory and sovereignty. *Geography Compass*, *3*(5), 1902–1919.

McConnell, F. (2009b). De facto, displaced, tacit: The sovereign articulations of the Tibetan Government-in-Exile. *Political Geography*, *28*(6), 343–352.

McConnell, F. (2012). Governmentality to practise the state? Constructing a Tibetan population in exile. *Environment and Planning D: Society and Space*, *30*(1), 78–95.

McConnell, F. (2016). Sovereignty. In K. Dodds, M. Kuus and J. Sharp (eds), *The Ashgate research companion to critical geopolitics* (pp. 109–128). London: Routledge.

MBBRACE (2021). Saving lives: Improving mother's care, lay summary 2021. Available at: www.npeu.ox.ac.uk/assets/downloads/mbrrace-uk/reports/maternal-report-2021/MBRRACE-UK_Maternal_Report_2021_-_Lay_Summary_v10.pdf (accessed 19 May 2023).

McKinnon, K. (2016). The geopolitics of birth. *Area*, *48*(3), 285–291.

Moisio, S. and Paasi, A. (2013). Beyond state-centricity: Geopolitics of changing state spaces. *Geopolitics*, 18(2), 255–266.

Mountz, A. (2003). Human smuggling, the transnational imaginary, and everyday geographies of the nation-state. *Antipode*, *35*(3), 622–644.

Nieuwenhuis, M. (2016). Introduction: Atmospheric politics and state governance. *Critical Studies on Terrorism*, *9*(3), 478–481.

Ohmae, K. (1995). *The end of the nation-state: The rise of regional economies*. New York: Free Press.

Painter, J. (2006). Prosaic geographies of stateness. *Political Geography*, *25*(7), 752–774.

Painter, J. and Jeffrey, A. (2009). *Political geography: An introduction to space and power*. London: Sage.

Peters, K., Steinberg, P. and Stratford, E. (eds) (2018). *Territory beyond terra*. London: Rowman & Littlefield.

Salah, H. and Tarnopolsky, N. (2018). Must reads: They're calling it the Kite War. How a simple plaything became a potent weapon in the Gaza Strip. *LA Times*, 18 June. Available at: www.latimes.com/world/la-fg-israel-gaza-kites-20180618-story.html (accessed 19 May 2023).

Satizábal, P. and Melo Zurita, M. de L. (2022). Bodies-holding-bodies: The trembling of women's territorio-cuerpo-tierra and the feminist responses to the earthquakes in Mexico City. *Third World Thematics: A TWQ Journal*, 1–23.

Weizman, E. (2012). *Hollow land: Israel's architecture of occupation*. New York: Verso Books.

Weizman, E. (2002). Control in the air. *Open Democracy*, 1 May. Available at: www.opendemocracy.net/conflict-politicsverticality / article_810.jsp (accessed 19 May 2023).

Williams, A. (2013). Re-orientating vertical geopolitics. *Geopolitics*, *18*(1), 225–246.

Yamamoto, L. and Esteban, M. (2010). Vanishing island states and sovereignty. *Ocean & Coastal Management, 53*(1), 1–9.

EIGHT

BORDERS: FROM STATE LINES TO THE BODY

Chapter Overview

This chapter explores one of the foundational objects and practices of political geography – the border. It explores thinking on borders that has evolved from static lines on a map through to the 'processual turn' which understands the border as a lively social construct that can be located in everyday life as much as at state boundaries. The chapter locates bordering practices in a wide range of spaces and contexts, thinking through how we might understand embodied borders, whilst also considering how violence is inextricably intertwined with bordering practices. The chapter moves to explore the 'offshoring' of borders and ends by reflecting on how we might imagine the border differently.

Learning Objectives

1. To understand that the border is more than a dividing line between states.
2. To think about where and how we might locate the border.
3. To critically engage with the concepts of 'bordering' and the 'borderscape'.

Read with: Chapter 10 (Mobilities), Chapter 7 (States and Territory), Chapter 9 (Nationalism)

For many, borders and boundaries are 'the most palpable political geographical phenomena' (Minghi in Van Houtum 2005: 672). They define the world map, shaping our geopolitical imaginations from a young age as we see black lines traced around the outlines of countries, providing definition and delineation to what would otherwise appear to be a messy system of colours and names. We might think of borders as being 'natural' phenomena, existing as inert features that 'run through the world' (Megoran 2021: 1). As Giudice and Giubilaro (2015: 81) write, 'lines are simple objects, so they simply exist'. Borders might also be seen as neat power containers that serve to delineate one sovereign territory from another, but as a number of geographers have noted, the border is far from being 'neat' and far from a passive infrastructure that shapes the world around us (Brambilla 2015, Cassidy et al. 2018, Paasi 2012). On the contrary, borders are acts of 'power and control' (Megoran 2021: 1) that have profound and often violent implications. Moreover, they are proliferating in the world around us like never before. Processes of globalisation have not eradicated borders but have instead led 'to a renewed demand for certainty, identity and security' (Brambilla 2015: 15). This has been accompanied by the spread of protectionist policies and 'feelings of anti-immigration' (Brambilla 2015: 15). For Megoran (2021: 1) 'the world has become more fenced and bordered than at any time in human history'. Events like the Covid-19 pandemic have only added further impetus to this, prompting an 'unprecedented and rapid proliferation and intensification of border controls with strikingly little critical debate or democratic deliberation' (Megoran 2021: 1). The growth and wide-ranging effects of borders mean that they demand our attention and critical awareness (Van Houtum and Van Naerssen 2002).

From Borders to Bordering

Contemporary border scholarship helps to provide us with the skills to undertake this critical work. Whereas border studies in the 1960s were preoccupied with the demarcation of boundaries and lines (much like the border between the US and Mexico, depicted in Figure 8.1), more recent scholarship shifts focus to understanding the process and practice of borders (Brambilla 2015). In other words, we might think about the border 'as

Figure 8.1 United States–Mexico Pacific Ocean border fence

Credit: Tony Webster (Creative Commons Attribution 2.0 Generic license) https://commons.wikimedia.org/wiki/File:United_States_-_Mexico_Ocean_Border_Fence_(15838118610).jpg

a verb' (Van Houtum 2005: 672). Understanding the border as a doing word implies that the border is actively enacted, produced, and always in process. This shift in how borders are understood also works to relocate *where* the border is located. Whilst borders may lie in some sense at the 'edge' of the nation state, borders are also a travelling and mutable discursive construct, located in the everyday lives of people across the world (Cassidy et al. 2018: 139). Brambilla (2015) and others refer to this 'shift' that began in the 1990s as the 'processual turn'. This turn combines expertise in political geography, human and cultural geography, anthropology and other allied fields and draws on the language of 'bordering' or 'borderscapes'. For Brambilla (2015) terms like 'borderscapes' speak to the need to find ways to critically engage with the fluid and shifting spatial complexities of the border. The border, as Brambilla (2015: 19) goes on to describe, might be established but at the same time is:

> continuously traversed by a number of bodies, discourses, practices, and relationships that highlight endless definitions and shifts in definition between inside and outside, citizens and foreigners, hosts and guests across state, regional, racial, and other symbolic boundaries.

We might therefore imagine the border not as a line but 'as a set of ideas, imaginations and relationships across space and time' (Brambilla 2021: 12). Mbembe (2019: 9) thinks of this in terms of 'borderisation', referring to the 'process by which certain spaces are transformed into uncrossable places for certain classes of populations, who thereby undergo a process of racialization'. The relational is key here. Drawing on feminist approaches (see Chapter 3), it draws our attention to different experiences of borders. How do bordering practices impact everyday lives? How are they embodied and felt, and how are bodies of different kinds drawn into bordering regimes in different ways? How do wider intersectional factors affect this (Cassidy et al. 2018)? Such work also urges us to ask: How do the mobile bodies of 'migrants, asylum seekers' and 'refugees' bring new possibilities to border spaces as they complicate and dislocate lines on the map (Giudice and Giubilaro 2015: 82)?

The 'big stories' of the nation matter here, but so do the 'small stories' that come from 'experiencing the border in day-to-day life' (Brambilla 2015: 25). For Brambilla (2021) and Cassidy et al. (2018), these relational questions are important, particularly if we are to capture the paradoxical nature of bordering practices as they produce spaces of both inclusion and exclusion, mobility and immobility, oppression and resistance (see Brambilla and Jones 2020: 298). This approach also opens up possibilities for bordering practices that can be otherwise. As Giudice and Giubilaro (2015: 82) write, if we understand the border as fixed and static in space, then we are unlikely to imagine it as something that can be changed in any way. On the contrary, when we think through bordering practices and borderscapes, we can be attentive to *how* borders are shaped, imagined, made, and enacted, and therefore how they can and might be re-shaped, reimagined, re-made, and re-enacted (see Brambilla 2015).

Over to You: Where is the Border?

Thinking broadly and creatively, spend 5–10 minutes creating a list of how the border, and bordering practices, affect your life.

Ask yourself, where have and might you encounter borders?

If you don't think that your life is impacted by bordering practices, what might this say about your positionality and privilege? How might your answers change if your race, nationality, or passport was different?

Revisit this list at the end of the chapter and see if your answers remain the same.

Violent Borderings

Understanding the border as a practice and a process is also important in recognising the border as an inherently violent construct. Borders, in everyday life or at the scale of the nation state, are inherently exclusive and concerned with spatial differentiation, often enforced through certain performances and practices of differentiation, including 'checking, verifying' and 'identifying' (Giudice and Giubilaro 2015: 85). For Brambilla and Jones (2020: 290), these are 'violent … acts of separation'. Indeed Reece Jones argues in his book *Violent Borders* (2016) that violence is not an effect of the border but that the border is a *source* of violence that creates differences between people and place – it does not merely reflect or represent these differences. This distinction is crucial as it highlights the role of borders and bordering practices in generating societal divisions that might otherwise be thought of as 'natural'. As Jones (2016: 297) argues, borders are dependent upon this violence and they are inherently premised on 'excluding other people from a particular area in order to claim the land, resources, and people there'. They afford certain rights of the 'in-group of citizens at the expense of noncitizens' (Jones et al. 2017: 1).

KEY TERMS: VIOLENT BORDERS

This is the idea (and title of the 2016 book by Reece Jones) that borders are by their nature violent constructs. Alongside the physical violence that takes places at borders, they are also premised on exclusion, the sorting of 'us' and 'them', and their extension into society produces multiple spaces of violence and 'othering'. For Megoran (2021: 1) border controls act as a form of 'global apartheid'. Such a system killed over 3,000 people worldwide in 2020 (International Organization for Migration, 2020 in Megoran 2021: 1). Borders are therefore never neutral, inert, or innocent.

Moreover, when border walls and bordering practices are enacted at particular sites, further layers of violence materialise. As we can see with the unfolding Mediterranean refugee 'crisis', people do not simply stop moving because borders exist (see Chapter 10). The effect is to funnel refugees and migrants to 'more dangerous routes and force them to rely on smugglers and human traffickers' (Jones 2016: 297). Stierl (2020) illustrates the profound and devastating effects of this. Writing on the 'crisis', he explores how the Covid-19 pandemic further hardened borders in the Mediterranean as European countries including Italy and Malta implemented a new strategy to reject migrants travelling on precarious boats on the premise that they were now unsafe. This left hundreds of people stranded at sea. As Stierl (2020) highlights, there was one group of 63 people who were left stranded when the boat's engine failed them. European authorities were informed of the distress but sent no help. As a result, 'some starved to death on board and others drowned' (Stierl 2020: n.p.).

We might also consider other complex spatial dimensions of the violent border. As Blanco (2022: 2) highlights, this may include 'bursts of exceptional violence' at bordering sites. No border site is exempt from violence. Viral images appearing to show US border agents charging at Haitian migrants on horseback while whipping them in 2021 is a case in point. A subsequent report stated that the border agents had used 'unnecessary force' and outlined how agents had yelled profanities and insults relating to the national origin of the border crossers as they attempted to re-enter the US with food (*Al Jazeera* 2022). Such examples highlight how the border is a 'permanent state of exception' which normalises violence at border sites (Salter 2008).

KEY TERMS: SPACES OF EXCEPTION

Originating with the work of Giorgio Agamben, states of exception traditionally refer to a sovereign state suspending legal protections to individuals in times of emergency. In the wake of the events of 11 September 2001 (9/11), for example, the US Government under George Bush argued that exceptional measures were needed to fight an 'unconventional enemy'. This was used to legitimise the protracted War on Terror and to enact strict and far-reaching border controls. Salter (2008) and Jones (2009) argue that the border is in a permanent state of exception, where exceptional measures are enacted to prevent and control the movement of people, and that the exceptional powers invoked after 9/11 have never really gone away.

Violence, as Giudice and Giubilaro (2015: 84) argue, is never 'an accidental feature of the border'. These are sites and spaces where the 'most fundamental contestations over identity occur', where physical harm and death can be commonplace outcomes, where lives are routinely 'judged to be undesirable', and where people are 'intentionally immobilised' and lives are 'shattered' (Mbembe 2019: 9).

Locating the Border
Borders and the Body

The violence associated with the border does not just exist at state lines. The border is sticky and embedded in everyday life in various ways too. Jones (2014: 530), for example, explores how the US TV series *Border Wars* reproduces the border in the 'homes of millions of Americans and viewers around the world every week'. The language of 'war' is itself a violent evocation and the series draws on guns, helicopters, dramatic music, and armed border agents to both create a sense that migration is a problem that warrants a violent response, and to locate such issues on everyday streets, as homes to be 'raided' and neighbours who may be 'illegal'.

Beyond this, Jackson (2016) powerfully illustrates how the border sticks to bodies and is difficult to shake off, even once the official border 'line' has been crossed. Drawing on feminist approaches that situate the body as a site of social process, action, and resistance (see Chapter 3), Jackson (2016) highlights how stereotyping is a practice and process through which particular bodily practices and performances are framed as producing and reproducing particular national and territorial identities. Drawing on the experiences of female expatriates and Foreign Domestic Workers (FDWs) in Singapore, Jackson (2016: 293–294) argues that 'particular stigmas surround the migrant body', often premised on 'class, race, ethnicity, and colonial histories'. This leads to bordering practices around migrant communities who are seeking to foster a sense of identity and belonging. One of Jackson's (2016: 296) participants, for example, described how they felt that there was a 'wall' between Singaporeans and migrants. Another, a Filipino FDW, described how she and her friends (also FDWs) were seen differently, and that they carried the sense with them that others thought they 'should not be there'. As a result, migrants often form expatriate communities where daily borders are maintained through language, food, dress, and the 'discounting of local routines' as a means of creating and maintaining cultural boundaries. Jackson (2016: 297–298) refers to these as practices and performances of 'border maintenance' as a reaction to being 'excluded emotionally and physically' from the 'host society'. Bodies, within this context and others, play an active role in the making of borders (Smith et al. 2016: 258). For Jackson (2016: 297), this cements the idea that the border is maintained and reproduced in the everyday, and the performance of bordering exemplifies the border as a multifaceted site of 'continual struggle and negotiation'.

Case Study: Intimate Borderings (Blanco 2022)

Blanco (2022) uses the term 'intimate borderings' to understand the intersections between border sites and the body. Drawing on feminist and Black geographies, Blanco 'sheds light on the intimate practices that weave, rupture and reconfigure relations' for Haitian domestic workers who live in Haiti and work in the border towns of the Dominican Republic. Blanco's work illustrates how significant the body and intimacy are in this process. Within this context, Blanco (2022) argues that the bodies of women crossing the border are gendered, racialised, sexualised, and rendered sites of inscription for the border. As Blanco explores, this is a legacy of violent and oppressive

(Continued)

histories, including slavery, which continue to have profound consequences in the present day. This takes many forms including everyday practices of racial profiling, structural exclusion such as being unable to access the documentation needed to undertake their jobs, and in and through forms of humiliation. Indeed one participant in Blanco's study described herself and her co-workers as being dehumanised and treated like 'dogs'. Moreover, their bodies are violently brought under this regime of power by the border guards who operationalise sexual assault as a means of control. Sexual harassment and intimate violence was experienced by a number of women in Blanco's study, both at official crossings and along smuggler routes. Knowing that the women rely on these crossings for their livelihoods, enduring such violence becomes an act of survival. As Blanco (2022: 7) writes, 'withstanding sexual harassment and groping is perceived as a form of Intimate Bordering imposed on women border crossers as a transaction linked to their mobility. Like bribery, sexual harassment is incorporated as one of the implicit costs of mobility'. The systematically gendered and racialised body is drawn into a spatial politics of exclusion here through intimate and violent bordering practices. The Black female body becomes the site and focus of the border regime that situates the border on the site of Black women.

Biometric Borders

A key development of recent years is the 'extent' to 'which border practices have taken a keen interest' in the human body as a means to 'achieve detailed control over movement' (Mbembe 2019: 9). Technology has been integral to this shifting focus. Since 9/11, there has been a significant shift in bordering practices whereby technologies, from contemporary border technologies to machine learning algorithms, have 'ushered in novel ways to sort, classify, group and assign risk to human mobilities' across borders (Amoore 2021: 5) (see also Chapter 13). These technologies collapse powerfully on the body as biometric practices of control intertwine 'individual physical characteristics with information systems' (Mbembe 2019: 9). In doing so, they effectively encode 'risk' on the body with significant implications for how borders are crossed and who can cross them. Within this framework, a subject is broken down into 'calculable risk factors' such as 'student', 'Muslim', 'woman', 'immigrant' (Amoore 2006: 339). This might also involve linking a person with other electronic traces, such as what airline tickets have been bought to ascertain where someone has travelled, how a credit card has been used and so on (Amoore 2006: 338). The idea behind this is that risk can be pre-determined based on a person's characteristics. Subjects and populations deemed to be too 'risky' have their mobility hindered, disrupted, and stopped (see Chapter 10 on mobilities). A range of electronic databases are used to do this and to encode passengers and people travelling 'according to degrees of riskiness' (Amoore 2006: 340). The origins of such practices largely lie in the wake of the events of 11 September 2001 (9/11) whereby a panel of technology experts were asked by the US Government how they might fight the War on Terror using 'risk profiling technologies' (Amoore 2006: 337). The bordering regimes that followed were premised on attaching bordering practices to the body. The border, through the body, is everywhere. It's 'carried by mobile bodies at the very same time as it is deployed to divide bodies at international boundaries, airports, railway stations, on subways or city streets, in the office or the neighbourhood' (Amoore 2006: 338).

Documents like passports carry information on our bodies too. In Figure 8.2 there are three passports from the UK, Iran, and Norway. Each looks different, each country has very different politics, but each passport has the same symbol at the bottom. The circle with a line on each side signifies that these, like most national passports, are biometric. This may speed up mobility through the airport but it also logs facial features (such as the distance between eyes) and other biographic information to link the carrier with the document, and thus also to the state (see Chapter 7). This is used with the view to 'fix and secure identity as a basis for prediction and prevention' (Amoore 2006: 337).

For Amoore (2006: 338), the 'biometric border is the portable border par excellence'. It is varied in each of us, the data of which is then deployed to divide us into categories of 'desirable' and 'undesirable', 'safe' and 'risky' at sites like airports, border crossings, stations, and even in city streets and neighbourhoods. As a result of this process, the ability of a person to cross and move relatively freely across a border is both fixed at and enacted

Figure 8.2a British passport

Credit: Swapnil1101 (This work created by the United Kingdom Government is in the public domain. This is because it is one of the following: It is a photograph taken prior to 1 June 1957; or It was published prior to 1973; or It is an artistic work other than a photograph or engraving (e.g. a painting) which was created prior to 1973. HMSO has declared that the expiry of Crown Copyrights applies worldwide) https://commons.wikimedia.org/wiki/File:British_Passport_2020.svg

Figure 8.2b Iranian biometric passport cover

Credit: Behniar (Creative Commons Attribution-Share Alike 3.0 Unported license) https://commons.wikimedia.org/wiki/File:Iranian_Biometric_Passport_Cover.jpg

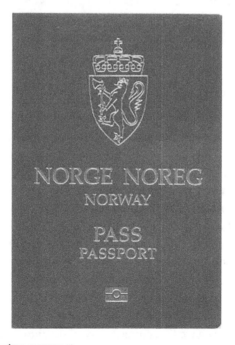

Figure 8.2c Norwegian passport

Credit: Noble (the copyright holder of this work releases this work into the public domain) https://commons.wikimedia.org/wiki/File:Norwegian_passport.jpg

well beyond the space of the border itself. It is fixed in terms of nationality, skin colour, gender, spending habits, travelling history, and many other everyday factors where electronic habits leave a 'trace' to be consumed by border agencies. The body emerges here as an agent in border making (Smith et al. 2016: 259), the effects of which, as the Case study below demonstrates, can be profound.

Case Study: The Body and the Border (Amoore 2021)

The collection of biometric data can be enforced in highly problematic ways. During the genocide in Myanmar, Rohingya Muslims fled to find safety and refuge in Bangladesh. At United Nations High Commissioner for Refugees (UNHCR) camps, refugees were faced with an 'intensive data collection exercise' (Amoore 2021: 4). The UNHCR collected facial images, thumbprints 'and a range of demographic and biographic information as part of the registration process'. There was little choice in the matter as the agency made it a requirement in order for refugees to receive a smart card and thus gain access to aid and basic services. The data was then shared by the UNHCR with the Bangladesh government who subsequently sent the records of '830,000 Rohingya refugees to the Myanmar government'. Those who had no choice but to flee violence had their identifying information and biometric data submitted to the perpetrators of genocide. As a result, 'many people were forced to flee the camp, to risk statelessness, and to go into hiding for fear of further violence' (Amoore 2021: 4). The biometric border, embodied by border crossers, is therefore powerful, violent, and renders many people insecure.

Re-materialising and Offshoring the Border

As has been explored in the sections above, the border is a complex practice and process that can be located in a range of contexts, sites, and bodies. For Megoran (2021: 2) 'borders increasingly rematerialize away from the literal edges of states'. As we have seen, this might be in the internal practices of border control, such as the use of biometric data, but the border also rematerialises in other ways too. The first is the location of the border in everyday spaces and contexts, such as classrooms, hospitals, workplaces, and universities. The university is a useful departure point here given that if you are reading this, you are most likely enrolled on or involved in a university course. The university is also a site, as Bagelman and Cinnamon (2018) highlight, where hostile border enforcement practices creep into everyday life. The resultant hostilities are produced in seemingly minor and banal, but nonetheless extremely consequential, ways (Bagelman and Cinnamon 2018). Jenkins (2014) explores this further in the context of the UK and the ways in which the UK Border Agency (UKBA) have transformed universities into border sites. This is premised on the requirement that if a university is to be able to teach non-EU students, then it must monitor these students to check that they are fulfilling visa conditions, as set by the UKBA. This data can then be shared with the UK Visa and Immigration division of the Home Office (Bagelman and Cinnamon 2018). 'The border-crossing student' is thus 'subjected to continual monitoring' and the university becomes partly responsible for 'administrating the national border'. This means that staff are enrolled as border agents doing the work of the state and that the 'student body becomes divided into a two tier system' (Jenkins 2014: 265). Importantly, such techniques of bordering also limit the mobility of certain students, 'tying them within a spatial and temporal ambit of the checkpoint' which might take the form of a register or meeting with a personal tutor (Jenkins 2014: 267). 'This downloaded responsibility' to monitor students undermines the duty of care staff have to students, radically changing the nature of university life and demonstrating the power of border in spaces we might not expect. In the UK, the media have also reported on doctors (Gentleman 2017) and landlords (Hamblett 2013) fulfilling similar Border Agency reporting functions with significant consequences – with landlords, for example, being unwilling or hesitant to rent to people with names that might not sound 'traditionally English'.

Beyond the border seeping and creeping into everyday and unexpected contexts, the state also powerfully relocates and offshores its borders to achieve certain geopolitical objectives. Indeed, Jones et al. (2017: 7) argue that the 'main geographical thrust in border enforcement has been to push borders and people trying to reach sovereign territory offshore'. State bordering practices do not simply end within the confines of the state; rather, in the name of security, they stretch and extend into the territories of other states and across borders (Paasi 2012). In the words of Paasi (2012: 2307), they are increasingly mobile and 'detached from the lines demarcating states'.

KEY TERMS: BORDER EXTERNALISATION

This refers to the 'enactment of domestic policies and bilateral/multilateral agreements that successfully enlist other countries, usually countries in the periphery of the State in question, in processing asylum seekers and enhancing their border controls with the ultimate goal of preventing asylum seekers from reaching the State enacting the putative externalization policies' (National Immigration Justice Centre 2021: 4).

Attempts to secure borders in the face of the so-called migrant 'crisis' in the Mediterranean Sea is a case in point. As Bialasiewicz (2012: 843) writes, the Mediterranean has long been a 'laboratory' in the policing of EU borders. Bordering practices in this space are very difficult to pin down, proceeding not through lines and clear demarcations but through a 'fluid assemblage of functions, mechanisms, and actors' (Bialasiewicz 2012: 843). A key mechanism within this assemblage is the offshoring of borders in an attempt to secure EU borders in spaces and contexts far removed from EU shores. The EU has for a long time provided specialist training to border guards in countries including Bosnia, Croatia, and Kosovo – each seen as a potential 'conduit to all sorts of illicit flows heading for European shores' (Bialasiewicz 2012: 846). For Bialasiewicz (2012: 847), neighbours of the EU are becoming the EU's policeman and border agencies. These practices of 'migration management' have extended beyond the European continent to the African continent. 2009–2010, for example, saw an offshoring of Italian borders to Libya. In a bilateral agreement, Italian coast guard vessels were permitted to operate in Libyan waters and the EU funded surveillance and monitoring equipment to be utilised along Libya's land and sea borders (Bialasiewicz 2012). Italian coast guard vessels also began taking migrants intercepted in international waters straight back to Libya – such practices are known as 'push back' operations. In the same week that this came into being, distress calls were sent from vessels in the Mediterranean with 230 migrants on board. The Italian coastguard took the people on board to Tripoli, Libya, 'without checking whether any individuals on board were in need of international protection or basic humanitarian assistance', or considering how such a 'push back' might negatively affect those on board (Bialasiewicz 2012: 852). Such behaviour, and the general disregard for life in the Mediterranean Sea, has been publicly condemned by the Office of the United Nations High Commissioner for Human Rights (National Immigration Justice Centre 2021).

Such practices exist all over the world but always most negatively impact those already marginalised. In Australia, for example, a brutal offshoring regime exists where

Figure 8.3 Libya and Italy locator

Credit: Elmondo21st (Creative Commons Attribution-Share Alike 2.5 Generic license) https://commons.wikimedia.org/wiki/File:Libya_Italy_Locator.png

the Australian Navy intensively patrol the seas, firing upon and forcibly boarding vessels suspected to be 'illegal', with the Navy permitted to use 'necessary force' to prevent asylum seekers setting foot on Australian soil (Perera 2006: 638, see also Little and Vaughan-Williams 2017). Two Pacific Islands and former Australian protectorates or colonies, Nauru and Manus, have been used as detention sites for migrants who have sought to enter Australia – a scheme known as the 'Pacific Solution' (National Immigration Justice Centre 2021: 31). We might also think about how the US has offshored asylum processing and immigration enforcement to Mexico and Central America within this framework. Wherever the case study may lie, the externalising of borders by wealthy Global North countries is a significant concern for political geographers. It not only carries with it significant human rights questions and abuses, but also fundamentally changes what the border is conceived to be and how it is violently enacted.

Over to You: Offshoring and Relocating Borders

Using the country that you call home as a starting point, do some research to identify how the government offshores borders. This can take many forms, including relocating migrants and refugees to other countries. Use the questions below to help you do this:

1. What is the government's attitude to refugees and migrants? Is it hostile, welcoming, or something in between?
2. How is this manifested in specific policies and through specific actors? (You might think of landlords and doctors, alongside bigger state-led projects within this framework.)
3. If your country does 'offshore' or 'relocate' their borders, where do they do this and what might this tell us?
4. What are the effects of these policies, both on those concerned and in wider society?
5. If you were to design an alternative, what would it look like?

Conclusion: Can the Border be Otherwise?

Whilst understandings of the border have evolved and changed within political geography, practices of bordering nonetheless remain a key concern. This is because borders and their associated politics have profound effects. On an international scale, the invasion of a country's borders can cause outcry and devastation, as seen only too clearly in the 2022 Russian invasion of Ukraine. In this contexts, troops are mobilised, equipment is sent across borders, the lines around Ukraine are shored up and defended – something people give their lives for. And yet at the same time, the border is also experienced in profoundly personal and everyday ways that are nonetheless geopolitical at their core. Borders travel through bodies, homes, TV screens; they are woven through clothing, mediated by passports and biometrics at the border, and shape how we see the world and those in it in important ways.

As this chapter explored, borders are also inherently violent. They are premised on exclusionary classifying, separating, and sorting. As we also explored, borders are always in process and unfolding, and here there lies hope for bordering practices. Understanding bordering as a process reveals borders for what they are – 'cultural artefacts and political formations' (Giudice and Giubilaro 2015: 81). In turn, this opens up spaces 'within which the organisation of new forms of the political and the social become possible' (Brambilla 2015: 18). For Giudice and Giubilaro (2015: 80) imagination is key if alternative 'visions and experiences of the border' are to be realised – 'filling the borderline with visions and experiences incompatible with its restrictedness' (Giudice and Giubilaro 2015: 85).

In the Field with Nick Megoran: Borders and Borderings

Nick Megoran is a political geographer at Newcastle University, England. His research is on post-Cold War nationalism and geopolitics, especially as viewed from border areas in Central Asia and northern Europe.

What drew you to research borders?

I've always been intrigued by political maps. As a child I would look at them and see, for example, France coloured in green and Germany in red. I used to ask myself: what colour are the people who live on the line – and who drew it in the first place, anyway?! Borders are places where state power is experienced most viscerally, but also where it is most absurd. Although geographically they are at the literal edge of the state, politically they are often at its heart. So they are great places to study the political geography of the world.

Can you imagine a world without them?

Yes, because international boundaries are very recent institutions and the borders that they produce change a lot over time. Contemporary border controls cement wealth inequalities and produce great violence. Yet many recent visions of borderlessness have also been violent, from Halford Mackinder's advocacy of a tariff-free British Empire to the more recent experiments of the EU (whose external borders are the deadliest on earth) and the Islamic State 'caliphate'. I'm drawn to Revd Martin Luther King's Christian humanist vision of 'the world house' – humanity working non-violently from existing starting points to share resources better and create 'the beloved community'. Boundaries may still exist on a map, but borders will then come to matter less. Who knows, we may even end up forgetting them.

(Continued)

> **What advice would you give undergraduates wanting to explore border worlds in their own research?**
>
> Go for it! Borders make for very good textual-analysis-based dissertations. They also make superb topics for fieldwork-based dissertations. I've seen undergraduate students go and spend a few weeks along interesting international borders to look at economic and identity-based topics. Internal borders have also proved excellent field sites. For example, my students have researched topics like the impact of Covid restrictions on life in the Anglo-Scottish borders, and the effects of county boundary changes. Borders are endlessly interesting because they tell us so much about the worlds that we make.

Summary

- Borders have always been a key concept and practice in political geography. Their importance has not diminished in the wake of globalisation.
- Understandings of borders have evolved significantly within political geography. Rather than understanding the border as a line on a map or a neat territorial container, the concepts of bordering or borderscaping speak to how the border is enacted and performed through a series of practices, actors, objects, and networks.
- Bordering practices are inherently violent, premised on exclusion and, as such, they disproportionately affect and impact marginalised people.
- Borders are embodied and felt in different ways. This may be through stereotyping or through biometric border regimes.
- Borders do not just exist along state lines. Borders are in many ways everywhere, existing within society and beyond the boundaries of nation states through off-shoring practices.

Follow-on Resources

Italian Limes: This project explores how climate change will affect border demarcations. Using the Italy–Austria border as a case study, it complicates ideas of 'natural borders'. See www.italianlimes.net/project.html

Border crossings: This project is an art and theatre based response to the bordering process. They seek to use art to facilitate mutual understanding, foster collaboration and to cultivate empathy. How might artistic interventions do this in ways that other interventions can't? See www.bordercrossings.org.uk/

Watch the Med: Watch the Mediterranean Sea is an 'online mapping platform to monitor the deaths and violations of migrants' rights at the maritime borders of the EU'. How does it seek to bring to justice to bordering practices on the Med? See https://watch-themed.net/

References

Al Jazeera (2022). US border agents used 'unnecessary force' on Haitians: Report. *Al Jazeera*, 8 July. Available at: www.aljazeera.com/news/2022/7/8/us-border-agents-used-unnecessary-force-on-haitians-report (accessed 19 May 2023).

Amoore, L. (2006). Biometric borders: Governing mobilities in the war on terror. *Political Geography*, *25*(3), 336–351.

Amoore, L. (2021). The deep border. *Political Geography*, 102547.

Bagelman, J. and Cinnamon, J. (2018). Border enforcement and the university: A conversation. *Society and Space*, *41*(2). Available at: http://societyandspace.org/2018/05/29/border-enforcement-the-university-a-conversation/ (accessed 19 May 2023).

Bialasiewicz, L. (2012). Off-shoring and out-sourcing the borders of Europe: Libya and EU border work in the Mediterranean. *Geopolitics*, *17*(4), 843–866.

Blanco, M. L. (2022). Intimate bordering: Intimacy, anti-Blackness and gender violence in the making of the Dominican border. *Political Geography*, *99*, 102743.

Brambilla, C. (2015). Exploring the critical potential of the borderscapes concept. *Geopolitics*, *20*(1): 14–34.

Brambilla, C. (2021). Revisiting 'bordering, ordering and othering': An invitation to 'migrate' towards a politics of hope. *Tijdschrift voor economische en sociale geografie*, *112*(1), 11–17.

Brambilla, C. and Jones, R. (2020). Rethinking borders, violence, and conflict: From sovereign power to borderscapes as sites of struggles. *Environment and Planning D: Society and Space*, *38*(2), 287–305.

Cassidy, K., Yuval-Davis, N. and Wemyss, G. (2018). Intersectional border(ing)s. *Political Geography*, *66*, 139–141.

Gentleman, A. (2017). Crackdown on migrants forces NHS doctors to 'act as border guards'. *The Guardian*, 20 April. Available at: www.theguardian.com/uk-news/2017/apr/20/crackdown-migrants-nhs-doctors-border-guards-immigration-undocumented-migrants (accessed 19 May 2023).

Giudice, C. and Giubilaro, C. (2015). Re-imagining the border: Border art as a space of critical imagination and creative resistance. *Geopolitics*, *20*(1), 79–94.

Hamblett, A. (2013). Private landlords should not be surrogate police or border officers. *The Guardian*, 16 May. Available at: www.theguardian.com/housing-network/2013/may/16/private-landlords-police-border-officers (accessed 19 May 2023).

Jackson, L. (2016). Experiencing exclusion and reacting to stereotypes? Navigating borders of the migrant body. *Area*, *48*(3), 292–299.

Jenkins, M. (2014). On the effects and implications of UK Border Agency involvement in higher education. *The Geographical Journal*, *180*(3), 265–270.

Jones, R. (2009). Agents of exception: Border security and the marginalization of Muslims in India. *Environment and Planning D: Society and Space*, *27*(5), 879–897.

Jones, R. (2014). Border wars: Narratives and images of the US–Mexico border on TV. *ACME: An International Journal for Critical Geographies*, *13*(3), 530–550.

Jones, R. (2016). *Violent borders: Refugees and the right to move*. London and New York: Verso.

Jones, R., Johnson, C., Brown, W., Popescu, G., Pallister-Wilkins, P., Mountz, A. and Gilbert, E. (2017). Interventions on the state of sovereignty at the border. *Political Geography, 59*, 1–10.

Little, A. and Vaughan-Williams, N. (2017). Stopping boats, saving lives, securing subjects: Humanitarian borders in Europe and Australia. *European Journal of International Relations, 23*(3), 533–556.

Mbembe, A. (2019). Bodies as borders. *From the European South, 4*, 5–18.

Megoran, N. (2021). Borders on steroids: Open borders in a Covid-19 world? *Political Geography*, 102443.

National Immigration Justice Centre (2021). Pushing back protection: How offshoring and externalisation imperil the right to asylum. Available at: https://immigrantjustice.org/sites/default/files/content-type/research-item/documents/2021-08/Offshoring-Asylum-Report_final.pdf (accessed 19 May 2023).

Paasi, A. (2012). Border studies reanimated: Going beyond the territorial/relational divide. *Environment and Planning A, 44*, 2303–2309.

Perera, S. (2006). 'They give evidence': Bodies, borders and the disappeared. *Social Identities, 12*(6), 637–656.

Salter, M. (2008). When the exception becomes the rule. *Citizenship Studies, 12*(4), 365–380.

Smith, S., Swanson, N. W. and Gökariksel, B. (2016). Territory, bodies, and borders. *Area, 48*(3), 258–261.

Stierl, M. (2020). How Europe is using coronavirus to reinforce its hostile environment in the Mediterranean. *Lacuna Magazine*, 20 May. Available at: https://lacuna.org.uk/migration/how-europe-is-using-coronavirus-to-reinforce-its-hostile-environment-in-the-mediterranean/ (accessed 19 May 2023).

Van Houtum, H. (2005). The geopolitics of borders and boundaries, *Geopolitics, 10*(4), 672–679.

Van Houtum, H. and Van Naerssen, T. (2002). Bordering, ordering and othering. *Tijdschrift voor economische en sociale geografie, 93*(2), 125–136.

NINE

NATIONALISM: FLAGS, FEARS, FICTIONS

Chapter Overview

Being part of a nation is perhaps something many of us take for granted. It is something 'natural', often assigned at birth, and more often than not, left unchallenged in our lives. This chapter shines a spotlight on ideas of the nation and nationalism. Far from being natural, it understands nationalism as a social construct – one with powerful and problematic implications for how we interact with the world, how we imagine it, and crucially, how exclusionary notions of 'us' and 'them' are constructed. It explores nationalism at a number of scales and across a range of contexts before thinking through how feminist approaches of care, welcome, and hospitality might challenge nationalistic sentiment.

Learning Objectives

1. To understand 'nationalism' as a complex concept that operates across multiple scales and contexts.
2. To think critically about manifestations of nationalism in our everyday lives.
3. To explore how notions of nationalism can be challenged and resisted.

Read with: Chapter 7 (States and Territory), Chapter 8 (Borders), Chapter 5 (Non-human Worlds), Chapter 3 (Feminist Geopolitics)

Expressions of nationalism are everywhere. From flags to postage stamps, reminders that you 'belong' to a nation abound within daily life. Rendered invisible by its ubiquity, nationalism is something that can easily be taken for granted and left un-analysed as we go about day-to-day life. The end of an era of nationalism, once prophesised alongside the demise of the nation state (see Chapter 7), 'is not remotely in sight' (Anderson 1983: 3). Indeed Anderson's (1983: 3) claim that 'nation-ness is the most universally legitimate value in the political life' still rings true many years later. Yet this idea of nation-ness is not natural, and ideas about the nation do come from *somewhere*. Far from being naturally occurring, nationalism is embedded within objects, it circulates through atmospheres, it is delivered in political speeches and constructed through language, and it waves in the wind through flags that adorn both state and everyday buildings. Nationalism and ideas of the 'nation' are not passive and inert backdrops to modern life, but rather are powerful drivers of identity politics and are ideologies for which people fight and die. Whether you identify strongly with a nation or not, nationalism commands profound power in the shaping of the world. This might be through the constructions of 'us' and 'them' that result from nationalistic sentiment, or the upswells of national pride that can galvanise communities and populations to invest and attach themselves to a national identity. Either way, nationalism matters in its capacity to mobilise people to think collectively in the pursuit of common goals, from waging war to hosting an Olympic Games (see Shin 2019).

What is Nationalism?

Whilst expressions of nationalism might be relatively straightforward to identify when you look for them, the concept itself is less straightforward to grasp and define (see Anderson 1983). A number of definitions, for example, pick up on the characteristics that might come to define a nation, with one of the earliest definitions of nationalism by French Philosopher Ernest Renan (1882) describing a nation as 'a soul' or a 'spiritual principle'. Within this soul, Renan described two key features that a population might share to think of themselves as a nation. The first is the 'possession of a rich legacy of memories'. In other words, a nation will have some sort of shared history. The second is 'present consent, the desire to live together, the desire to continue to invest in the heritage we have jointly received'. For Renan, this shared history carries through to the present, and is moved forward by a collective sense of togetherness. Similar sensibilities emerge in a range of other engagements with what makes a 'nation'. Shin (2019: 1), for example, writes of a nation being a 'community of people who share language, culture, and a sense of common history and destiny'. Smith (1991 in Jones et al. 2004: 83) picks up on these themes too, writing that a nation should be viewed as a 'named population sharing an historic territory, common myths, and historical memories'. While it is difficult to pin down, a nation represents a shared sense of collectivity, or what Benedict Anderson (1983: 6) refers to as an 'imagined community'. For Anderson, the community is imagined in that even within the smallest of states or territories, you will never meet and know everyone, and yet you might imagine yourself as being part of something with that group of people. The advent of print capitalism was key here – connecting national communities and allowing people to relate to each other in profoundly new ways (Anderson 1983). A national football match would be a contemporary example of an imagined community. You will never meet the vast majority of people in a football stadium, and yet you imagine yourself to be sharing the same sense of national identity or national affiliation – that you share a 'deep, horizontal comradeship' (Anderson 1983:

7). This sense of belonging always implies a sense of detachment from those 'outside' of this group (Militz and Schurr 2016).

National Atmospheres

These imagined communities are enacted, practised, and brought into being through a range of 'social activities, discourses, and cultural practices' (Shin 2019: 2). In this sense, they are much more than 'imagined'. As Merriman and Jones (2017: 602) assert, we might better understand nations as 'relational, networked, or performed socio-material constructions'. As Closs (2016: 191) writes, national feelings 'can stick to many different kinds of objects, materials, and bodies' and 'things' that may be charged with national atmospheres in one moment but not in the next. At a football match, for example, nationalism might be felt and experienced through the shared practices of singing the national anthem, flag waving, shirt wearing, cheering, or collective despairing. It cannot be traced back and does not emanate from a single source, rather it must be traced through 'multiple constituencies as part of a nebulous, diffuse atmosphere' (Closs 2016: 182).

Unpacking *how* this comes into being is extremely important. In the words of Closs (2016: 182), we need to understand how nationality becomes 'installed in the soft tissues of affect, emotion, habit, and posture'. How does it take hold? How can we pin something that can seem so ephemeral and ubiquitous? Closs explores these questions in relation to the London 2012 Olympic Games, finding that a range of affective logics come together to produce the nation at any given time. This ranged from slogans like 'we make the games!' – 'we' implying a sense of bounded community, to an Olympic torch relay that travelled round the United Kingdom, to the opening ceremony which told a particular story about Britain and its national history, celebrating things like the National Health Service (NHS). A healthy budget of £32 million was also allocated to 'dress town centres in the Olympic spirit'. The main venue, lit up in the colours of the Union Jack (see Figure 9.1), served as a focal point for nationalistic sentiments to emerge. For Closs (2016: 184), the 2012 Olympics served as an example of affective nationalism, whereby an atmosphere came to define the national mood. This was informed by 'sound, music, colours, ... postures and gestures'. In other words, it was actively constructed and reproduced by those that adopted this mood and national sensibility.

However, these feelings and affective dispositions are not singular or universal. As Closs (2016: 185) writes, nationalism can be experienced in a range of ways by different people at different times. These might be premised on attachment and detachment, generosity and hospitality, competition and hostility, or anything in between. If we are to understand nationalism as something that is constructed, that circulates between people and objects, then it will never be experienced in the same way by everyone. As Merriman and Jones (2017) highlight, events, spaces, and practices may for one person be mundane and banal, whilst for others, experienced intensely. The resonance of nationalism is variable. For Antonsich et al. (2020: 4), 'the idea that some will be moved, while others may feel excluded or even just plain bored' by a particular context, encourages us to pay attention to the politics of nationalism.

Figure 9.1 Olympic stadium and The Orbit during London Olympics opening ceremony 2012

Credit: Alexander Kachkaev (Creative Commons Attribution 2.0 Generic license) https://commons.wikimedia.org/wiki/File:Olympic_stadium_and_The_Orbit_during_London_Olympics_opening_ceremony_(2012-07-27)_2.jpg

In the Field with Angharad Closs: Nationalism and Atmospheres

Angharad Closs Stephens is Senior Lecturer in Human Geography at Swansea University and author of *The persistence of nationalism: From imagined communities to urban encounters* (Routledge, 2013) and *National affects: The everyday atmospheres of being political* (Bloomsbury, 2022).

What drew you to researching nationalism?

I was lucky to have a PhD supervisor who encouraged me to begin and keep returning to the questions I had about the world. 'Keep staring at the question' was one of his catchphrases. I was drawn to researching nationalism because I had questions about where ideas about 'us and them' had come from, how they became so powerful, and how so many debates seem tied up in reproducing that binary. I was drawn to read and write about nationalism because I felt frustrated and often enraged with this way of seeing the world. And I wanted to find ways of getting past those ideas. This felt like a very intense and urgent need for me at the time.

(Continued)

How did you go about researching feelings and atmospheres that aren't necessarily tangible?

I remember watching the London Olympic Games of 2012 on television with a friend I have known most of my life. She is a keen fan of watching sports on television – indeed, her whole family is. We therefore watched the Games, as I expected we would, and of course that meant watching the feelings and atmospheres that were visible on the screen, but which also surpassed the screen and echoed in the special events put on in the city I lived in at the time, the decorations placed in the local supermarket and on the streets, and in social media initiatives. At this time, I had just completed my book on *The persistence of nationalism: From imagined communities to urban encounters* (Routledge, 2013). I remember realising that in that book, I hadn't really engaged with people's feelings. Suddenly this felt ridiculous: how could I write about the nation and not engage with affects and feelings? Although these are not very tangible, they are nevertheless palpable and undeniable.

What role do geographers have in making sense of current nationalistic trends?

I feel I was so lucky to come across Human Geography, and to find a job being employed as a geographer. In geography, I found a discipline that had a much more open and grassroots understanding of what 'politics' is, and an intense interest in asking, *how do people live?* That is, geographers often start from the empirics, asking what is taking place on the ground, and from there, develop concepts and ideas. When I listen to or read theories of global politics now, I find myself wondering how a strikingly well-developed conceptual framework comes up against the incoherence of things on the ground – the messiness of how people live and how people can hold viewpoints that are at the same time, completely contradictory. This is of course also a huge contribution of affect theories for me – how they offer rich readings of everyday life – something that geography and geographers first showed me.

The messiness and complexity of nationalism was laid bare in a number of ways at the Olympics. The 'British' status of national hero Mo Farah, for example, was always held in tension (Closs 2016). Whilst celebrated, his status as a Somali-born British citizen revealed anxieties about difference. As Closs (2016: 189) highlights, Farah was 'repeatedly asked in television interviews about his feelings of belonging to Britain'. He was at once emphatically celebrated as British, yet the 'depth of his Britishness' was constantly being called into question. Nationalism, as is explored later in the chapter, is always premised on 'underlying assumptions of "hosts" and "guests", "insiders" and "outsiders" … and bounded notions of membership' of a national citizenry (Aparna and Schapendonk 2018: 2). Within this framework, 'who is a "migrant", who is a "guest", who is a "citizen", who is a "host", who is a "resident alien", who is a "stranger" is highly situational, highly contested, and comes to be produced and transformed' in specific situations, like the Olympics where Britishness was seen to be at a premium (Aparna and Schapendonk 2018: 228). We also saw how the then British prime minister, David Cameron, sought to extend the affective nationalisms that emerged during the Olympics. Closs (2016: 191) highlights how Cameron returned to the Olympic Park after the Olympics to make a speech on the Scottish independence referendum. The site was supposed to represent British unity, rather than division, making it a significant choice on behalf of Cameron and his team. Nationalism does, after all, provide legitimacy to the state (see Chapter 7). Nationalism is continually made and remade here through relationships between people, objects, and particular places. In seeking to deconstruct nationalism we can acknowledge the different forms it takes, think about how it travels and how it finds form, and explore the dissonances that occur with any kind of nationalistic sentiment or feeling.

Over to You: Imagined Nations

As with the example of Mo Farah, nationalism is premised on ideas of who belongs and who does not. States are active in shaping these imaginaries and in deciding who gets to join a national citizenry and who is excluded from doing so.

Do some research and find out what it means to obtain citizenship in the country you were born in.

- Is there a test?
- What kinds of questions make up the test?
- Would you pass?
- What do these tests/questions say about the construction of a national imaginary and identity?
- How does it relate to ideas of inclusion, exclusion, and belonging?

Nationalism and the Everyday

Beyond grand displays of nationalism, such as the Olympic Games, we can also consider nationalism as an everyday practice. As Antonsich et al. (2020) and others argue, nationalism is underpinned by everyday processes and feelings that manifest in a number of ways. Michael Billig's (1995) seminal work on *Banal nationalism* is very helpful here. For Billig (1995: 6) many of the 'ideological habits, by which our nations are reproduced as nations, are unnamed and therefore unnoticed'. Billig cites the national flag hanging outside public buildings in the United States as a prime example (see Figure 9.2). The flag, he writes, 'attracts no special attention. It belongs to no special, sociological genus' (Billig 1995: 6). In other words, it is so non-descript and omnipresent that it forms part of the background of everyday life. As a result, this reproduction of (US) nationalism is never identified or critically interrogated.

In this sense, nationalism is not something that exists 'out there' or something that is performed by extremists and far right nationalists. On the contrary, Billig (1995: 6) argues

Figure 9.2 US Utah Ogden High School 2019

Credit: Thomas Wozniak (Creative Commons Attribution-Share Alike 4.0 International license) https://commons.wikimedia.org/wiki/File:US_Utah_Ogden_High_School_2019.JPG

that 'the world of nations is the world of the everyday'. Everyday objects and practices including coins, bank notes, and weather forecasts are used by Billig to highlight how the nation is continually 'flagged' to populations. We might think of street names and signs (see Azaryahu and Kook 2002), postage stamps (see Raento and Bruun 2005), and a whole host of other everyday 'flaggings' within this framework, each serving as an almost sub-conscious reminder of the nation and by association, the state. Merriman and Jones (2017: 606) incorporate other unlikely actors within this system of flaggings and nationalism. Roads, railways, flight corridors, shipping routes, and other infrastructures are not only responsible for networking nations but they do so in very particular, often nationalised ways. No two countries' infrastructures will be the same, 'leaving different traces in national space' and shaping our national experience in 'distinctive ways' (Merriman and Jones 2017: 606). The visualisations of these infrastructures are particularly important. Maps, whether in Google Maps, an atlas, or a route planner, circulate understandings of mobility and travel and are the ways many people traverse and inhabit national space. Despite their importance, they are often taken for granted and thought of (if at all) as 'ordinary, banal, insignificant' (Merriman and Jones 2017: 612). These objects, artefacts, and infrastructures perform cultural and political work as they are brought into relationships with people, other objects, and various affects and atmospheres.

As scholars such as Benwell (2014) and Jones and Merriman (2009) have highlighted, however, it is also important to look beyond mindless 'flaggings'. Many reproductions of the nation might occur in everyday contexts but are very deliberate, thoughtful, and force-ful interventions that exist alongside the unremarkable and banal expressions outlined by Billig. For Benwell (2014), it is important to consider these other everyday expressions and to better understand where nationhood is learned and communicated. Such approaches 'foreground the significance of people's everyday practices and feelings in underpinning national forms of organisation, identification, and expression' (Antonsich et al. 2020: 2). Benwell (2014) explores this in relation to the Falkland Islands, researching how school students are actively taught about their nation and identity as citizens of a British Overseas Territory through the national curriculum, but also through activities like visits to local and national memorials, sporting events, and writing poetry. Militz and Schurr (2016) explore everyday nationalism in relation to national dancing in Azerbaijan, highlighting how other practices, including the cooking and eating of traditional or national dishes, might also be understood as everyday and atmospheric reproductions of the nation at the scale of the body. Meanwhile, Jones and Merriman (2009) explore the campaign for bilingual road signs in Wales as a form of everyday, hard-fought nationalism. Some people may not have noticed or cared, but for others single language English signs were seen as an affront to Welshness and the Welsh language. The previous monolingual English signs were seen as an oppressive imposition of 'Englishness' on Wales. Road signs are an incredibly everyday form of nationalism and representation but the 1960s and 70s campaign to change the signs to bilingual (Welsh and English) served as an important reminder of the everyday contexts within which nationalism is reproduced and fought for (Jones and Merriman 2009).

In short, the 'nation does not somehow stand apart from other aspects of our everyday lives' (Antonsich et al. 2020). This is important to note as it radically changes what nationalism is, and how we challenge understandings of it as a fixed and stable entity. If we understand nationalism as already and always entangled within our experiences and everyday lives, then we can understand nationalism as being contingent in those contexts. It is only as prominent and powerful as the reproductions that embody it. Nationalism is thus malleable, changeable, and never fixed. In the words of Antonsich et al. (2020: 3), it reveals the 'very instability' of nationalism. Far from being grounded, fixed, stable, and operating in a single direction, nations and nationalism might better be understood as in constant movement, open to change, and in flux.

Case Study: Extra-Territorial Nationalism (Shin 2019)

Whilst nationalism is often associated with a particular space or state, we might think about how this can be complicated to better grapple with its complexity as a concept and practice. Shin (2019: 1), for example, explores practices associated with extra-territorial nation building – that is practices 'that build a nation as a collective identity and imagined society outside the national territory'. This involves nation building and nationalism from the 'bottom-up', separate from the practices and performances of the state. Shin explores this through the nation-building practices of North Korean refugees living in New Malden in the UK, the largest North Korean community in Europe.

(Continued)

> The research provides an insight into practices of nationalism and nation building 'free from all state interference'.
>
> Shin found that North Korean refugees undertake a variety of strategies to maintain a sense of 'North Koreaness'. This includes strategies to disengage with South Korean migrants (reflecting a state-level policy where face-to-face contact between North and South citizens is technically banned). Whilst schools might be mixed, Shin noted that North Korean and South Korean parents 'do not mingle', and North Korean language schools, churches, restaurants, shops, and associations provided spaces to practise being North Korean. This functions as a form of border maintenance, whereby a distinction is made between migrants and the host society (see Smith et al. 2016). One participant in Shin's research stated that they were 'afraid our North Koreaness will disappear'. Material practices of nation-making and place-making are crucial in maintaining this sense of national identity 'outside the national physical territory' (Shin 2019: 2).

The Divisive Logics of Nationalism: 'Us' and 'Them'

Whilst phrases like 'We make the Games!' at the London Olympics may seem to be relatively innocent, more broadly the process of drawing boundaries around groups of people through language like 'we', 'us', and 'them' is less so. As Jones et al. (2004: 82) highlight, one of the main 'ideological foundations of nationalism is to encourage us to believe that it is possible to draw boundaries around homogenous groupings of people'. The effects of this manifest on multiple scales and are made starkly apparent in moments of geopolitical ruptures like 9/11. Indeed 9/11 was a watershed moment in reifying ideas of the American nation and American nationalism and this took place against an outside other. As you can see from the following excerpts from a speech by then president, George W Bush (2001), distinct language was used to draw a boundary around America as a nation:

> Tonight, we are a country awakened to danger and called to defend freedom. Our grief has turned to anger and anger to resolution. Whether we bring our enemies to justice or bring justice to our enemies, justice will be done.
>
> All of America was touched on the evening of the tragedy to see Republicans and Democrats joined together on the steps of this Capitol singing 'God Bless America'.
>
> Americans have many questions tonight. Americans are asking, 'Who attacked our country?'

The words 'we' and 'our' are extremely powerful here. They denote a community, drawing clear lines around America as a united entity, providing a clear sense of belonging for those that feel a part of the America being described by Bush. Note that Bush also states that 'all of America was touched on the evening of the tragedy', suggesting that to be un-touched by the events of 9/11 was to be un-American and to stand outside of national interests. Bush went on to ask, 'why do they hate us?', before stating:

> These terrorists kill not merely to end lives, but to disrupt and end a way of life. With every atrocity, they hope that America grows fearful … They stand against us because we stand in their way.
>
> Every nation in every region now has a decision to make: Either you are with us or you are with the terrorists.

In addition to drawing a line around the American nation, Bush is also framing the nation in opposition to an outside other. Words like 'they' imply a group that is beyond the American nation. The final statement takes this to an extreme, dividing a world into us and them, pro-American and anti-terrorist or anti-American and pro-terrorist. Drawing on a long history of American exceptionalism, such divisive ideologies were most likely long present in the psyche of George Bush, but 9/11 gave them an opportunity to erupt with profound and destructive consequences.

KEY TERMS: 'OTHER'

The notion of the 'other' and 'othering' originates from Edward Said's work, *Orientalism* (1978). Said used the phrase orientalism to describe how in Western ways of thinking, a distinction is made between the Occident (self) and the Orient (other). The idea of the 'other' and 'othering' is now widely used to describe practices, ideologies, and belief systems where stark boundaries are made between the self (usually White, Western) and other people or groups of people who are seen to be outside that 'norm'. The 'other' is often painted as being dangerous, a threat, and undesirable in some way, and such binary distinctions are inherently and problematically premised on race.

It became very difficult, for example, to voice any critical opinions of America and the subsequent War on Terror in the immediate aftermath of 9/11. Moreover, pre-existing expressions of nationalism, such as the pledge of allegiance performed by school children every morning, took on a very different tone. This was a kind of nationalism writ large, and to stand outside of it had significant social consequences. As Antonsich et al. (2020: 11) state, affective nationalism is 'made through affective economies of fear and love' – in this case this was love of country and fear of the other. As Saeed (2011) highlights, the consequences of this are deeply personal, lived, and experienced. For Saeed, a British Muslim, the hostility he experienced after 9/11 made him question his own 'notions of identity and belonging'. He felt a need to emphasise his 'Britishness', constantly treading the stark binary of being British or Muslim, whilst simultaneously being constructed as a 'false national' and othered (Saeed 2011: 210–213). The panic and fear around 9/11, and later attacks including the 7/7 London Underground bombings empowered far-right political communities who loudly shouted for a return to a '"core national culture", alongside stricter immigration and policing controls' (Saeed 2011: 211). The racism and Islamophobia that followed (including widespread racial profiling by the police), is 'premised on generalising human beings' existence and experiences into simple homogenous groupings' (Saeed 2011: 211) – in other words it is premised on the idea and practice of nationalism. The nation here becomes located on the body with the colour of skin, and choice of clothing and dress serving as fuel for far-right nationalists to generate mistrust and racism (see Hopkins 2007).

Beyond Terrorism

We do not need to go as far back as 11 September 2001 to see how racism and nationalism so often go hand in hand (see Tolia-Kelly in Antonsich et al. 2020). Such dynamics unfold the world over, with stark examples emerging from the Russian invasion of Ukraine which began in 2022 and, at the time of writing, is far from over. Who was allowed to leave Ukraine was very much determined along racist lines. Black and Indian people, for example, reported widespread racism as they sought to leave Ukraine after the Russian invasion (Pietromarchi 2022, UN 2022). Meanwhile, whilst European states opened their arms to White Ukrainian refugees, Yemeni, Syrian, and other refugees from the Middle East and Africa are not afforded the same welcome. White bodies are clearly privileged. In a different context, we see similar ideologies pushed to tragic extremes. The genocide of Rohingya Muslims in Myanmar, for example, is premised on underlying assumptions of self and other, belonging and exclusion.

Conclusions: Beyond Nationalism?

As the chapter has explored, nationalism is a powerful social construction that infuses life across multiple scales – from the national to the everyday. It is something that emerges through relationships, whether that be between people, objects, or infrastructures, and it powerfully shapes how people see themselves in relation to the 'other'. Moments of crisis like 9/11 bring these feelings to the fore, demonstrating in the process that nationalism is always and inherently exclusive. As it also explored, nationalism can be complicated and it is not always attached to the state. It is precisely because nationalism is complex, and anything but stable that we can speculate on how nationalism might look differently in the future. National futures are not set in stone in any context, leaving room to imagine how they might be otherwise, premised on inclusivity and generosity as much as suspicion and aggression (Antonsich et al. 2020: 6).

As is highlighted in the introduction to this textbook and as will be explored in the final chapters, political geography offers opportunities to think about how geopolitical phenomenon might be otherwise. Drawing on feminist approaches (see Chapter 3), Dowler (2013) demonstrates how a politics of welcome might unsettle nationalistic sentiment that draws boundaries around 'them' and 'us'. For Dowler, a politics of hospitality that is reciprocal and grounded can minimise this binary (Dowler 2013: 780). Hospitality can of course be understood in many ways. As Craggs (2014) highlights, it is both something that takes place at a national scale through practices of diplomacy, or might be understood in terms of the hospitality industry. Dowler (2013: 783), however, understands hospitality on a more intimate and everyday scale whereby practices of

POLITICAL GEOGRAPHY

welcome are adopted in spaces that minimise the distance between self and other, host and guest. These are spaces of care that are sheltering and nourishing, subverting state 'entry' practices that might involve visa applications, interactions with border forces and other mechanisms through which the state imposes itself on people (see Chapter 7).

For Gill (2018), in order to reimagine what it means to belong, and to do away with the exclusive and divisive logics that so often accompany nationalism, we must think beyond simply permitting entry to people or just meeting practical needs like food, drink, and shelter. It must entail human warmth, it cannot be 'mechanistic and unfeeling'. It needs to be underpinned by emotion, relationality, and shared vulnerability between the host and welcomer – in the words of Gill (2018: 91), 'it demands intimacy' (see also Darling 2011). Whilst this may seem apolitical, Popke highlights the political potential of this approach. For Popke (in Darling 2011: 408), 'Care is more than simply a social relation with moral or ethical dimensions; it can also be the basis for an alternative ethical standpoint, with implications for how we view traditional notions of citizenship and politics'. In other words, the feminist logics of care and welcome can be geopolitically transformative. Campaigns like #RefugeesWelcome in response to the Mediterranean refugee 'crisis' in 2014 is one example of how campaigners sought to challenge the national narrative in the UK around who is welcome and who is not. The campaign, for Gill (2018: 89), meant that the questions of belonging that surround the 'refugee' took centre stage 'in the collective consciousness of ordinary Europeans' and the matter of borders shifted, albeit briefly, from a state issue to a grassroots 'geosocial' issue. In practice this might have taken a variety of forms, including people opening their homes, or wider collectives partaking in 'City of Sanctuary' initiatives that provide practical and emotional support to refugees.

Acts of welcome and care might take other forms too. In 2012 for example, an Islamic Tartan was created in Scotland. Tartan is the national dress of Scotland and a symbol of Scottish nationalism and identity. The Islamic Tartan was created to acknowledge that many Muslims in Scotland identify as Scottish nationals and thus it was intended 'to celebrate ... communities with dual heritage' and to try and overcome intolerance and cultural discrimination (Islamic Tartan 2012: n.p.). The colours on the Tartan are symbolic, materially weaving together Scottish nationalism and Islam. In the process, Scotland also brand their own national identity as welcoming and open – suggesting that to be otherwise is to be 'un-Scottish'. Whether or not this is the experience of refugees, it is an example of the practices of place branding associated with nationalism.

Case Study: Welcome in the Baddawi Refugee Camp (Fiddian-Qasmiyeh 2015)

We often conceptualise 'welcome' as something that is extended from wealthy nations or people to less wealthy nations and people. But, as Gill (2018: 93) highlights, striking instances 'of welcome in recent years have been south–south, refugee to refugee'.

(Continued)

This might be Acehnese fishermen rescuing hundreds of displaced Rohingya who were stranded in the Andaman Sea in 2015 (Missbach 2015), or as Fiddian-Qasmiyeh (2015) highlights, something that occurs in Lebanon's Baddawi refugee camp.

Home to between 25,000–40,000 refugees, the Baddawi camp largely consists of Palestinian refugees. The camp has offered 'protection and assistance to tens of thousands of new arrivals from Syria since 2011' (Fiddian-Qasmiyeh 2015), including to Syrian nationals who have fled violence and who may have been displaced multiple times. Whilst European states debated how to respond to the crisis, vital support was given in Lebanon, Jordan, and Turkey by local communities. This is an example of what Fiddian-Qasmiyeh (2015) refers to as 'south–south humanitarianism' – that is assistance offered by Global South countries to those in need. Refugees in the Baddawi camp have been offering support and protection to refugees from Syria. Whilst there are many complexities in this process, the act of hospitality defies the 'widely held assumption that refugees are passive victims who need outsiders to care for them' and provides a shared space of solidarity and togetherness for refugees regardless of nationality.

We have seen in recent years, however, how notions of welcome can be problematic. A number of issues animate this, including the power dynamics associated with the host/stranger (Ramadan 2008) and the shifting dynamics of social relations – when is a guest no longer a guest? (Aparna and Schapendonk 2018). Most importantly perhaps, is the question of who gets to receive welcome, as explored above. Whilst not diminishing these problems, the underlying premise of welcome and hospitality, founded as it is on 'interdependence and relationality' (Darling 2011: 410), has potential in challenging future nationalistic exclusionary logics. While it requires 'hard work, commitment, and a desire to welcome others' (Darling 2011: 410), welcome and the intimacies it entails can also 'ground global events'. In other words, it brings wider geopolitical events and contexts into the everyday, generating openness and solidarity in the process (Gill 2018: 91). How this can be achieved is open to debate, but it is certainly an important pursuit.

Over to You: Questioning Welcome (See Gill 2018: 88)

Can you find an example of a welcoming practice that challenges ideas of nationalism?

- What is your example and who is involved?
- How does it disrupt nationalistic ideas?
- How does it make you think about the politics of welcome?
- Does it help us imagine the world differently?

Summary

- While we often take being part of a nation for granted, belonging to a nation is far from a 'natural' thing.
- This chapter explores nationalism as a social construct, drawing attention to both national and elite displays of the nation, as well as everyday practices of banal nationalism, to demonstrate how these collectively shape national belonging.
- Importantly, in shaping our experiences in the world, nationalism is not a singular thing. Rather, it is rooted in understandings of 'us' and 'them', friend and foe. Nationalism is thus both inclusionary and exclusionary.
- While definitions of nationalism are challenging, feminist approaches centred on care and compassion offer alternative practices which can challenge problematic nationalistic sentiments.

Follow-on Resources

The Great Campaign: This is a soft power campaign by Great Britain. Explore the site and examples and critically reflect on how Britain is being represented. How can you read this critically? See www.greatcampaign.com/

Islamic Tartan: As of 2012, an Islamic Tartan was added to the Scottish Register of Tartans. Tartan is an important material marker of national identity in Scotland and can encompass a sense of national pride. Explore the Islamic Tartan site and reflect on how this might be understood within the frameworks of nationalism and welcome. See www.islamictartan.com/

How sport affects nationalism: Drawing on the examples of Kenya and Tanzania in the Africa Cup of Nations, this *Conversation* article explores how sporting events impact nationalism and attitudes towards refugees. Do the results surprise you? See https://theconversation.com/kenya-and-tanzania-how-sport-affects-nationalism-and-attitudes-towards-refugees-159646

References

Anderson, B. (1983). *Imagined communities*. London: Verso.

Antonsich, M., Skey, M., Sumartojo, S., Merriman, P., Stephens, A. C., Tolia-Kelly, D. P., Wilson, H. and Anderson, B. (2020). The spaces and politics of affective nationalism. *Environment and Planning C: Politics and Space*, *38*(4), 579–598.

Aparna, K. and Schapendonk, J. (2018). Shifting itineraries of asylum hospitality: Towards a process geographical approach of guest-host relations. *Geoforum*, *116*, 226–234.

Azaryahu, M. and Kook, R. (2002). Mapping the nation: Street names and Arab-Palestinian identity: Three case studies. *Nations and Nationalism, 8*, 195–213.

Benwell, M. C. (2014). From the banal to the blatant: Expressions of nationalism in secondary schools in Argentina and the Falkland Islands. *Geoforum, 52*, 51–60.

Billig, M. (1995). *Banal nationalism*. London: Sage.

Bush, G. (2001). President Bush's address to a joint session of Congress and the nation, 20 September. Available at: www.washingtonpost.com/wp-srv/nation/specials/attacked/transcripts/bushaddress_092001.html (accessed 19 May 2023).

Closs, A. (2016). The affective atmospheres of nationalism. *Cultural Geographies, 23(2)*, 181–198.

Craggs, R. (2014). Hospitality in geopolitics and the making of Commonwealth international relations. *Geoforum, 52*, 90–100.

Darling, J. (2011). Giving space: Care, generosity and belonging in a UK asylum drop-in centre. *Geoforum, 42*(4), 408–417.

Dowler, L. (2013). Waging hospitality: Feminist geopolitics and tourism in West Belfast Northern Ireland. *Geopolitics, 18*(4), 779–799.

Fiddian-Qasmiyeh, E. (2015). Refugees helping refugees: How a Palestinian camp in Lebanon is welcoming Syrians, *The Conversation*, 4 November. Available at: https://theconversation.com/refugees-helping-refugees-how-a-palestinian-camp-in-lebanon-is-welcoming-syrians-48056 (accessed 31 January 2018).

Gill, N. (2018). The suppression of welcome. *Fennia, 196*(1), 88–98.

Hopkins, P. (2007). Global events, national politics, local lives: Young Muslim men in Scotland. *Environment and Planning A, 39*(5), 1119–1133.

Islamic Tartan (2012). A timely and powerful symbol of the recognition by Scotland's Islamic communities of their national identity. Available at: www.islamictartan.com/ (accessed 19 May 2023).

Jones, M., Jones, R. and Woods, M. (2004). *An introduction to political geography*. London: Routledge.

Jones, R. and Merriman, P. (2009). Hot, banal, and everyday nationalism: Bilingual road signs in Wales. *Political Geography, 28*, 164–173.

Merriman, P. and Jones, R. (2017). Nations, materialities and affects. *Progress in Human Geography, 41*(5), 600–617.

Militz, E. and Schurr, C. (2016). Affective nationalism: Banalities of belonging in Azerbaijan. *Political Geography, 54*, 54–63.

Missbach, A. (2015). *Troubled transit: Asylum seekers stuck in Indonesia*. ISEAS-Yusof Ishak Institute.

Pietromarchi, V. (2022). More African students decry racism at Ukrainian borders, *Al Jazeera*, 2 March. Available at: www.aljazeera.com/news/2022/3/2/more-racism-at-ukrainian-borders (accessed 19 May 2023).

Raento, P. and Brunn, S. D. (2005). Visualizing Finland: Postage stamps as political messengers. *Geografiska Annaler Series B, 87*, 145–163.

Ramadan, A. (2008). The guests' guests: Palestinian refugees, Lebanese civilians, and the war of 2006. *Antipode, 40*, 658–677.

Renan, E. (1882). What is a Nation?, text of a conference delivered at the Sorbonne, 11 March 1882, in Ernest Renan, *Qu'est-ce qu'une nation?* Available at: http://ucparis.fr/files/9313/6549/9943/What_is_a_Nation.pdf (accessed 19 May 2023).

Saeed, A. (2011). 9/11 and the increase in racism and Islamophobia: A personal reflection. *Radical History Review, 111*, 210–215.

Said, E. (1978). *Orientalism.* London: Routledge.

Shin, H. (2019). Extra-territorial nation-building in flows and relations: North Korea in the global networks and an ethnic enclave. *Political Geography, 74*, 102048.

Smith, S., Swanson, N. W. and Gökariksel, B. (2016). Territory, bodies, and borders. *Area, 48*(3), 258–261.

UN (2022). Ukraine: UN expert condemns racist threats, xenophobia at border. Press release, 3 March. Available at: www.ohchr.org/en/press-releases/2022/03/ukraine-un-expert-condemns-racist-threats-xenophobia-border (accessed 19 May 2023).

TEN
MOBILITIES: GEOPOLITICS IN MOTION

Chapter Overview

From the micro-mobilities of our everyday lives to the movement of troops and tanks across borders, the politics of movement matters. Power seeps in and out of our mobile lives, defining where we feel safe, where we feel out of place, in danger, or at home. As Cook (2018: 137) notes, it's an 'inescapable and fundamental fact of life', underpinning both the 'extraordinary and the everyday'. Who and what can move, and who is forced to stop, to wait, and to stay in place are fundamentally geopolitical questions, as movement is unevenly accessed and experienced. Through the lens of different moments and experiences of passage, this chapter explores mobility as an important concept. It also highlights that to think about mobility is to consider immobility too. From being forced to stop and halt at detention centres or migrant camps, to stopping and occupying a protest space, both immobility and stillness are inherently political experiences and practices too.

Learning Objectives

1. To gain an understanding of what mobility is and why it matters as a geopolitical concept.
2. To develop an understanding of different forms of immobility and the ways that it can impact and interrupt everyday life.
3. To facilitate the independent application of the concepts of mobility and immobility to case studies.

Read with: Chapter 5 (Non-human Worlds), Chapter 8 (Borders), Chapter 3 (Feminist Geopolitics)

Our world is constantly on the move. From human migration to flows of goods and pollution, geopolitical worlds are composed by and alive with mobilities. Climate change has and will only exacerbate this, with mobilities becoming 'a keyword for the twenty-first century' (Hannam et al. 2006: 1). This was made readily apparent in the wake of the 2020 outbreak of Covid-19. Mobility was halted, curtailed, and shifted in a range of ways, from lockdowns to social distancing, to the growing popularity of video-conferencing, to the disconnections related to uneven vulnerabilities of encountering a mobile, yet invisible, virus (Ho and Maddrell 2020, Sparke and Anguelov 2020). We might also think of the war in Ukraine as an example of a highly publicised mobility politics. The movements of troops, tanks, and soldiers was carefully surveyed from the air, refugees were tracked and monitored as they moved across borders, whilst wider global concerns were sparked about food and supply shortages as the war affected the movement of energy, grain, and other staple materials consumed by people thousands of miles outside of Ukraine.

Defining and Interrogating Mobility

How can we interrogate these events that are at once global and local, through the framework of mobilities? What does it offer? As Tim Cresswell (2010: 552) writes, 'mobilities research thinks about a variety of things that move, including humans, ideas and objects'. To adopt a mobilities lens, then, is to 'interrupt the taken-for-granted world of flows', at once 'questioning how things move' and the meanings afforded to these movements (Cresswell 2014: 712). In exploring mobility, it is important to note that mobility is more than simply mapping journeys from A to B, but rather involves considering the social and political complexities of movement (Cresswell 2010: 552). Before exploring in greater detail, it is helpful to dig a little further into how geographers have defined mobility. While acknowledging that mobility is a challenging and contested concept (Adey 2017), the list below shows four central ways scholars have explored mobility as everyday and embodied, material, spatialised and moderated, and political and uneven.

1. **Mobility is everyday and embodied**: We enact and encounter mobility in our everyday lives, and experience mobility through our bodies. Everyday mobilities, including walking, driving, cycling, and sitting on the train, are accessed and experienced differently, by different people.
2. **Mobility is material**: Mobile materials aid our mobility, accompany, and sustain us. For example, aircraft carry us, viruses travel within and around us, and materials such as water and energy flow into our homes.
3. **Mobility is spatialised and moderated**: There are particular spaces and sites associated with mobility, such as airports, railways, and borders. Mobility is moderated, controlled, and policed at and beyond such sites.
4. **Mobility is political and uneven**: Forms and experiences of mobility are not uniform or singular. Geopolitical factors, such as identity, impact who and what can and can't move. Considering mobility requires attention to difference.

Mobility as Everyday and Embodied

Understanding everyday and embodied mobilities has been key to exploring the power dynamics of mobile lives (Binnie et al. 2007: 165). After all, we both enact and encounter mobility in our everyday lives, and experience mobility in our bodies through practices like walking, taking the bus, and cycling. Each of these forms of everyday mobility are 'high on policy agendas', following desires to enable and 'adopt more sustainable modes of transport' and travel (Middleton 2011: 90). These forms of everyday mobility are thus inherently political.

In addition, as we move, we feel this in our bodies. As Simon Cook (2021: 1) writes of run-commuting, a 'rapidly growing mobile practice in which people run between work and home', a desire to make time for running often drives this desire for movement, one that is both 'effortful and intensely embodied' (further information about Simon Cook's work can be found in the 'In the Field' box below; see also the discussion of bodies in Chapter 3). When considering the 'experiential dimensions' of everyday mobilities (Middleton 2011: 91) we can also think about different bodily experiences of movement through drawing attention to the 'diverse' ways that differently-abled bodies move (Hall and Wilton 2017, see also Bissell 2009). As we will explore further in the discussion of mobility as uneven below, mobility is differently experienced and impacted by difference. A wheelchair user, for example, will experience a city in very different ways to a non-wheelchair user.

In the Field with Simon Cook: Running Geographies

Simon Cook is a geographer whose work explores geographies of mobility through the lens of running. Read more on Simon's blog, 'Jographies' (https://jographies. wordpress.com/).

What does mobility mean to you?

My understanding of mobility is influenced by Tim Cresswell's early work on the topic, particularly through ideas of mobility = movement + meaning + power. For me, this illuminates the complex ways movement connects and divides within and between societies. Mobility is affected by and effects differentiated social relations in the extraordinary and the everyday that make it a potent concept for political geography.

How and why did you approach the study of mobility through running?

Running has become the focus of my mobilities thinking a) because I am a runner, and b) because running aligns well with mobilities' desire to understand movement as more than functional. In running, the start and end points are often the same, so

(Continued)

> understanding this movement requires asking a different set of questions, which for me has often meant exploring the micro-politics of moving in cities.
>
> ### Do you have any top tips for a student interested in undertaking research on mobility?
>
> Mobility is a tangible concept yet one difficult to pin down and research. Mobilities are inherently bound up in other mobilities in ways that are hard to unpick. To help refine your research interests, take the mobile phenomenon under question and try asking: What if it didn't move? What if it moved differently? What if other people/things moved instead? Thinking through the implications of mobility changes and disruptions like this can highlight key aspects for your enquiries.

When thinking about everyday bodily experiences of movement we can also consider the social dimensions of movement. Writing of 'everyday bus travel', Wilson (2011: 634, 635) turns attention to 'bodily orientations' and 'public codes of conduct', arguing that the bus is a 'space of extraordinary intimacy' in which 'bodies are pressed up against each other, seats are shared, and personal boundaries constantly negotiated'. Reflecting specifically on the bus as a site of 'everyday multiculture' in which mobile bodies 'negotiate difference on the smallest of scales', Wilson (2011: 635) argues that 'physical mobility can powerfully combine social mobility and belonging' too. Mobility, then, is both social and political in interesting ways.

Mobility as Material

Second, we can understand mobility as material. Mobile materials both aid our mobility, accompany, and sustain us. Non-humans such as viruses can also accompany our mobile bodies. As Adey et al. (2021: 3) write of mobility in the time of the Covid-19 pandemic, 'the diseased body and the mobile body appear almost as one', arguing that 'we can think of mobile bodies as vehicles for viruses, and viruses as passengers of sorts'. We can also consider the mobility of non-humans such as water and energy – materials whose flows are vital to sustaining our geopolitical worlds. For example, Peter Forman (2018: 231, 238) draws attention to the movements of natural gas within pipelines, material mobilities that at once 'traverse diverse terrains and multiple countries', and whose circulation are 'productive of variety of forms of (in)security'. For example, while mobile gas has become 'normalised' and 'mundane' – enabling us to 'prepare food, warm water and generate electricity', so too does it 'introduce threats to everyday environments' – from the 'possible escape and ignition of gas' to igniting questions of its 'negative effects on global climate' (Forman 2020: 144). Here, in drawing attention to the significance of mobile materials, Forman (2020: 144) highlights that natural gas can be 'generative of geopolitical effects at different scales' – from local explosions to international 'geopolitical crises' over energy supplies.

Mobility as Spatialised and Moderated

Thirdly, we can understand mobility as both spatialised and controlled in different ways. Particular spaces and sites – such as airports and borders – shape how mobility is encountered, moderated, controlled, and policed (we explore these issues further in Chapter 8). Each space has its 'own grammar which can direct or limit mobility' – and as such, each should be considered not simply as a 'context', but as 'actively' producing and 'produced by the act of moving' (Cresswell and Merriman 2011: 7). In other words, spaces where mobility is foregrounded are not simply backdrops, but rather act to inform, control, enable, and limit our experiences of movement in important ways. For example, when boarding a train you will move through a barrier, you may have your ticket checked, and you will almost certainly be subject to CCTV, your movements and actions recorded and monitored. You may also hear security announcements on the train, such as the 'see it, say it, sorted' motto. Through this campaign, the British Transport Police (n.d.) encourage 'all passengers and people who use railway stations to help keep themselves and others safe by reporting unusual items or activity on the railway'.

Mobility as Political and Uneven

In addition to demonstrating how mobilities are monitored and controlled in different ways, we also need to be aware of how such practices may be unevenly applied and experienced. While we might understand the above British Transport Police scheme as encouraging 'vigilance', the 'see it, say it, sorted' campaign featured a poster with a 'dark-skinned bearded person wearing a coat in front of a light-skinned female onlooker', reproducing harmful associations between skin tone and terrorism (Emerson 2019: 287).

As Jennifer Hyndman (2004: 177) writes, 'race, ethnicity, and gender mark people in particular ways that affect mobility'. For example, 'mobilities are differently accessed', meaning that our identities can 'make a difference to our ability to access and enjoy certain forms of mobility' (Adey 2017: 106). This can be evidenced through phrases such as 'driving whilst Black', used to denote the 'unequal treatment Black drivers have received' as police forces in and beyond the United States racially profile, stop and search Black drivers (Adey 2017: 106). As Hannam et al. (2006 in Adey et al. 2021: 2) argue, mobility is 'differential', meaning that people are differently able to travel, a fact which both reflects and reinforces 'structures and hierarchies of power'. After all, while 'freedom of mobility' has both historically and 'long been denied' to particular groups, no group 'has been denied freedom of movement as completely as African Americans' (Macek 2021: n.p.). This is evidenced in a 14-year study in North Carolina (USA) which found that Black drivers were '63% more likely to be stopped by police than White drivers, even though Black people on average drive 16% less' (Macek 2021: n.p.). Such practices of policing form part of a racialised system of 'surveillance and control', working to 'reproduce' the (historic) 'spatial confinement of Black communities' (Hawthorne 2019: 7).

> ## Case Study: Dollar Cabs and the Mobility of Caribbean Immigrants (Best 2016)
>
> Exploring the mobilities of 'postcolonial subjects', Best (2016: 442) draws on her experience undertaking a six-month ethnography of 'dollar cabs', taxis that you find in 'predominantly Caribbean neighbourhoods' in Brooklyn, New York (USA). Best (2016: 442, 443) notes that these taxis, recognised not by their 'exterior color or medallion but by the way they blow their horns', are an interesting form of 'quasi-public transportation' because their mobilities act to reveal a 'critical site of sociality' for the individuals and communities using them. She argues that 'dollar cabs' are more than cars transporting their passengers, rather they 'make the strange familiar' through bringing a popular mode of travel from the Caribbean to the United States – an action 'allowing Black immigrants to inhabit the space through the everyday practice of getting around it' (Best 2016: 443). In other words, the dollar cabs enable and open up a familiar form and experience of movement for the Caribbean community in the USA. While aware of the ways in which 'surveillance and control' punctuate 'Black life', this account demonstrates how Black communities exceed as well as 'resist and creatively subvert' such power relations (Hawthorne 2019: 7) by offering 'a sense of place to those whose bodies' are otherwise 'treated as out of place'.

Collectively, this growing geographical work on mobilities demonstrates the emergence of what has been described as a 'mobilities paradigm' (Cresswell 2010: 551). This 'mobilities turn' 'focuses on, and holds mobility centre stage' in distinct and critical ways (Cresswell 2010: 551), examining mobility across a 'range of forms, practices, scales, locations and technologies' (Blunt 2007: 684). In so doing, it identifies and interrogates the 'flows which make up the spatial and social complexity' of our worlds (Binnie et al. 2007: 165).

KEY TERMS: MOBILITY TURN OR PARADIGM

The mobility turn or paradigm refers to a shift in geographical thinking which places mobility at the centre of our critical accounts. Here, attention is centrally placed on where, how and by whom mobility is 'given meaning' (Adey 2017: 66), and how it is both differently practised and experienced.

Unpacking Air Travel Mobilities

Air travel provides a good opportunity to apply these understandings of mobility. We live in a globalised, interconnected, compressed world (Das and Bridi, 2013: n.p.). Encompassing the movement of 'people, commodities, capital, knowledge, cultural values, and

Figure 10.1 Airport

Credit: Jorge Diaz (Attribution-ShareAlike 2.0 Generic (CC BY-SA 2.0)) www.flickr.com/photos/xurde/4731815658/

environmental pollutants' alike, globalisation is understood to have 'economic, political, cultural, spatial, and environmental' dimensions (Das and Bridi 2013: n.p.). The growth of air travel is a central aspect and enabler of globalisation, with the number of global flights 'increasing steadily since the early 2000s and reaching 38.9 million in 2019' (Statista 2022: n.p.).

KEY TERMS: 'TIME–SPACE CONVERGENCE'

This refers to both the falling costs of mobility over time and the shrinking of the separation between places (Gregory et al. 2009: 467). It is often used in conjunction with globalisation.

In approaching air travel through the lens of mobility, we can first note that 'passengers are embodied' (Adey 2007: 439). From feeling stressed at the length of the security queue, feeling anxious as you pass through security check points, feeling fearful or unwell as an aircraft in flight moves in turbulence, or feeling excited when you reach a destination, our bodies experience air travel in diverse ways. Drawing upon historical records of passenger experiences of travel by air during the 1920s and 1930s, Budd (2011) explores a range of 'diverse kin/aesthetic and affective experiences of flight' – including 'bodily (dis)comforts, fears, and anxieties' – to highlight both the bodily experience of flight and the ways in which aerial travel has 'transformed what it means to be mobile'.

We can also understand mobile air travel as material. For example, arriving at the airport, you are greeted with automatic doors, CCTV, passport checks, and barriers. These are apparatus of the state, intended to sort and filter moving bodies under the overarching objective of 'security'. Far from spaces that are 'free' and 'open to mobility', airports have a range of 'surveillance practices' in place designed to both 'control and differentiate movement, bodies, and identities' (Adey 2004: 1365). As explored in Chapter 8, technologies and techniques used at airports to 'identify specific body parts, such as faces, eyes, and palms, which are unique to every individual' bring the body into contact with the state in profoundly embodied ways (Adey 2004: 1370). As such, the body becomes a site of 'observation, calculation, prediction and action' (Adey 2009: 274). The spread of Covid-19 entrenched these intersections. As Covid-19 devastated the travel industry, technologies like temperature monitors were introduced to add a further layer of bodily surveillance.

Importantly, across all examples, mobility is not singular. It is plural – meaning it is differently and unevenly accessible and experienced. As Mimi Sheller (2015: 15) powerfully writes:

> Mobility may be considered a universal human right, yet in practice it exists in relation to class, racial, sexual, gendered, and disabling exclusions from public space, from national citizenship, and from the means of mobility at all scales. These barriers to access and controls over mobility are implemented via formal and informal policing, borders, gates, passes, clothing, rules, and surveillance systems that limit the right to move, filter entry and exit, and selectively apply the protection of the state.

The airport is a site which starkly reminds us of this fact. In order to travel you must bring an identity document, often a passport, in order for your mobility and passage to be permitted. Documents such as passports and visas can be understood as key 'documents of mobility', which enable and limit movement (Salter 2009). Further, as Cresswell and Merriman (2011: 9) note, moving is 'associated with distinctive subject positions'. By this they mean our experience as passengers is impacted by both our 'rights to move' and 'the particular nations to which we belong'. Such issues are brought into sharp relief when we consider the distinct and different experiences of the tourist either freely travelling or travelling on a visa to a holiday destination, and that of the refugee encountering myriad challenges as they seek to journey – each are 'mobile' but their experiences are underpinned by different positions, practices, and passages (Cresswell and Merriman 2011: 9). As Peter Adey (2017: xv) writes, for some mobility is 'a desperate passageway full of hope' while for others it is 'banal and forgettable'. In applying and analysing mobility as a concept, keep in mind these diverse and uneven experiences.

> ## Over to You: Understanding Your Own Mobility
>
> Think about a typical weekday for you. Make a note of the types of mobilities you use, rely on, or encounter. Are there mobilities you take for granted? (see Cook 2018: 137). Focus on one example from your list and reflect on the following:
>
> 1. What was your embodied experience of this mobility? Reflect on how bodies with different abilities might differently experience your example.
> 2. Think about your example in relation to the material. What non-humans are involved in your example (e.g., train tracks, data flows)? How do they impact and/or shape your example?
> 3. Reflect on if and how your example of mobility may be unevenly accessed, encountered, or experienced by others (e.g., in another location, with a different socio-economic background).
> 4. Finally, how does your discussion link back to wider geopolitical themes? How might your mobility, for example, bring you into contact with the state?

Immobility, Waiting, and Stillness

Entangled within questions of movement are those of stillness and immobility (Creswell and Merriman 2011: 7). As Cresswell (2012: 645) argues, to think of movement is to think of different 'forms of stillness' too. From stopping (being halted or strapping in), to being forced to queue in an immigration line, to being told to take cover and keep still in a warzone, attention to the spaces and ways in which we may be stationary or still remain important (Cresswell and Merriman 2011: 7, see also Cresswell 2012). Think, for example, about immobility and stillness at detention and refugee camps, where mobility is at once regulated, interrupted, and stalled in 'fearful and wretched' ways (Adey 2017: 13, Creswell 2012). The refugee camp is a 'distinctive political space' (Ramadan 2013: 65). Writing in the context of Palestinian refugee camps in Lebanon, Ramadan (2013: 65) highlights that the camp is at once a space of 'shelter' and a space in which refugees are temporarily halted and held 'until a durable solution can be found to their situation'. For Brankamp (2021: 3, 2) the camp is a space of 'control, concentration and suspension of people and time'. Here immobility is enforced, challenging, and fraught.

Alongside forced stopping and halting, when considering our vocabularies of (im) mobility, we can also consider stillness and the range of political dispositions this act entails and enacts. For example, in their work foregrounding stillness in a mobile world, David Bissell and Gillian Fuller (2011 in Adey 2017: 13) highlight how often we think of stillness as something to 'overcome or be done away with', associating it with something negative, from standing in lengthy lines to sitting in frustration in traffic, but it can also be crucial to 'moments of resistance' (Adey 2017: 13). Being stationary can be a powerful mode of protest. The Occupy Wall Street protest in New York, USA, is a prime example.

Following an online post by Adbusters (an activist hub) calling for an end to 'the influence money has over our representatives in Washington – for Democracy not Corporatocracy', a march and rally was organised in New York in September of 2011 (Chappell 2011: n.p.). Protesters refused to move after they gathered and 'set up a temporary city in lower Manhattan's Zuccotti Park' (Chappell 2011: n.p.), aiming to place 'debates about class inequality at the centre of political debate' (Kinna et al. 2016: n.p.). The group quickly created an informal infrastructure with their 'own newspaper, food supply chain and wi-fi' (Chappell 2011: n.p.). This enabled people to 'stay together for longer periods of time: to eat, sleep and share daily routines with fellow protesters' (Frenzel 2017: n.p). The semi-permanence of the protest camp enabled discussion, reflection, and resistance. Here, the Occupy protest camp, as with many others like it, became a stationary protest that sought to challenge, contest, and resist. As Sheller (2015: 27) reminds us, stillness is vital to the contestation of mobility.

Mobility and the 'Migrant Crisis'

The so-called Mediterranean 'Migrant Crisis' lays some of the geopolitical considerations of mobility bare. Red flags were raised in 2015 when over 1,000,000 migrants arrived in the European Union (EU), 'having taken perilous journeys across the Mediterranean Sea in search of safety' (Crawley n.d.). There were '4,000 recorded deaths as people drowned in overloaded and unseaworthy boats' (Crawley n.d.). As migrant mobilities made the front pages of newspapers around the world, politicians described the migration as an 'unprecedented event' (Crawley et al. 2016: n.p.) and the EU 'declared the movement' as a 'crisis' (Tazzioli 2018: n.p.). While the crossings of 2015 were presented as an 'unprecedented crisis', it should be noted that there remains a 'long history of migration via the Mediterranean', with thousands crossing each year – and the Mediterranean Sea being a site 'where irregular migration to Europe' is perhaps 'most visible' (Missing Migrants n.d.). The real 'crisis' thus lies in how migrants are received and treated.

In the case of the 2015 crossings, conflict in countries neighbouring Europe was a significant factor in the rise of migrant mobility (Crawley n.d.), with many migrants pursuing risky mobilities in order to seek safety and/or to 'build or rebuild a life due to a lack of rights or opportunities' (Crawley et al. 2016: n.p.). These fraught and fatal mobilities thus demand 'attention to unequal relations of power' (Adams-Hutcheson et al. 2017: 2).

The 'Crossing the Mediterranean Sea by Boat' research project is helpful in locating embodied mobilities in this crisis. The project explored lived experiences of migration policy, foregrounding those 'making – or contemplating making – the dangerous journey across the Mediterranean Sea', while developing insight into the 'journeys, understandings, expectations, concerns and demands of people on the move' (University of Warwick 2019). In examining lived experiences, the project found migrants both emphasised their 'inability to access legal routes to safety', while describing encounters and experiences of violence from both smugglers and authorities alike (Squire et al. 2017: 64). The migrant participants described witnessing and experiencing 'robberies, kidnappings,

Figure 10.2 Migrant boat

Credit: CSDP EEAS (Public Domain Mark 1.0) www.flickr.com/photos/eeas-csdp/22548071545/
in/photolist-AmuL7e-EzDHTm-EzDKcd-Dr25NT-4NwpqY-bkMHGM-DPU1iH-4LB6gx-KDjkee-
KtTTR9-2bmhSeq-KtWNTC-A9bpUx-2b4zVmg-2bmhLhL-29FJKhq-2csm9aF-AKPERe-yp4W-
3K-Y5HwT1-Ef9HQR-uDzK5w-A4Zng2-Anua6T-8gX8MS-22GSEyH-xSQ9WC-29Bziiy-Em5rCY-
qbrNDn-KmkVS2-g36WFg-2csmc5P-NG3v3z-2csmeT4-AGx1my-29FJPGh-2cnTzSb-2b4zZ6v-
wxtHyy-4LFgGh-NG3oz4-QjvnvJ-NG3p5H-2bmhUwb-29FJMXL-zMNyEY-21dkdQN-NfVL4R-
2jMgpa1

beatings, dehydration, starvation, and death threats', as well as detailing dire living conditions including 'inadequate food and clothes provision, a lack of sanitation facilities and items, overcrowding and lack of privacy' (Squire et al. 2017: 66, 67).

Other factors also affect these mobilities. As UNICEF (2017: 4) found, half of the women interviewed described experiencing 'sexual violence or abuse during their journey'. Similarly, they found that 'nine out of ten children who crossed the Mediterranean were unaccompanied' (UNICEF 2017: 2). A total of 25,846 children made the crossing, 'which is double the previous year' (UNICEF 2017). Of those interviewed, 'three quarters of the migrant children said they had experienced violence, harassment or aggression at the hands of adults' (UNICEF 2017: 4). As such, in understanding uneven mobilities, we must remain attentive to the ways in which identity can inform, impact, and shape experiences of mobility in significant ways. The material geopolitics of this are also key. Many of the objects and technologies used on these journeys can tell us much about wider geopolitical concerns. The boats, as a prime example, are often not fit for such a crossing and lack sufficient fuel. Lifejackets are unevenly distributed and again, may not be fit for purpose. Meanwhile, the state deploys its own technologies to police the sea. Drones have been key here. Following the wider growth of the use of drones for border control over land and at sea (Jumbert 2018), drones have been deployed by Frontex (on behalf of the European Border and Coastguard Agency) to 'monitor migrants from afar' (Ahmed 2020: n.p.). Following reports of instances where migrants hear the noise of a drone engine, 'waving for help' without realising the drone's operator is several thousand miles away 'watching their final moments' (*The Guardian* 2019: n.p.), concerns have been raised about the resourcing of 'eyes in the sky' without 'hands on the sea' (Zwijnenburg in Ahmed 2020: n.p.).

While it is common to see migrant journeys presented as linear on maps appearing on the television or in news stories, as Campos-Delgado (2018: 489) notes, such 'met-anarratives of state-centric maps' fail to communicate the complexities discussed above. Nor do they communicate the experiences and 'stories of courage, negotiation, anguish, physical pain, solidarity, and resilience'. After all, in their passage, migrants encounter different acts and spaces of bordering (see Chapter 8). The camp is again a clear example of this. As Davies and Isakjee (2015: 93) write, the 'Calais Jungle' camp in France (2015–2016) became a 'bottleneck' space for 'people seeking to reach the UK' (Mould 2016). The camp space 'unleashed privation and mortality on countless migrant bodies' (Davies and Isakjee 2015: 93) – its conditions of immobility highlighting and enacting 'precarity' and 'despair' (Mould 2018: 393). Here we can see that just as mobility is uneven, so too are experiences of 'stopping, waiting' (Sheller 2015: 17).

Over to You: Immobility in Motion

There are lots of ways we can think about immobility. The experiences of seafarers further complicate the understandings of immobility we've outlined. Seafarers working aboard container ships are responsible for keeping the global economy moving. Over 90% of the things in your room right now will have travelled to you by sea. And yet, whilst being constantly mobile and moving through the seas, seafarers experience immobility in a range of ways. Take a look at the issues seafarers face on the Mission to Seafarers website (www.missiontoseafarers.org/about/our-issues). Focus your attention on the first three: fatigue, communication, and abandonment.

1. How do these issues speak to the themes outlined in this chapter?
2. Seafarers are both moving and immobile at different times. Can you find a specific example of this?
3. How might you apply mobilities thinking more widely to investigate and understand this workforce?

Conclusion

In this chapter, we've explored the value of approaching political geography through the lens of mobility. As Peter Adey (2017: 106) argues, 'mobility produces and distributes power' and does so in uneven ways. As he continues, 'how we are placed differently in relation to' mobility can act to 'radically shape' our lives – the 'chances' we might get, the 'services we may have access to', and the ways in which we might feel 'part of' or 'excluded' by the society and space within which we live (Adey 2017: 106). Mobility, then, is a 'fundamental process' (Adey 2017: 11) that we can explore through attention to different actors (both human and non-human) and across different scales (from the body to the national and international). In this chapter we have drawn particular attention to the human and embodied dimensions of mobility in order to demonstrate both that bodies experience mobilities differently, and that approaching mobility at the scale of the body enables us to consider the experiences and politics of everyday life anew. Further, the chapter explored the ways in which non-humans (from viruses to suitcases, and passports to natural gas) both travel and travel with us – acting to accompany as well as to shape and interrupt our mobilities. Immobility and stillness emerge as key concerns here too. Mobility and immobility are two sides of the same coin. As Lin (2013: A1) writes, a 'geopolitics of immobility is emerging at the global scale'. As Lin (2013: A1) continues, while some enjoy developments in civil aviation – flying freely around the world – the abilities of others to 'traverse' as such are 'hampered' and halted in violent ways. (Im) mobility, then, is also inherently geopolitical.

Summary

- We live in a world defined by movement in different ways. Mobilities is a way of thinking that helps us get to grips with the politics of movement, and the power dynamics that underpin it.
- These power dynamics are important. A range of intersectional issues shape how or when people can move. These include gender, race, and age. The 'migrant crisis' lays bare these complexities.
- There are certain spaces that significantly impact mobility, the airport being a prime example. Here, people are monitored, checked, sorted, and sometimes prevented and stopped from moving.
- Alongside movement, mobilities thinking also prompts us to consider stillness and a lack of motion. This might be in the form of the refugee camp, but also the mobilisation of immobility in and as protest and resistance.

Follow-on Resources

The Green Book: A guidebook first published in 1936, *The Green Book* was dubbed 'the bible of Black travel'. Written in the context of the Jim Crow laws, it had the aim of identifying and sharing 'services and places relatively friendly to African-Americans so they could find lodgings, businesses, and gas stations that would serve them along the road' (Library of Congress n.d.) (see also the film, *Green Book*, 2018).

Comics and graphic novels: As Nijdam (2021: n.p.) writes, there has been 'renewed interest in comics representing migrant experience'. Through its foregrounding of 'personal stories', such media, Nijdam (2021: n.p) argues, can 'articulate the complexity of refugee experience'. Alongside offering a useful critical reflection on several comics, Nijdam also reflects on the wider ethical questions surrounding comics and graphic novels 'not by refugees but about refugees'. To consider these issues further, look at the comics and graphic novels featured on Positive Negative (https://positivenegatives.org/). What do such visual accounts tell you about (experiences of) mobility and immobility?

Watch the Med: Watch the Med is an online mapping platform designed to monitor both the deaths and violations of migrants' rights at maritime borders. The project began as part of the 2012 Boats4People campaign in the Central Mediterranean, and now involves a wide network of organisations, activists, and researchers. Learn more at: https://watchthemed.net/

References

Adams-Hutcheson, G., Thorpe, H. and Coleborne, C. (2017). Introduction: Understanding mobilities in a dangerous world. *Transfers*, *7*(3), 1–5.

Adey, P. (2004). Surveillance at the airport: Surveilling mobility/mobilising surveillance. *Environment and Planning A, 36*, 1365–1380.

Adey, P. (2007). Airports, mobility and the calculative architecture of affective control. *Geoforum, 39*, 438–451.

Adey, P. (2009). Facing airport security: Affect, biopolitics, and the preemptive securitisation of the mobile body. *Environment and Planning D: Society and Space, 27*, 274–295.

Adey, P. (2017). *Mobility (2nd edn)*. London and New York: Routledge.

Adey, P., Hannam, K., Sheller, M. and Tyfield, D. (2021). Pandemic (im)mobilities. *Mobilities, 16*(1), 1–19.

Ahmed, K. (2020). EU accused of abandoning migrants to the sea with shift to drone surveillance. *The Guardian*, 28 October. Available at: www.theguardian.com/global-development/2020/oct/28/eu-accused-of-abandoning-migrants-to-the-sea-with-shift-to-drone-surveillance (accessed 21 March 2022).

Best, A. (2016). The way they blow the horn: Caribbean dollar cabs and subaltern mobilities. *Annals of the American Association of Geographers, 106*(2), 442–449.

Binnie, J., Edensor, T., Holloway, J., Millington, S. and Young, C. (2007). Mundane mobilities, banal travels. *Social & Cultural Geography, 8*(2), 165–174.

Bissell, D. (2009). Conceptualising differently-mobile passengers: Geographies of everyday encumbrance in the railway station. *Social and Cultural Geography, 10*(2), 173–195.

Blunt, A. (2007). Cultural geographies of migration: Mobility, transnationality and diaspora. *Progress in Human Geography, 31*(5), 684–694.

Brankamp, H. (2021). Feeling the refugee camp: Affectual research, bodies, and suspicion. *Area, 00*, 1–9.

British Transport Police (n.d.). See it, say it, sorted. Available at: www.btp.police.uk/police-forces/british-transport-police/areas/campaigns/see-it-say-it-sorted/#:~:text=If%20you%20see%20something%20that,or%20text%20us%20on%2061016, (accessed 2 November 2022).

Budd, L.C.S. (2011). On being aeromobile: Airline passengers and the affective experiences of flight. *Journal of Transport Geography, 19,* 1010–1016.

Campos-Delgado, A. (2018). Counter-mapping migration: Irregular migrants' stories through cognitive mapping. *Mobilities, 13*(4), 488–504.

Chappell, B. (2011). Occupy Wall Street: From a blog post to a movement. *NPR,* 20 October. Available at: www.npr.org/2011/10/20/141530025/occupy-wall-street-from-a-blog-post-to-a-movement?t=1655804329801 (accessed 10 April 2021).

Cook, S. (2018). Geographies of mobility: A brief introduction. *Geography, 103*(3), 137–145.

Cook, S. (2021). Geographies of run-commuting in the UK. *Journal of Transport Geography, 92,* 103038.

Cook, S. (n.d.). Jographies: Geographical perspectives on running [blog]. Available at: https://jographies.wordpress.com/ (accessed 10 November 2022).

Crawley, H. (n.d.). Unravelling the Mediterranean migration crisis. *The Royal Geographical Society.* Available at: www.rgs.org/schools/teaching-resources/mediterranean-migration-crisis/ (accessed 1 December 2022).

Crawley, H., Duvell, F. and Siogna, N. (2016). No direct flight: New maps show the fragmented journeys of migrants and refugees to Europe. *The Conversation,* 2 November. Available at: https://theconversation.com/no-direct-flight-new-maps-show-the-fragmented-journeys-of-migrants-and-refugees-to-europe-67955 (accessed 3 June 2022).

Cresswell, T. (2010). Mobilities I: Catching up. *Progress in Human Geography, 35*(4), 550–558.

Cresswell, T. (2012). Mobilities II: Still. *Progress in Human Geography, 36*(5), 645–653.

Cresswell, T. (2014). Mobilities III: Moving on. *Progress in Human Geography, 38*(5), 712–721.

Cresswell, T. and Merriman, P. (2011). Introduction: Geographies of mobilities – practices, spaces, subjects. In T. Cresswell and P. Merriman (eds), *Geographies of mobilities: Practices, spaces, subjects* (pp. 1–18). Surrey, UK: Ashgate.

Das, R.J. and Bridi, R. (2013). Globalization. *Oxford Bibliographies.* Available at: www.oxfordbibliographies.com/view/document/obo-9780199874002/obo-9780199874002-0018.xml (accessed 10 September 2022).

Davies, T. and Isakjee, A. (2015). Geography, migration and abandonment in the Calais refugee camp. *Political Geography, 49,* 93–95.

Emerson, R. G. (2019). Vigilant subjects. *Politics, 39*(3), 284–299.

Forman, P. (2018). Circulations beyond nodes: (In)securities along the pipeline. *Mobilities, 13*(2), 231–245.

Forman, P. (2020). Security and the subsurface: Natural gas and the visualisation of possibility spaces. *Geopolitics, 1*, 143–166.

Frenzel, F. (2017). Political intents: How protest camps are reviving social movements around the world. *The Conversation*, 7 June. Available at: https://theconversation.com/political-intents-how-protest-camps-are-reviving-social-movements-around-the-world-78789 (accessed 20 November 2022).

Gregory, D., Johnston, R., Pratt, G., Watts, M. and Whatmore, S. (2009). *The dictionary of human geography* (5th edn). New York: Wiley-Blackwell.

Hall, E. and Wilton, R. (2017). Towards a relational geography of disability. *Progress in Human Geography, 41*(6), 727–744.

Hannam, K., Sheller, M. and Urry, J. (2006). Editorial: Mobilities, immobilities and moorings, *Mobilities, 1*(1), 1–22.

Hawthorne, C. (2019). Black matters are spatial matters: Black geographies for the twenty-first century. *Geography Compass*, 13e124468.

Ho, E. L. and Maddrell, A. (2020). Intolerable intersectional burdens: A COVID-19 research agenda for social and cultural geographies. *Social and Cultural Geography, 22*(1), 1–10.

Hyndman, J. (2004). The (geo)politics of mobility. In L. A. Staeheli, E. Kofman and L. J. Peake (eds), *Mapping women, making politics: Feminist perspectives on political geography* (pp. 169–184). New York: Routledge.

Jumbert, M. G. (2018). Control or rescue at sea? Aims and limits of border surveillance technologies in the Mediterranean Sea. *Disasters, 42*(4), 674–696.

Kinna, R., Prichard, A. and Swann, T. (2016). Anarchy in the USA: Five years on, the legacy of Occupy Wall Street and what it can teach us in the Age of Trump. *The Conversation*, 10 November. Available at: https://theconversation.com/anarchy-in-the-usa-five-years-on-the-legacy-of-occupy-wall-street-and-what-it-can-teach-us-in-the-age-of-trump-68452 (accessed 17 April 2022).

Lin, W. (2013). A geopolitics of (im)mobility? *Political Geography, 36*, A1–A3.

Macek. S. (2021). Mobility, race, citizenship and driving while Black. A journal of cities and culture. *Mediapolis*, 6 April. Available at: www.mediapolisjournal.com/2021/04/mobility-race-citizenship-and-driving-while-black/ (accessed 31 May 2023).

Middleton, J. (2011). Walking in the city: The geographies of everyday pedestrian practices. *Geography Compass, 5*(2), 90–105.

Missing Migrants (n.d.). Migration within the Mediterranean. Available at: https://missingmigrants.iom.int/region/mediterranean (accessed 12 November 2022).

Mould, O. (2016). Aid and instability: An urbanist's perspective on the Calais Jungle. *The Conversation*, 17 February. Available at: https://theconversation.com/aid-and-instability-an-urbanists-perspective-on-the-calais-jungle-54604 (accessed 10 September 2022).

Mould, O. (2018). The not-so-concrete jungle: Material precarity in the Calais refugee camp. *Cultural Geographies, 25*(3), 393–409.

Nijdam, B. (2021). Comics and graphic novels are examining refugee border-crossing experiences. *The Conversation,* 14 June. Available at: https://theconversation.com/comics-and-graphic-novels-are-examining-refugee-border-crossing-experiences-158257 (accessed 3 July 2022).

Ramadan, A. (2013). Spatialising the refugee camp. *Transactions of the Institute of British Geographers, 38,* 65–77.

Salter, M. B. (2009). Borders, passports, and the global mobility. In B. Turner and R. Holton (eds), *The Routledge International Handbook of Globalization Studies* (2nd edn). London, UK: Routledge.

Sheller, M. (2015). Uneven mobility futures: A Foucauldian approach. *Mobilities, 11*(1), 15–31.

Sparke, M. and Anguelov, D. (2020). Contextualising coronavirus geographically. *Transactions of the Institute of British Geographers, 45,* 498–508.

Squire, V., Dimitriadi, A., Perkowski, N., Pisani, M., Stevens, D. and Vaughan-Williams, N. (2017). Crossing the Mediterranean Sea by boat: Mapping and documenting the migratory journeys and experiences. Final project report. Available at: https://warwick.ac.uk/fac/soc/pais/research/projects/crossingthemed/ctm_final_report_4may2017.pdf (accessed 10 November 2022).

Statista (2022). Number of flights performed by the global airline industry from 2004 to 2022. Available at: www.statista.com/statistics/564769/airline-industry-number-of-flights/ (accessed 29 November 2022).

Tazzioli, M. (2018). Migration: new map of Europe reveals real frontiers for refugees. *The Conversation.* Available at: https://theconversation.com/migration-new-map-of-europe-reveals-real-frontiers-for-refugees-103458 (accessed 19 June 2023).

The Guardian (2019). Once migrants on Mediterranean were saved by naval patrols. Now they have to watch as drones fly over. *The Guardian,* 4 August. Available at: www.theguardian.com/world/2019/aug/04/drones-replace-patrol-ships-mediterranean-fears-more-migrant-deaths-eu (accessed 21 February 2022).

UNICEF (2017). A deadly journey for children: The central Mediterranean migration route. Available at: www.unicef.org/eca/reports/deadly-journey-children#:~:text=A%20Deadly%20Journey%20for%20Children%3A%20The%20Central%20Mediterranean,into%20Libya%20and%20across%20the%20sea%20to%20Italy (accessed 1 October 2022).

University of Warwick (2019). Crossing the Mediterranean Sea by boat. Available at: https://warwick.ac.uk/fac/soc/pais/research/projects/crossingthemed/ (accessed 20 September 2022).

Wilson, H. F. (2011). Passing propinquities in the multicultural city: The everyday encounters of bus passengering. *Environment and Planning A, 43,* 634–649.

ELEVEN

VIOLENCE: PRACTICE AND EXPERIENCE

Chapter Overview

This chapter introduces and explores political geographies of violence. It reflects on what violence is, who and what practises and perpetrates it, and diverse experiences of violence as they occur across a wide range of scales and spaces. It explores these themes by examining historical and ongoing experiences of violence, first through the political geographies of war, second in the context of settler colonialism, and third by tracing everyday occurrences of violence across different spaces and contexts. Violence is sadly embedded in society in multiple ways. This chapter provides a language and framework to engage with this, as well as to understand the importance of political geography in such discussions.

Learning Objectives

1. To introduce the political geographies of violence.
2. To gain an understanding of why the political geographies of violence matter, and the ways in which they unevenly impact different communities and peoples.
3. To develop understanding of different actors, scales, sites, histories, and spaces of the political geographies of violence.

Read with: Chapter 3 (Feminist Geopolitics), Chapter 12 (Peace and Resistance), Chapter 7 (States and Territory), Chapter 8 (Borders)

We live in a troublingly violent world. Whether it's a news story on an ongoing war, represented on social media, shared in the experiences of friends, or streamed into living rooms, violence is inescapable and it is something, in the words of Mountz (2018: 765), that we 'must attend to'. Indeed, Mountz (2018: 765) argues that 'there is no more important issue for geographers to study'. This chapter introduces violence, exploring how

168 | POLITICAL GEOGRAPHY

geographers understand and think about it, while drawing on case studies to illustrate why violence remains an important concept for political geographers.

This section grapples with violence as a concept. As Springer and Le Billon (2016: 1) note, violence has been understood as a 'confounding concept' that is difficult to define. While taking many forms, at its core, violence 'prevents individual or collective access to space, security, or life sustaining resources' (Fluri 2022: 698). Taking the form of an 'action' or 'inaction', violence is understood as a practice or condition which negatively impacts 'the material and non-material conditions' of another person or peoples, 'reducing their potential to survive' (Tyner and Rice 2015: 9).

──────── KEY TERMS: VIOLENCE ────────

Violence is a practice or process that negatively impacts someone or something's conditions and world, preventing them from living safely, securely, or at all. Violence might refer to a particular action (e.g. striking someone), or it may refer to an 'inaction' or failing to act on an issue (Tyner and Rice 2015: 9).

Geographical thinking on violence shares several common themes (Springer and Le Billon 2016: 1). First, that we should consider violence as both a form of power and a situation or condition where unequal power relations are made visible. As Springer and Le Billon (2016: 1) write, while we can imagine 'power relations free from violence', it remains difficult to 'imagine violence free from power'. Here, it's important to distinguish between different kinds of violence. 'Violent geopolitics' refers to 'visceral, embodied acts' – such as a 'punch to the gut or shot in the head' (Philo 2017: 256). This refers to 'direct' violence that is encountered in an immediate and first-hand way, and is often associated with an 'identifiable actor' (Tyner and Rice 2015: 2), for example, someone who punches someone else. This is different to 'geopolitical violence', referring instead to the processes by which 'violence' comes to occur (Philo 2017: 256). Attention is drawn away from the 'immediate act' (the punch) and instead to the systems and institutions that produce 'structural' violences and inequalities over time (Philo 2017: 256). Here violence isn't perpetrated by one sole or identifiable individual, but instead is part of a wider 'structure' producing 'unequal power' (Tyner and Rice 2015: 2). This understanding of violence would consider an attack on a Black individual not only as a form of direct and embodied violence, but also in relation to the 'violence of the broader systemic conditions of racism' (Christian and Dowler 2019: 1067). It's also useful here to think about violence and time. For example, Nixon (2011) argues that while discussions of violence often 'focus on spectacular, sensational and rapid explosions of force', it's also important to think beyond such 'hot' direct violence and instead to consider 'slow violence' (Christian and Dowler 2019: 1068). Nixon (2011) draws attention to slow 'invisible' forms of violence, such as the violences of environmental toxins or climate change, the effects of which creep over time, with profound consequence. In this sense, we should understand violence as a 'process' and something that is 'unfolding', rather than only as an 'act' or 'outcome' (Springer and Le Billon 2016: 2).

Second, we should be concerned with violence as it works and is experienced across different scales, from the everyday to the global (Springer and Le Billon 2016: 1) (see Chapter 3). Political geography tends to focus on the scale of the global when exploring violence. Pain (2014: 544) argues that studying violence 'close to home' through the example of domestic violence is just as important. Such work highlights the importance of examining violence at the scale of the body, how it is experienced in everyday life, and the ways in which violence is unevenly experienced along lines such as gender and race (Springer and Le Billon 2016: 2).

Geographies of Violent Warfare

As a discipline, geography remains entangled with military operations and practice (see Chapters 2 and 4). Central to military operations is the ability to 'see the terrain' (Galgano 2017: n.p.). Here, 'geospatial methods and tools' were 'invented, perfected, and used' as 'valuable strategic' assets for militaries around the globe (Galgano 2017: n.p.). The practice of geography, then, has long been enrolled into battlefield spaces and operations, deployed in service of the state. While this relationship is now well-known and critiqued, this was not always the case. Lacoste (1973) famously argued that geography is first and foremost for the waging of war. Through the example of the US bombing of dikes in the densely populated Red River Delta region of Vietnam, Lacoste critiqued the powerful role of 'geographical information and thinking' as an enabler of the 'strategic knowledge' deployed in the perpetration of violence (Lacoste 1973: 3, 4; O'Tuathail 1994: 326).

Such work opened the door to wider critical interventions tracing the discipline's colonial and imperial ties (Rech et al. 2015). This work is often collectively known as critical military geographies, and the sub-field continues to grow (Forsyth 2019). While multi-faceted, this work draws attention to several key themes.

==== KEY TERMS: CRITICAL MILITARY GEOGRAPHIES ====

This branch of geography recognises the entanglement of the wider discipline of geography with the historical and ongoing perpetration of military violence (Rech et al. 2015), and seeks to understand the spatialities and embodied experiences of warfare, and the ideologies and practices through which military interventions are legitimated and normalised.

First, work in critical military geographies explores the (shifting) geographical dimensions of the battlefield, attentive to its spatialities and scales. As we have seen, the '21st century has been variously defined by the War on Terror' and its associated military interventions and divisive politics (Forsyth 2019: 1). Importantly, the War on Terror is also 'characterised by particular spatialities' which are at once 'located in particular sites (military interventions), everywhere (the battlefield loosening to becoming a pervasive battlespace), and nowhere (the use of black spots and stripping of citizenship)' (Forsyth 2019: 1; see also Gregory 2011a). This includes attention to the 'footprints' of military intervention, both in terms of their environmental costs and impacts (Belcher et al. 2020) and with regard to their spatial footprints. For example, explorations of the 'extent of US military activities in Africa' highlight that while there is a comparatively small US 'military footprint on the continent', the military presence is 'masked' by 'the extensive use of private military contractors, covert special operations forces, and secret facilities' (Moore and Walker 2016: 686). It is thus argued that 'perhaps more than anywhere else in the world', US operations in Africa demonstrate the 'blurring of the traditional geographies of warfare' (Moore and Walker 2016: 687). Such work also draws attentions to the US military's mobilisation of African bases to 'expand' its 'network of drone' activities and their reach (Moore and Walker 2016: 693), demonstrating Gregory's (2011a) notion of the 'everywhere war' in action. This refers to the idea that there are no longer only 'clear battlefields and officially recognised combat zones', rather more 'multidimensional, fluid and shadowy' conflicts have emerged (Moore and Walker 2016: 687). Technologies such as drones are crucial here, and as such particular attention is paid to the 'processes and technologies by which contemporary conflicts are being waged' (Forsyth 2019: 1).

Case Study: Drone Warfare

The deployment of military drones by a growing number of countries globally raises key questions about contemporary practices of military violence. While military drones range in size considerably, geographical attention to these technologies of war has focused on large drones capable of expansive surveillance operations and striking targets with missiles (Gregory 2011b). It has also focussed on the vast infrastructures and networks – both human and non-human – that enable the drone's functioning, and the experiences of drone operators enacting violence that is mediated through a screen (Gregory 2011b).

The drone also changes the spatialities of warfare as it expands, extends, and blurs battlefield and conflict boundaries (Gregory 2011a). However, Akhter (2019: 64) argues that such theorisations can be nuanced further by placing the drone within a 'lineage of colonial technologies of pacification'. Labelling drones as a 'game-changing military technology' acts to 'obscure histories of war, state violence, and imperialism' within which drones remain entangled (Akhter 2019: 68). By tracing these histories and lineages, we can situate military drones and the spaces and populations unevenly 'subject to state violence, surveillance, and/or control based on racialized assumptions' (Parks 2016 in Akhter 2019: 65) within wider discussions of 'colonial state power at multiple scales' (Akhter 2019: 65).

Second, this work foregrounds embodied experiences of war's violences. Gregory's (2014: 33) work on 'corpographies', namely the soldier's embodied ways 'of knowing, ordering and navigating the space of military violence', reflects on how bodies in war encounter the battlefield through their senses. Baghel and Nüsser (2015: 24, 25) for example, explore corporeal experiences of soldiers navigating mountainous heights in the Siachen conflict between India and Pakistan, arguing that the 'natural conditions' of the Himalayas 'are deadlier for soldiers than enemy action'. In this 'high altitude and extreme climate' frost-bite sets in, cerebral oedema encroaches, oxygen availability decreases – human bodies reach their limits (Baghel and Nüsser 2015: 24, 25).

Third, critical military geographies examine the legitimation and normalisation of military interventions and practice. The concepts of 'militarism' and 'militarisation' are central. 'Militarism' refers to 'ideologies which prioritize military capabilities in the resolution of conflicts', while 'militarisation' refers to the range of 'social, cultural, economic, and political processes and practices' that together aim to garner 'elite and popular acceptance for the use of military approaches' (Rech et al. 2015: 48). While militarism relates to ideology, militarisation relates to the practices and processes that promote and normalise such ideologies. Geographers have explored militarisation across diverse sites and forms, from the spectacle of airshows (Rech 2015) and military recruitment in popular culture (Rech 2014), to objects such as military paraphernalia (Rech 2020).

Over to You: Encountering Militarisation

Open Kaplan et al. (2020) (see references). The editors' letter reflects on how militarism features in 'everyday landscapes and locations'. In the first paragraph you'll find an overview of pieces in the wider essay collection, those spanning diverse militarisations from 'walking amidst landmines in Colombia, to harvesting kelp to make explosive munitions, to re-occupying Indigenous land for recreational hiking, to recovering the military history of a university arboretum, to the social media of military recruitment' (Kaplan et al. 2020: n.p.). Pick one essay and read it. Reflect on the following questions:

- Who are the key actors in your example?
- How does militarism feature in your example?
- How does your example relate to the types of violence we've explored in the chapter?

Feminist work has also been pivotal in exploring the violences of war, those which function across multiple scales, and exceed spaces of combat. It has drawn attention to militarised violence both in terms of its 'gendered experiences, impacts, meanings and dynamics', and its unfolding at the scale of everyday life and the body (Brickell and Cuomo 2020: 456). Following the recognition that many earlier accounts of the military body were 'overwhelmingly White boys' stories of the natures of war' (Gregory 2016: 39), feminist work seeks to widen this focus. Christian et al. (2016: 64) draw attention to US soldiers' experiences of sexual violence. Bringing feminist geopolitics into conversation with banal nationalism (see Chapter 9), they argue that while sexual assault is often 'depoliticized through its banalization' (Christian et al. 2016: 64), this form of everyday violence is nonetheless entangled with the scale of the nation and the context of war.

Others also decentre the body of the military soldier and foreground experiences of civilians caught in military violence. In exploring attempts by the US military to 'secure' against Taliban insurgency in the Pashtun population in Kandahar and Helmand, Afghanistan, Belcher (2018: 96) details practices of 'direct intervention' into homes and relations and spaces of kinship, with the aim of 'controlling the population'. Attention is shifted from occupying military bodies to the scale and 'level of the Afghan household', foregrounding the lived and 'intimate' experiences of civilians (Belcher 2018: 97, 96). In this vein, Woon (2011: 285) centres local responses to the 'geographical extension of the US-led War on Terror to the Philippines'. While arguing that 'framings of terrorism' have enabled a manipulation of 'fear to justify destructive strategies for the eradication of imminent threats', Woon (2011: 285) highlights the importance of considering everyday non-violent responses and the wider range of emotions accompanying these.

Violent Legacies: Settler Colonialism and Indigenous Experiences

Gregory and Pred (2007: 2) assert the importance of 'being sensitive to the fractured histories of violence, predation and dispossession – as material fact, as lived experience, and as resonant memory erupting in the present'. As explored in Chapters 2 and 4, this involves a responsibility to 'reflect on our discipline's colonial history' (de Leeuw and Hunt 2018: 1). One aspect of this is to consider the experiences of Indigenous peoples that have been, and continue to be, shaped by violent colonial legacies. Colonialism is often understood as 'a form of domination' where colonisers 'seek to exploit a set of benefits' that 'they believe to be found in the territories of one or more other indigenous societies already living there' (Whyte 2016: n.p.). As Smiles (2021: n.p.) writes of Indigenous communities in the USA, there is a 'distinct form of colonialism' known as 'settler colonialism'. This 'form of colonialism is built upon the settlement of a geographic space by non-native people and the displacement of the Indigenous communities who lived in that space' (Smiles 2021: n.p.). This settlement is typically forceful, with Indigenous peoples dispossessed, 'displaced and marginalized as their homeland was taken by treaty, sale, guile and theft' (Short 2022: n.p.). It is about 'control over space' – through both the 'occupation and the remaking of space' (Smiles 2020: n.p.). The term 'settler colonialism' urges us to understand this 'project' as both historical and ongoing (Grote and Johnson 2021).

'Postcolonial theory' and decolonisation frameworks are operationalised 'to understand the perpetuation of colonial norms within the present' while 'emphasizing how they affect Indigenous peoples' (Coombes et al. 2012: 691). As we saw in Chapter 4, decolonisation refers to a 'theoretical framework' and practice critiquing 'colonial projects' that have 'produced worlds of violence, dispossession and erasure for Indigenous, Black, and minority populations' (Gergan 2020: 2). 'Decolonizing research' can thus 'open more space for the perspectives and feelings of Indigenous peoples in the geographic record' (de Leeuw 2016: 16).

We continue to see battles over stolen land and 'unceded territories' in the news, demonstrating the ongoing and structural violence of settler colonialism. In the context of the USA, Congress 'officially has plenary (absolute) power over tribes', controlling 'how Indigenous peoples govern themselves internally and their territories as Tribal Nations' (Whyte 2016: n.p.). As such, ongoing tensions are laid bare through particular issues – such as the case of the 2016 events at Standing Rock, North Dakota.

The proposed construction of the Dakota Access Pipeline (DAPL), connecting 'production fields in North Dakota to refineries in Illinois' while passing through the lands of the Standing Rock Sioux Tribe, garnered considerable attention (Whyte 2016: n.p.). While often presented in 'one-dimensional' terms by the media, the Tribe raised diverse concerns around the pipeline, from 'tribal sovereignty, economic vulnerability, and climate change' impacts, to the risk of oil leaks 'threatening water quality' (Grote and Johnson 2021: 1, Whyte 2016: n.p.). In order to resist the pipeline's development 'through their lands, waterways, and sacred sites', the Tribe, along with allies, coordinated marches and protests (de Leeuw and Hunt 2018: 2; see Figure 11.1). They 'gathered in the ancestral territories' and deployed 'nonviolent' protest in an attempt to 'stop the building' of the pipeline (Whyte 2016: n.p.). This, however, resulted in the Indigenous peoples

Figure 11.1 Protest against the Dakota Access Pipeline

Credit: Fibonacci Blue (Attribution 2.0 Generic (CC BY 2.0)) www.flickr.com/photos/fibonacciblue/29630653446/

experiencing violence of different kinds, from 'police attacking elders, young people and children with rubber bullets' (Radcliffe 2018: 436), being 'denied nourishment' (Whyte 2016: n.p.), to 'mass arrests for protesting' (de Leeuw and Hunt 2018: 2). Such events remind us that the violence of settler colonialism is ongoing and contested, direct and immediate, and structural and slow.

In response to such violences, geography is increasingly interested in 'opening spaces for Indigenous peoples and Indigenous ways of knowing and being' (de Leeuw and Hunt 2018: 1). This involves recognising the ways that Indigenous peoples have been violently 'erased' from historical accounts, that their erasure continues into the present, and as such, that we need to enable 'fuller understandings of our history' through making space for their voices (Smiles 2021:.n.p.).

KEY TERMS: INDIGENOUS GEOGRAPHIES

Indigenous geographies foreground the histories, knowledges, and experiences of Indigenous peoples and communities. As a result of colonialism, Indigenous peoples from diverse communities and spatial contexts have experienced violence – both in their expelling and dispossession from land, their 'erasure' from historical accounts, and from the discounting and devaluing of their 'knowledges and ways of being' in and by the Western academy (de Leeuw and Hunt 2018: 1, Smiles 2021: n.p.). Indigenous geographies respond to these violences and erasures, 'opening spaces' for Indigenous histories, voices, and experiences (de Leeuw and Hunt 2018: 1).

Indigenous geographies also powerfully reflect on and respond to physical and embodied violences. In exploration of the 'removal of Indigenous children from their families' in British Columbia, Canada, Sarah de Leeuw (2016: 21, 14) highlights that colonial violence is evident not only 'at the level of territories, maps, and resources' but also in and through 'geographies of Indigenous homes, families, and bodies'. By way of context, a series of 'policies and legislation' impacting Indigenous communities in Canada emerged and 'evolved' in relation to 'practices of assimilation' (Sinclair 2016: 9). These included childcare and schooling, with at least '150,000 indigenous children' being 'separated from their families and forced to attend residential schools between the 19th century and the 1990s' (Chavez and Joseph 2021: n.p.). Scholarship on the violences of this context argues that 'Indigenous women and children' were subject to particular 'controls over parenting' by the state, and that this can be understood as 'visceral' forms and 'experiences of colonialism' (De Leeuw 2016: 21, 15).

Lastly, it's important to note that violence against Indigenous peoples does not just take human form. Many Indigenous peoples have belief systems that exceed the human, with spirits and deities playing a central role, often in ways that challenge Western modes of thinking (Radcliffe 2018: 441). We see this play out in a small Eastern Himalaya state in India when Indigenous communities were profoundly affected by a hydropower dam initiative (Gergan 2020). Not only was it seen to 'threaten regional ecology and Tribal land ownership', but Indigenous people argued that subsequent earthquakes were a direct consequence of the dam, 'linked to the desecration of sacred landscape' and the angering of 'deities residing in the hillsides and mountains' (Gergan 2020: 5). In highlighting an 'Indigenous spirituality', Gergan (2020: 5) reminds us that violence can take many forms, including against beings and spiritual belief systems.

Feminist Geographies of Violence: Uneven, Embodied, and Operating Across Scales

The final key strand of geographical work on violence is feminist work on violence beyond the battlefield. Building on the assertion that for too long gendered violence has remained 'the silent elephant in the room' rather than a 'mainstream concern within geographical research and thinking' (Brickell and Maddrell 2016: 206), feminist geographers highlight the prevalence of gendered violence as it is 'intimately interwoven' into geopolitical contexts and relations (Pain and Staeheli 2014: 344). Such work understands violence as 'a multi-faceted and multi-sited force – interpersonal and institutional, social, economic and political, physical, sexual, emotional and psychological' (Pain and Staeheli 2014: 344), something which spans diverse contexts, experiences, and spaces.

This section advances the approaches we introduced in Chapter 3, while also highlighting several key intersecting themes feminist geographers have explored in writing on violence. These include how identity politics shapes violence, attention to the scales and registers of violence, and attention to where violence takes place.

Identity Politics and Violence

As Fluri and Piedalue (2017: 537) write, 'geographic explorations of violence lay bare the ways in which raced, sexed and gendered bodies experience extensive vulnerabilities that are ignored or rendered invisible'. Identity is key here, with significant implications for how violence is lived and experienced. Violence against women is one area where this can be explored further. Martin and Carvajal (2016) turn attention to the issue of femicide, namely the killing of women on account of their gender, in Oaxaca, Mexico. In Mexico more widely, there 'are between 10 and 11 femicides each day' (Jones 2022: n.p.). In their investigation, Martin and Carvajal (2016: 989) explore femicide as 'act and process'. This distinction echoes earlier discussions of violence as direct and structural – women are violently murdered in an act, but so too do 'multifaceted processes' enable this structural phenomenon to (re)occur (Martin and Carvajal 2016: 989).

Attention is also drawn to how other aspects of identity impact experiences of violence. Consider sexual orientation. As Igonya (2022: n.p.) notes, 'same-sex relations are criminalised in 37 countries' in the African continent, continuing that 'even where the law is grey or it is legal, sexual and gender minorities are plagued by social exclusion, stigma and discrimination'. Research on 'sexualities in the Global South' emphasises the violences and challenges faced by LGBTQ+ groups 'due to discrimination' (Tucker 2019: 683).

In pursuing a 'glocal' approach 'relating the global to the local scale', we can also think about everyday experiences of violence in relation to religious identity (Listerborn 2015: 97). Listerborn (2015: 94) foregrounds the experiences of Muslim women who wear the hijab in Malmö, Sweden, demonstrating that many are 'exposed to violent public encounters' which deeply impact them.

Over to You: Identity Politics and Violence

In this exercise we'd like you to reflect further on the violences facing a predominantly Afro-Colombian community in Buenaventura, Colombia. As Jenss (2020: 1) writes, Buenaventura is a 'rapidly expanding Pacific port' and 'simultaneously a city of violence'. Read the open access article Jenss, A. (2020). Global flows and everyday violence in urban space: The port-city of Buenaventura, Colombia. *Political Geography*, 77, 102113. Reflect on the following questions:

1. What types of violence can you identify in this context? Think back to the discussion of direct and structural violence.
2. Are the experiences of violence described even? How might identity politics inform and shape the experiences discussed?
3. Is the violence resisted? If so, how? If not, why?
4. How and why does the author discuss the scale of the everyday?

Scales and Registers of Violence

As we saw in Chapter 3, a central aspect of feminist geography is its attention to scale. This is echoed in feminist work on violence too, which explores 'geopolitical violence' at scales 'from the site of the body to international politics' (Fluri 2009: 259). While we have seen that violence can be examined at the scale of the military and state (Gregory and Pred 2007), feminist geographers have highlighted the need to consider violence at the scale of the body too. This is important in order to understand 'the insidious violence of entrenched inequalities' and to recognise how different bodies experience violence differently (Fluri and Piedalue 2017: 537).

In this vein, feminist geographers have drawn attention to the ways that people employ their bodies to 'counter violent politics, to resist' (Fluri 2009: 260). Writing of the 'Revolutionary Association of the Women of Afghanistan' (RAWA), an organisation that secretly documented and shared photographs of state and military violence, Fluri (2009: 261) highlights an 'alternative epistemology of violence from below'. RAWA members hiding cameras in their chadari (burqas) to challenge state and military surveillance demonstrates the importance of the body as a site of geopolitical violence (Fluri 2009). Further, such 'resistance' highlights how the scale of the body is tied to the site of the international, as the group share images to 'reach beyond control of the state' (Fluri 2009: 264).

Alongside attention to multiple scales of violence, feminist geographers have also argued for a consideration of violence as experienced and enacted through different registers. Pain and Staeheli (2014: 344) argue that while violence is often understood in relation to 'physical harm to bodies', it also 'works through intimate emotional and psychological registers' – it shapes and is shaped by our emotional reactions. By thinking across these scales and through the lens of intimacy, we see both the 'rejection of scalar spatial hierarchy' (Pain 2015: 72) and the 'enriching' and 'turning inside out' of geopolitical analysis (Pain and Staeheli 2014: 435). For example, differently-abled people can 'experience fear, harassment and violence in an array of public and private spaces' (Hall 2019: 249). Here, we can identify violence as at once direct, structural, and intimate and emotional too.

Case Study: Gender-Based Violence in Delhi Slums

Datta (2016) explores violence in everyday life in the slums in Delhi, India (see Figure 11.2). In recent years 'incidents' of gender-based violence, including rape, have brought the issue of a gendered 'right to the city sharply onto the geographical agenda' (Datta 2016: 323). Greater scrutiny has been afforded to 'how the actions' of those accused of such forms of violence 'were shaped by their immediate environment in the Delhi slums' (Datta 2016: 323). Datta (2016: 323) argues for the importance of attention to the 'slum as a space where the violence of an exclusionary city is woven into its intimate material and social conditions, but where this violence is also domesticated and rendered as part of the everyday'. Exploring violence across the scales of cities and homes alike, Datta (2016: 323) foregrounds stories of the 'intimate lives' of those living in the slums as a way to explore how women show 'agency' through 'living with intimate violence'. Here, Datta (2016: 323) presents a form of 'urban subjectivity' in which women 'acquire' and practise 'knowledge' of their 'bodily terrain in order to limit' the violence to which they are subjected. Datta details a participant's experience of reporting gendered violence to the police with limited effect. This demonstrates both how experiences and perceptions of violence extend beyond the home and into the city, and how 'intimate violence is reinforced within the walls of state institutions and through the bodies of the state' too (Datta 2016: 332). Gendered violence, then, is everyday, operates in and between different scales, and is interrupted by women exerting agency as they 'attempt to lead an ordinary life within a framework of violence' (Datta 2016: 230).

Sites of Violence

Feminist geographers have also explored different sites and spaces of violence, as exemplified in work on domestic violence and the home. While geographers once had 'little to say about domestic or sexual violence' (Pain 2015: 64), it's now receiving growing attention (as we saw in Chapter 3). Domestic violence can be understood as a 'pattern of coercively controlling behaviour' by an abuser who uses 'a variety of tactics' to inflict 'emotional, psychological and physical violence' (Cuomo 2019: 61).

Figure 11.2 Delhi slums

Credit: Pál Baross (Creative Commons Attribution-Share Alike 3.0 Unported) https://commons.wikimedia.org/wiki/File:Delhi-slum-improvement-IHS-98-01-1983.JPG

In the Field with Katherine Brickell: Domestic Violence

Katherine Brickell researches domestic violence, with a specific focus on Cambodia. This has involved long-term collaborations with NGOs and involvement with both policy and legal actors.

How have you approached the study of domestic violence?

I have been driven by the study of the political geographies of domestic violence, refusing to see this everyday and gendered form of physical and/or emotional violence as apolitical. In recent years my collaborative writing, particularly on 'feminist geolegality' (Brickell and Cuomo 2019), has tried to push beyond the predominant focus of scholarship on international lawfare and military conflict in political geography to think more about the ever-evolving battlefields of everyday life in and through which laws (and sometimes their own violence) take both shape and form. I have found feminist geopolitical scholarship especially fruitful in this endeavour.

Can you share any top tips for a student interested in developing a project exploring the geographies of domestic violence?

Ethical considerations are absolutely paramount when researching domestic violence, especially with survivors, and this encompasses a keen need for thinking about safeguarding. Consider tailored training on these and also think about working in collaboration with an organisation.

Such work importantly explores the spatialities of violence through the site of home (Brickell 2012). However, while the site of home plays a crucial spatial role in the perpetration and experience of domestic violence, domestic violence also occurs beyond it. For example, while domestic violence is 'widely researched', there remain 'limited studies' that explore its spatial complexities, such as through journeys (Bowstead 2017: 110). As such, Bowstead (2017: 108, 110) foregrounds 'women's journeys to escape domestic violence in England', exploring the mobilities and politics of 'leaving' and 'relocating'. In addition, Cuomo (2019) turns attention to the site of the 'exchange and visitation center' where abuser and survivor meet in a controlled setting, highlighting that domestic violence also harms others too. Staff working at the centre, for example, can experience 'vicarious abuse', namely 'witnessing the coercively controlling tactics of a domestic violence abuser' (Cuomo 2019: 59). The fears that staff experience also remind us that domestic violence is a 'public safety concern' beyond the site of home (Cuomo 2019: 59).

Conclusions: What Can Political Geographies of Violence Reveal?

While it is clear that 'no single' discussion 'could encompass the violence that animates our world' (Gregory and Pred 2007: 1), in this chapter we've explored some of the ways in which violence is diversely understood and encountered across different sites, scales, and contexts. Alongside grappling with the challenges of defining violence, we have encouraged you to think about violence through different lenses, from the violences of military intervention and war, to the ongoing legacies of violent settler colonialism on Indigenous peoples, to feminist approaches revealing how violence unfolds at different scales and with uneven impact. In doing so, we have demonstrated that violence is pervasive, working at scales from the international to the body, and is practised, witnessed, experienced, and resisted in our everyday lives. As political geographers it is important to be aware of such violences, and the power relations and dynamics that enable and amplify them.

Summary

- This chapter introduced violence as an importance concept for political geographers.
- After exploring geographical definitions of violence, we examined its geographical dimensions in three ways. We first explored geographies of violent warfare, examining questions of the spatialities of violence, embodied experiences of war's violences, and the processes and practices through which military intervention is normalised in everyday life.
- Second, we explored historical and ongoing legacies of settler colonialism, examining violence against Indigenous peoples, and highlighting responses to this – from practices of resistance to forms of scholarly intervention.

Follow-on Resources

Forensic Architecture: In collaboration with journalists at Bellingcat, Forensic Architecture have 'geolocated and verified over a thousand incidents of police violence, analysing them according to multiple categories, and presented the resulting data in an interactive cartographic platform'. See https://forensic-architecture.org/investigation/police-brutality-at-the-black-lives-matter-protests

Women Doing Fieldwork Network: This group of academics run 'a collaborative project to collect literature about gender-based violence that women researchers experience during data collection'. See www.zotero.org/groups/2737349/gbv_during_data_collection

Stolen relations: This 'community based' archival project is designed as a 'collaborative effort to build a database of enslaved and unfree indigenous people throughout time all across the Americas in order to promote greater understanding of the historical circumstances and ongoing trauma of settler colonialism'. This resource encourages you to think about recovering the erased histories, legacies, and stories of Indigenous violence. See https://indigenousslavery.org/

References

Akhter, M. (2019). The proliferation of peripheries: Militarized drones and the reconfiguration of global space. *Progress in Human Geography, 43*(1), 64–80.

Baghel, R. and Nüsser, M. (2015). Securing the heights: The vertical dimension of the Siachen conflict between India and Pakistan in the Eastern Karakoram. *Political Geography, 48*, 24–36.

Belcher, O. (2018). Anatomy of a village razing: Counterinsurgency, violence, and securing the intimate in Afghanistan. *Political Geography, 62*, 94–105.

Belcher, O., Bigger, P., Neimark, B. and Kennelly, C. (2020). Hidden carbon costs of the 'everywhere war': Logistics, geopolitical ecology, and the carbon boot-print of the US military. *Transactions of the Institute of British Geographers, 45*(1), 65–80.

Bowstead, J. C. (2017). Women on the move: Theorising the geographies of domestic violence journeys in England. *Gender, Place & Culture, 24*(1), 108–121.

Brickell, K. (2012). 'Mapping' and 'doing' critical geographies of home. *Progress in Human Geography, 36*(2), 225–244.

Brickell, K. and Cuomo, D. (2019). Feminist geolegality. *Progress in Human Geography, 43*(1), 104–122.

Brickell, K. and Cuomo, D. (2020). Geographies of violence: Feminist geopolitical approaches. In A. Datta, P. Hopkins, L. Johnston, E. Olson and J. Maria Silva (eds),

Routledge international handbook of gender and feminist geographies (pp. 297–307). London and New York: Routledge.

Brickell, K. and Maddrell, A. (2016). Gendered violences: The elephant in the room and moving beyond the elephantine. *Dialogues in Human Geography*, 6(2), 206–208.

Chavez, N. and Joseph, E. (2021). Canada set to pay billions to Indigenous children removed from their families, court rules. *CNN*, 30 September. Available at: https://edition.cnn.com/2021/09/30/americas/canada-indigenous-children-compensation/index.html (accessed 10 November 2022).

Christian, J. M. and Dowler, L. (2019). Slow and fast violence: A feminist critique of binaries. *ACME: An International Journal for Critical Geographers*, 18(5), 1066–1075.

Christian, J., Dowler, L. and Cuomo, D. (2016). Fear, feminist geopolitics and the hot and banal. *Political Geography*, 54, 64–72.

Coombes, B., Johnson, J. T. and Howitt, R. (2012). Indigenous geographies II: The aspirational spaces in postcolonial politics – reconciliation, belonging and social provision. *Progress in Human Geography*, 37(5), 691–700.

Cuomo, D. (2019). Domestic violence, safe space and vicarious abuse: Inside a Pennsylvania exchange and visitation center. *Gender, Place & Culture*, 26(1), 59–74.

Datta, A. (2016). The intimate city: Violence, gender and ordinary life in Delhi slums. *Urban Geography*, 37(3), 323–342.

de Leeuw, S. (2016). Tender grounds: Intimate visceral violence and British Columbia's colonial geographies. *Political Geography*, 52, 14–23.

de Leeuw, S. and Hunt, S. (2018). Unsettling decolonizing geographies. *Geography Compass*, 12, e12376.

Fluri, J. (2009). Geopolitics of gender and violence 'from below'. *Political Geography*, 28, 259–265.

Fluri, J. (2022). Political geography II: Violence. *Progress in Human Geography*, 46(2), 698–704.

Fluri, J. L. and Piedalue, A. (2017). Embodying violence: Critical geographies of gender, race, and culture. *Gender, Place & Culture*, 24(4), 534–544.

Forsyth, I. (2019). A genealogy of military geographies: Complicities, entanglements, and legacies. *Geography Compass*, 13, e12422.

Galgano, F. A. (2017). Military geography. *Oxford Bibliographies*. Available at: www.oxfordbibliographies.com/view/document/obo-9780199874002/obo-9780199874002-0029.xml (accessed 1 October 2022).

Gergan, M. D. (2020). Disastrous hydropower, uneven regional development, and decolonization in India's Eastern Himalayan borderlands. *Political Geography*, 80, 102175.

Gregory, D. (2011a). The everywhere war. *Geographical Journal*, 177, 238–250.

Gregory, D. (2011b). From a view to a kill. *Theory, Culture and Society*, 28(7-8), 188–215.

Gregory, D. (2014). Corpographies: Making sense of modern war. *Geographical Imaginations*. Available at: https://geographicalimaginations.files.wordpress.com/2012/07/gregory-corpographies.pdf (accessed 8 September 2022).

Gregory, D. (2016). The natures of war. *Antipode, 48*(1), 3–56.

Gregory, D. and Pred, A. (2007). Introduction. In D. Gregory and A. Pred (eds), *Violent Geographies: Fear, Terror, and Political Violence* (pp. 1–7). London and New York: Routledge.

Grote, K. M. and Johnson, J. T. (2021). Pipelines, protectors, and settler colonialism: Media representations of the Dakota Access Pipeline protest. *Settler Colonial Studies, 11*(4), 487–511. Available at: https://doi.org/10.1080/2201473X.2021.1999008 (accessed 2 June 2023).

Hall, E. (2019). A critical geography of disability hate crime. *Area, 51*(2), 249–256.

Igonya, E. K. (2022). Rwanda: LGBT rights are protected on paper, but discrimination and homophobia persist. *The Conversation,* 16 May. Available at: https://theconversation.com/rwanda-lgbt-rights-are-protected-on-paper-but-discrimination-and-homophobia-persist-182949 (accessed 2 December 2022).

Jenss, A. (2020). Global flows and everyday violence in urban space: The port-city of Buenaventura, Colombia. *Political Geography, 77*(102113), 1–12.

Jones, S. (2022). 'No clarity, no justice': Mother of murdered Mexican photojournalist seeks answers. *The Guardian,* 10 July. Available at: www.theguardian.com/world/2022/jul/10/no-clarity-no-justice-mother-of-murdered-mexican-photojournalist-seeks-answers (accessed 3 December 2022).

Kaplan, C., Kirk, G. and Lea, T. (2020). Editors' letter. Everyday militarisms: Hidden in plain sight/site. *Society and Space,* 8 March. Available at: www.societyandspace.org/articles/editors-letter-everyday-militarisms-hidden-in-plain-sight-site (accessed 7 February 2022).

Lacoste, Y. (1973). An illustration of geographical warfare: Bombing of the dikes on the Red River, North Vietnam. *Antipode, 5*(2), 1–13.

Listerborn, C. (2015). Geographies of the veil: Violent encounters in urban public spaces in Malmö, Sweden. *Social & Cultural Geography, 16*(1), 95–115.

Martin, P. M. and Carvajal, N. (2016). Feminicide as 'act' and 'process': A geography of gendered violence in Oaxaca. *Gender, Place & Culture, 23*(7), 989–1002.

Moore, A. and Walker, J. (2016). Tracing the US military's presence in Africa. *Geopolitics, 21*(3), 686–716.

Mountz, A. (2018). Political geography III: Bodies. *Progress in Human Geography, 42*(8), 759–769.

Nixon, R. (2011). *Slow violence and the environmentalism of the poor.* Cambridge, MA: Harvard University Press.

O'Tuathail, G. (1994). The critical reading/writing of geopolitics: Re-reading/writing Wittfogel, Bowman and Lacoste. *Progress in Human Geography, 18*(3), 313–332.

Pain, R. (2014). Everyday terrorism: Connecting domestic violence and global terrorism. *Progress in Human Geography, 38*, 531–550.

Pain, R. (2015). Intimate war. *Political Geography, 44*, 64–73.

Pain, R. and Staeheli, L. (2014). Introduction: Intimacy-geopolitics and violence. *Area, 46*(4), 344–360.

Philo, C. (2017). Less-than-human geographies. *Political Geography, 60*, 256–258.

Radcliffe, S. A. (2018). Geography and indigeneity II: Critical geographies of indigenous bodily politics. *Progress in Human Geography*, *42*(3), 436–445.

Rech, M. (2014). Be part of the story: A popular geopolitics of war comics aesthetics and Royal Air Force recruitment. *Political Geography*, *39*, 36–47.

Rech, M. (2015). A critical geopolitics of observant practice at British military airshows. *Transactions of the Institute of British Geographers*, *40*(4), 536–548.

Rech, M. (2020). Ephemera(l) geopolitics: The material cultures of British military recruitment. *Geopolitics*, *25*(5), 1075–1098.

Rech, M., Bos, D., Jenkings, N. K., Williams, A. and Woodward, R. (2015). Geography, military geography, and critical military studies. *Critical Military Studies*, *1*(1), 47–60.

Short, J. R. (2022). Settler colonialism helps explain current events in Xinjiang and Ukraine – and the history of Australia and US, too. *The Conversation, 14 March*. Available at: https://theconversation.com/settler-colonialism-helps-explain-current-events-in-xinjiang-and-ukraine-and-the-history-of-australia-and-us-too-176975 (accessed 1 June 2023).

Sinclair, R. (2016). The indigenous child removal system in Canada: An examination of legal decision-making and racial bias. *First Peoples Child & Family Review*, *11*(2), 8–18.

Smiles, D. (2020). The settler logics of (outer) space. *Society + Space*, 26 October. Available at: www.societyandspace.org/articles/the-settler-logics-of-outer-space (accessed 17 September 2022).

Smiles, D. (2021). Erasing indigenous history, then and now. *Origins*, *15*(1). Available at: https://origins.osu.edu/article/erasing-indigenous-history-then-and-now (accessed 1 June 2023).

Springer, S. and Le Billon, P. (2016). Violence and space: An introduction to the geographies of violence. *Political Geography*, *52*, 1–3.

Tucker, A. (2019). Geographies of sexualities in sub-Saharan Africa: Positioning and critically engaging with international human rights and related ascendant discourses. *Progress in Human Geography*, *44*(4), 683–703.

Tyner, J. A. and Rice, S. (2015). To live and let die: Food, famine, and administrative violence in Democratic Kampuchea, 1975–1979. *Political Geography*, *48*, 1–10.

Whyte, N. (2016). Why the Native American pipeline resistance in North Dakota is about climate justice. *The Conversation*, 16 September. Available at: https://theconversation.com/why-the-native-american-pipeline-resistance-in-north-dakota-is-about-climate-justice-64714 (accessed 17 July 2022).

Woon, C. Y. (2011). Undoing violence, unbounding precarity: Beyond the frames of terror in the Philippines. *Geoforum*, *42*, 285–296.

TWELVE

PEACE AND RESISTANCE: DECENTRING WAR

Chapter Overview

War and violence often dominate the news. They also dominate and frame the study of political geography. Practices of peace and resistance are vital in destabilising these narratives. More importantly, they also help us to imagine how the world might be less violent and more equitable. This chapter grapples with peace and resistance in various ways, including thinking through social movements and protest at various scales, including the everyday and the body. It explores the power dynamics that move and flow through peaceful practices, challenging us to think about the peaceful and with peoples and citizens pursuing and fighting for social justice, alongside and in tension with dominant narratives of war.

Learning Objectives

1. To introduce geographies of peace and resistance, and to understand why they matter.
2. To explore practices of peace and resistance (e.g., activism, protest) and to understand how these are experienced across different scales (e.g., global, local, body).
3. To think about the role of the non-human within such processes and practices.

Read with: Chapter 3 (Feminist Geopolitics), Chapter 11 (Violence), Chapter 7 (States and Territory), Chapter 9 (Nationalism)

We only have to open a news page to see the prevalence of war or conflict in the world. War is far from being consigned to the history books. The Russian invasion of Ukraine in 2022 exemplifies this all too clearly. Analysing such events has been, in many ways, the bread and butter of political geography. As Williams et al. (2014) note, political geographers have done much to shed light on how 'war is waged and violence legitimized'.

Accounts of peace and peaceful practice have historically featured much less strongly. For Megoran (2011: 178), geographers 'have been better at studying war than peace', maintaining a 'focus on male, weaponised, miltarised, bodily violations'. As such, peace is often presented as either the absence of war (Megoran, 2013: 190) or the 'end product after war' (Megoran et al. 2014). As this chapter will demonstrate, the reality is far more complex than this and it is increasingly important to think about and 'contribute to the various ways in which peace and justice are built' (Koopman 2016: 354; see also Kobayashi 2009). The first challenge is to understand 'what we mean by peace' (Megoran 2011: 178) and to move beyond vague definitions and instead towards careful and critical modes of analysis. (Koopman 2011, Megoran 2013).

Defining Peace

First and foremost, geographers have argued that we should understand peace as more than its relation to war. They have argued that while peace may refer to 'the absence of war', it also refers to the 'possibility of maximising human potential' (Flint in Megoran 2011: 182). Peace is therefore understood as 'a process' (Loyd 2012: 477), something that is actively performed by people and 'shaped by the spaces in which it is made' (Koopman 2017: n.p.). Peace – and efforts to achieve it – can include a range of actions and activities, including resistance, which will be discussed later in the chapter. Moreover, peace means different things to different people, at different times (Koopman 2017: n.p.). This is important, Koopman (2011: 194) argues, because when peace is 'portrayed as a mythical singular' thing, it arguably 'becomes abstract' and 'unobtainable'. In developing our understandings of peace, we must therefore recognise that peace is 'not the same everywhere any more than war is' (Koopman 2017: n.p.).

KEY TERMS: PEACE

Peace is both a concept and an action. It is not simple or romantic, rather it means different things to different people, at different times. Peace is a 'process' and can be sought through 'conscious or unconscious actions', both by everyday people like you or me, and by 'powerful geopolitical actors' (Williams et al. 2014). It may refer to a 'yearning for a radically new and just social order', or may be employed as a tactic 'by the powerful to resist exactly such change' (Williams et al. 2014).

In addition to recognising that peace exists in many forms (Megoran 2013: 190), questions of power are also key to understanding peace. As Williams et al. (2014: n.p.) note, 'the construction of peace is a political act that is both underpinned by, and reproduces, particular practices of power'. A number of important questions emerge here: Who gets to name peace? Who gets to define what kind of peace? Where is it made and how is peace realised? What does peace feel like? In order to 'take peace to pieces', Koopman (2011: 194) argues that we need to reflect on peace as a 'doing' – something that is practised and experienced in different ways at both elite and on the ground contexts. We should therefore consider peace as it is 'grounded' in particular places (Koopman 2011: 194). Finally, in seeking to define peace, it is important to think about it in a range of contexts. Beyond war, Koopman (2017: n.p.) reminds us that peace can also be considered 'in relation to the concepts of justice, development, security, and human rights', as each of these can involve and inform peaceful practices, action, and experience. As such, a 'small' but 'growing' body of work in political geography is seeking to engage with these complexities (Koopman 2016: 534).

Practising Peace

In addition to understanding and exploring peace as a *concept*, political geographers have also argued for further attention to the discipline's role 'in achieving peace' (Kobayashi 2009: 819). In other words, there is a need not just to study peace but to 'build it' (Koopman 2011: 193). The idea here is that geographers should welcome and pursue the 'fusion of theory and practice' (Routledge 2009a: 7), committing to peace through both 'research and activism' (Megoran 2011: 178, Takahashi 2009: 2). This action can take different forms. It may be in relation to research which involves practices of solidarity with those resisting and challenging 'oppressive power relations' (Routledge 2009a: 7). In other words, as political geographers interested in peace, we should seek to foster it through our actions. We will see examples of this throughout the chapter.

Geographies of Resistance

When we think about peace, it is important to consider the related concept of resistance. As Sparke (2008: 423) notes, the 'basic idea' of resistance refers to 'people pushing back' against a thing, situation, event, act, or belief. Resistance can be understood as an 'umbrella' term, including a range of 'resistant activities' such as 'activism, counter-conduct, social movements, and subversive tactics' (Hughes 2020: 1142). Resistance and power are linked and entangled. When we engage in 'resistant politics', against, for example, 'class exploitation, gender, racial, sexual (and other) forms of domination and oppression' (Routledge 2009b: 646), we are often understood to 'have a fixed position' within a 'particular configuration of power' (MacLeavy et al. 2021: 1566). In other words, when we resist something, our resistance is understood as intentional (i.e., we want to resist this thing, in this way, with this desired effect).

Cindi Katz's work on 'resistance, reworking and resilience' is important here (Sparke 2008: 424). As Sparke (2008: 424) details, Katz (2001) understands resistance as that which is 'oppositional' and achieves 'emancipatory change'. Resistance might include 'resistive practices' such as 'informal walkouts, joining a trade union or organising strikes' (Salmon 2021: 2), and can be compared to related ideas of resilience – that which 'enables people to survive' without necessarily 'changing the circumstances that make such survival so hard' (Katz in Sparke 2008: 424). Collectively, such work encourages attention to grounded 'accounts of agency' that consider different practices of resistance, their limitations, and uneven impacts (Sparke 2008: 424).

Such frameworks also add complexity to settled understandings (see Hughes 2020). Like peace, geographers have raised concerns about resistance being somewhat 'romanticised' and idealised (Sparke 2008). In response, Hughes (2020) complicates the concept through the idea of resistance as 'emergence'. Hughes (2020) turns to the example of the 2017 Women's March in Washington DC, USA (see Figure 12.1) whereby hundreds of thousands of women marched in protest against the inauguration of the then President, Donald Trump, and his 'misogynistic views' (Hartocollis and Alcindor, 2017, Hughes 2020). As Hughes (2020: 1141) notes, participants 'could not fully know' what their presence might mean for 'future claims' made about the size, power, and force of the march.

In other words, while the end result or effect of such resistance was unclear, there was and is power in the process (Hughes 2020: 1143). Within this framework, resistance emerges; it is not always pre-determined. We can find examples of emergent resistance around the world. Consider, for example, the 'wave of demonstrations' in Iran following the death of 22-year-old Mahsa Amini who 'died in Tehran while in the custody of Iran's morality police' (Hooman 2022: n.p.). As Hooman (2022: n.p.) describes, the morality police deploy 'coercive force compelling women to comply with the mandatory hijab law through physical and verbal violence and humiliation – all part of a systematic effort to suppress and control their bodies'. Following women bravely removing their headscarves at Mahsa's funeral, protests erupted across Iran, with women 'turning their bodies into arenas of resistance against the ideology and intervention of the state' (Hooman 2022: n.p.).

Figure 12.1 Women's march on Washington DC, USA (2017)

Credit: Mobilus In Mobili. (Creative Commons Attribution-Share Alike 2.0 Generic) https://commons.wikimedia.org/wiki/File:Women%27s_March_on_Washington_(32593123745).jpg

Resistance, then, is not just understood as 'fighting back or in opposition', but as emerging and changing in and through the 'everyday challenges that people' encounter and respond to (MacLeavy et al. 2021: 1566).

Practising Resistance

Activism refers to 'the practice of political action by individuals or collectives' (Routledge 2009c: 5). It encompasses different practices (from social movements to protests) and is undertaken by different groups including non-governmental organisations, community groups, charities, and citizens. While activism can be presented in 'restrictive' ways, as 'physical' and 'macho' action (Routledge 2009c: 6), the geographies of activism include a wide range of activisms, with different purposes, goals, and scales (Takahashi 2009).

KEY TERMS: ACTIVISM

Activism refers to practices of political action designed to 'effect social change' (Routledge 2009c: 5). Activism takes a range of forms, including social movements and protest, and occurs in a variety of spaces – from the streets to digital picket lines.

A focus on activism brings together the concepts of peace and resistance. Activism is both a form of resistance and can be an important way in which peace is pursued (Megoran 2011). As Routledge (2009c: 5) charts, stemming from the 'advent of radical and Marxist geography in the 1960s', geography advocated for research concerned with understanding and aiding the 'solving of social problems'. Here, geographers of activism have encouraged us to consider activism across multiple scales, from 'the sites of international politics to everyday' and embodied contexts (Askins 2013, Williams 2014: n.p., Williams and McConnell 2011).

We might think of The Black Panther Party for Self-Defence (commonly known as the 'Black Panthers') as a form of everyday activism (see Figure 12.2). Formed in 1966 in Oakland, USA as a grassroots organisation, they aimed to 'collectively combat White oppression' and 'confront corrupt systems of power' (Saunders 2019, Workneh and Finely 2018: n.p.). Co-founders Huey P. Newton and Bobby Seale considered the Black Panthers not as something they had 'thought up', but rather as a 'continuation of earlier African American movements that grappled with oppression and exploitation' (Tyner 2006: 108). With the protection of 'Black men and women from state-sanctioned violence' at its core (Workneh and Finley 2018: n.p.), the group shared 'personal experiences and observations' in the building of community (Tyner 2006). Efforts to effect change were therefore 'actively forged through the everyday spaces and lives of ordinary people' (Williams 2014: n.p.). While beginning as a local organisation, the group went on to achieve 'national and international prominence through their local activities and global ideas' (Tyner 2006: 105). Their activism included both the provision of education and direct action.

Figure 12.2 Women in the Black Panther Party

Credit: Rainalee111 (Creative Commons Attribution-Share Alike 4.0 International) https://commons.wikimedia.org/wiki/File:Black.Panthers.Women.jpg

Direct action can be non-violent or violent, and refers to techniques that 'seek to effect change' (Hail 2019: 38). The Black Panthers undertook a range of direct action, from rebellions and so-called guerrilla tactics to community food provision programmes (Tyner 2006: 106, see also Heynen 2009). In so doing, they sought to perform 'an alternative geopolitics' (Hail 2019: 37). While presented by some as 'radical militants' (Tyner 2006: 106), the Black Panther Party emerged as one of 'the most significant radical political movements in US history', forging and performing 'grassroots organizing' and community building and based 'survival programs' (Heynen 2009: 411). As such, the party demonstrates both the role and power of 'direct action' in the face of systemic racialised inequalities (Heynen 2009: 411), and the value of attention to the scale of everyday life and practice as a space and site to 'build hoped-for futures in the present', while equally recognising that this 'process is experimental, messy and contingent' (Chatterton and Pickerill 2010: 475).

Understanding Activism

One key form of activism is protest. Protest refers to a range of forms of 'mobilisation', from 'demonstrations and riots, to strikes' (Fox and Bell 2016: 54). Protests seek to disrupt spaces and flows, 'making marginalized people visible' and challenging 'elite norms' (Salmenkari 2009: 239). Protests also seek to lay claim to, occupy, and mobilise public space (Awcock 2019). Motivations for undertaking protest vary, but there remains a 'long list of causes to protest against', including 'war, autocratic government, privatisation and commodification of land and natural resources, climate change, corporate greed, social oppression and violence on the basis of gender, sexuality, ethnicity, and ability' (Askins 2013: 529).

PEACE AND RESISTANCE | 191

===================== KEY TERMS: PROTEST =====================

Protest refers to the mobilisation and gathering of people in activities such as public demonstrations, riots, or strikes. Protests are designed to (visually, spatially, and socially) claim and disrupt spaces and contexts, and to communicate messages or goals in order to urge and prompt action.

We can see the complexities of protest clearly through the 2017 Women's March in the USA. Understood as a 'kind of counter-inauguration', the protest was sparked by a post on Facebook (Hartocollis and Alcindor 2017: n.p.). While seeking to bring together demonstrators 'around issues like reproductive rights, immigration and civil rights' (Hartocollis and Alcindor 2017: n.p.), the march featured many women wearing 'pink knitted "pussy hats", as a gesture to the [then] president's boasts of assaulting women' (Hughes 2020: 1141). By showing up, marching and wearing these hats, women resisted, 'organising opposition to a configuration' of gendered 'power relations' (Hughes 2020: 1141).

In addition to protests on the ground, we are, of course, also increasingly seeing protesters mobilising, networking, and flooding digital space and social media. In March 2021, for example, the hashtag #RippedJeans trended in India. The so-called 'ripped jeans' online protest emerged following a negative remark from Uttarakhand Indian Chief Minister, Tirath Singh Rawat, regarding a woman he witnessed 'wearing ripped jeans' on a flight (Dewan 2021). The Minister stated that he 'took issue with her exposed knees' (Dewan 2021). The 'shaming tone' of the remark (Dewan 2021), one echoing those of previous 'prominent politicians who connected rape and sexual assault to women's outfits' (Pandey 2021), struck a powerful chord, with a clip of the remark 'going viral' online (Dewan 2021). As many women have sadly encountered, sexual harassment and assault frequently enter 'public spaces, restricting women's mobility and creating fear' (Bhattacharyya 2015: 1340). In the case of the 'ripped jeans' protest, women across India responded to the video 'with alacrity and speed as they posted photos of themselves in ripped jeans on social media. Some even cut holes into their jeans before posting the defiant images' (Dewan 2021: n.p.).

Collectively, such protests remind us that 'big issues' can be encountered, resisted, and explored at the scale of 'everyday life' (Mott 2016), both on the ground and in the digital realm (see Chapter 13). While beneficial to appreciate particular forms and practices of activism and resistance, geographers have reminded us that activism is practised, experienced, and embodied by people.

What, or Who, is an Activist?

Take a moment to consider what you imagine when you hear the word 'activist'. Perhaps imagining an activist conjures up an image of a 'loud, attention-grabbing and disruptive' protester (Steele et al. 2021: n.p.). Perhaps you think of someone you've seen in the news. Greta Thunberg might spring to mind for some, following her 'Skolstrejk för klimatet (school strike for climate)' outside the Swedish Parliament in 2018 (see Figure 12.3), prompting 'worldwide protests' using similar tactics (Lundberg and Heidenblad 2021: n.p.).

Figure 12.3 Skolstrejk för klimatet

Credit: Derek Read (Creative Commons Attribution 2.0 Generic) https://commons.wikimedia.org/wiki/File:%22Skolstrejk_f%C3%B6r_klimatet%22_(48812129197).jpg

KEY TERMS: ACTIVIST

Alongside understanding activism (see previous Key Terms box), it's also important to reflect on who and what we imagine when we think of the 'activist' (Askins 2013: 528). Activists participate in activism. Just as activism takes a range of forms, so too do activists take many forms. They can be young or old, and their identities cross a range of intersectional demographics.

These included a 2019 strike in which hundreds of thousands of students in over '1664 cities across 125 countries' walked out of their schools and colleges in strikes urging action on the climate crisis (Haynes 2019: n.p.). The 'growing climate crisis has shown how children and young people can be a political force to be reckoned with' (Skovdal and Benwell 2021: 259). This is echoed in the term 'Youthquake', referring to 'a significant cultural, political, or social change arising from the actions or influence of young people', and one recognised as the *Oxford Dictionaries 2017* word of the year (Cain 2017: n.p.). An activist, therefore, is never just one thing.

Over to You: Thinking Critically About the 'Who' of Activism

Read the (paraphrased) except below from Morten Skovdal and Matthew Benwell's (2021) paper 'Young people's everyday climate crisis activism: New terrains for research, analysis and action'.

(Continued)

> Climate change has been described as one of the greatest threats facing humanity, and a defining issue of our time. Children and young people are at the forefront of experiencing the devastating impacts of the climate crisis … However, children and young people are not only victims of climate change. (Skovdal and Benwell 2021: 259)

Online, search for the phrase 'youth climate protest'. Select a story or page that focuses attention on a youth movement, group or one specific protest. Pay particular attention to examples from the Global South. Do a wider search on that youth movement or protest and find and read one additional news story covering their actions.
Reflect on the following questions:

1. What are the youth climate activists you have selected protesting?
2. Why are they protesting? What form does their protest take (e.g., on the ground, digital)?
3. Who are the youth climate activists you have selected? What motivates them?
4. How are they and their actions presented in the accompanying news story (e.g., as political agents, as disruptive, as victims)?

While activists like Greta Thunberg may capture global headlines, other 'largely hidden', activist stories, unfolding in our homes, in our schools, and in local communities warrant further attention too (Skovdal and Benwell 2021: 259). This might include facing the 'insurmountable' climate crisis by undertaking more 'manageable' actions 'such as eating less meat, recycling, and consuming less' (Skovdal and Benwell 2021: 263). These 'quieter' forms of activism 'refer to small, quiet, everyday actions which can also be very impactful in generating change' (Steele et al. 2021: n.p.). By re-approaching activism in more 'gentle' and 'quiet' terms, we see that 'political actions need not always be noisy and disruptive' (Hall 2020: 243). For example, writing of fieldwork in a 'befriending scheme' pairing refugees and local residents, Askins (2014: 353) examines a 'quiet' and 'unassuming' politics of 'encounter embedded in intimate relationships'. Foregrounding everyday acts like 'gentle hands on shoulders' as a form of 'remaking place and community in inclusive ways' (Askins 2014: 354, Askins 2015: 475), Askins draws upon Horton and Kraft's (2009) discussion of 'small acts and kind words'. Their work calls for attention to the dimensions of activism that are 'personal, quotidian and proceed with little fanfare' (Horton and Kraft 2009: 14).

Resistance in Action: Being an Activist Geographer

As Paul Routledge (2009c: 5) notes, geographers have long critiqued the 'separation' between the discipline of geography and the practice of activism. Here, we – as political geographers – are urged to become more 'politically engaged outside of the academy', and to take seriously the 'social responsibility' to 'make a difference on the ground' (Routledge 2009c: 5, 6). Activist geography can therefore be understood as a form of 'critical praxis' driven by the desire to expose and challenge 'socio-spatial processes that (re)produce inequalities' through action both in and beyond the academy (Routledge 2009c: 6). Activist geography, or 'action research', thus 'personalizes academic geography and professionalizes personal geographies' (Ward 2007: 698).

Case Study: Activist Geographies at the US–Mexico Border

US Customs and Border Protection reported over 977,500 encounters with migrants at the US–Mexico border in 2019, and over 458,000 in 2020 (Customs and Border Protection n.d.). Here, 'encounters' refer to migrants both being taken into custody to 'await adjudication', and to immediate expulsions back to the migrant's 'home country' (Pew Research Center 2021: n.p.). The number of migrants encountered at the border in the month of July 2021 'exceeded 200,000 for the first time in 21 years' (*BBC News* 2021: n.p.). While many are 'processed' as above, others tragically die during attempts to cross the border. It was reported that in 'fiscal year 2021' there were 557 migrant deaths at the US Southern border, a higher total 'than in any prior year on record' (*CNN* 2021: n.p.). Within this tragic landscape, allegations have emerged against Border Patrol agents who have reportedly intentionally destroyed food and water supplies for border crossers (Amnesty International 2019: n.p.).

Alongside research on processes of bordering and migration, scholar-activists such as Scott Warren seek 'to do away with the academic/activist divide' (Ward 2007: 696). Warren is an activist at US faith-based border aid group 'No More Deaths' and has been part of projects offering humanitarian aid (food, water, shelter) to migrants in the border area. While seeking to challenge and 'right the wrongs' of bordering's oppressions (Routledge 2009a: 8), Warren's activism faced challenges, including his arrest in January 2018. Facing charges of 'harbouring migrants' (Amnesty International 2019: n.p.), he subsequently went through two trials before being acquitted. After the verdict was read, Professor Warren stated 'the Government failed in its attempts to criminalize basic human kindness' (NPR 2019).

It's not just professors or lecturers who are geographer activists. It's important also to recognise the pivotal role of students (geographers and otherwise) who participate in different forms of activism. Consider, for example, the 2019 protests that erupted in Chile following the government proposal to increase the price of metro tickets. As Riethof (2019: n.p.) writes, students responded by 'dodging metro fares, jumping the turnstiles en masse and setting metro stations on fire'. These protests began in Santiago and spread to other Chilean cities, leading to the then President, Sebastian Piñera, to declare a ' state of emergency' and imposing curfews (Riethof 2019: n.p.). Eighteen people died and several thousand were arrested (Riethof 2019). These protests emerged quickly, it is argued,

PEACE AND RESISTANCE | 195

because of the backdrop and 'economic and ideological' legacies of 'the Pinochet era' which saw 'high inequality' embedded into the Chilean landscape (Riethof 2019: n.p.). Students here were pivotal in communicating and contesting a 'growing dissatisfaction with high levels of inequality and a high cost of living' (Riethof 2019: n.p.).

Disobedient Objects and Technologies

Whilst substances like tear gas can be used to disable protests and activism – as noted in Chapter 5 – disobedient objects are key to understanding resistance and protest, playing a 'powerful role in movements for social change' (Victoria and Albert Museum n.d.). More broadly, we can understand objects and technologies as important in understanding resistance and activism, raising important questions about 'social difference and unequal power relations' (Panelli 2009: 79). This is evident when we consider the role of digital technologies, from smartphones and social media to encrypted communications, in the planning of protests. Moreover, as Oliver (2021) writes in relation to veganism, platforms like social media are vital to spreading and disseminating campaigns. Drawing on everyday objects, Hannah Awcock's (2021a) work on protest stickers demonstrates the power of the material in everyday contexts. Awcock (2021b: n.p.) recalls walking through Edinburgh, Scotland and catching her eye on 'a small, round sticker on a rubbish bin'. Upon closer inspection, the text on the sticker read 'No To – Mandatory Masks – Mandatory Vaccines – No More Lockdowns'. Awcock (2021b: n.p.) subsequently researched this sticker, tracing it back to a 'non-political grassroots movement' set up in opposition to 'measures taken to fight Covid-19'. As Hannah Awcock (2021b: n.p.) argues, protest stickers are important geopolitical objects – both 'cheap to produce and distribute' and 'a common tactic of social movements' across the political spectrum.

In the Field with Hannah Awcock: Protest Stickers

In this section we hear from Dr Hannah Awcock about her work exploring activism, protest, and resistance through the lens of the sticker.

What does resistance mean to you?

Resistance is expressing discontent with a more powerful individual, group, or ideology. It can range from overt, attention-grabbing acts like protest marches and riots, to covert, everyday actions like putting up a sticker, or taking a slightly longer break at work. Resistance is about demanding a voice when you have been denied one, and taking action when you feel powerless. Resistance is always present to greater or lesser

(Continued)

extents, but I think it is particularly important that we pay attention to it at times like this, when so many groups of people, rightly or wrongly, feel disenfranchised.

How and why did you approach the study of protest through stickers?

I started studying protest stickers because I think they are wonderful objects that hardly any academics were paying attention to. They are concentrated bursts of human creativity and expression. I am fascinated by the way that they are a common part of the urban fabric, but go unnoticed by so many. I started photographing protest stickers in 2014, an odd hobby that has developed in the intervening years into my main research interest. At the moment I use visual and material analysis to study stickers, but I want to start doing interviews with people who make, put up, and interact with stickers as well.

Any top tips for a student interested in undertaking research on protest objects?

There are a huge variety of protest objects, ranging from riot shields and tear gas canisters to stickers and placards. There are also so many research methods you can use with them, including visual, textual, and material analysis, interviews, participant observation, and ethnography. So get creative, think beyond the obvious options, and you might be surprised what insights into resistance you could provide!

Case Study: Anti-Government Protests in Hong Kong

As Hou (2020) explores, we can also see the use of sticky objects – this time post-it notes (shown in Figure 12.4) – in anti-government protests in Hong Kong. Following the proposition of a controversial bill that would have enabled extradition from Hong Kong to mainland China, a wave of protests were sparked across Hong Kong. Hou (2020: n.p.) reflects on the spatial dimensions and effects of such protests, drawing attention to the ways 'citizens and activists made use of the urban environment during the movement'. In doing so, Hou (2020: n.p.) foregrounds the use of 'Lennon walls' such as that shown in Figure 12.4. These sticky-note adorned spaces 'sprung up on buildings, walkways, sky bridges, underpasses and storefronts' across the city and were the bearers of 'messages like "Hong Kongers love freedom", "garbage government", and "We demand real universal suffrage"' (Hou 2020: n.p.). As Hou (2020: n.p.) traces, such creative displays originated in Prague following the murder of the Beatles band member and musician John Lennon, and were historically spaces to share messages of love and remembrance. However, 'Lennon walls' have since morphed, 'becoming a location for community-generated protest art that endures – yet is ever-changing'

(Continued)

Figure 12.4 Hong Kong Lennon Wall in 2014

Credit: Ceeseven (Creative Commons Attribution-Share Alike 4.0 International) https://commons.wikimedia.org/wiki/File:Close_view_of_Hong_Kong_Lennon_Wall_on_2014-11-08.JPG

to this day (Hou 2020: n.p.). Importantly, such 'simple and highly adaptable' resistant practices enable 'multitudes of citizens, visitors and tourists to participate in the movement and the political debate' (Hou 2020: n.p.). Whether or not they support the state, messages can be left and views shared, with the 'community developing a tacit agreement that people won't take down or cover over messages they disagree with' (Hou 2020: n.p.).

Conclusions: Peace and Political Geography

While there may be 'no utopian end of warfare in sight' (Kobayashi 2009: 819), by foregrounding geographies of peace and resistance, this chapter highlights the varied practices by which people seek to challenge and change geopolitical worlds. While we recognise that peace and violence remain entangled, through for example nation states 'drawing up and enforcing international boundaries and security in the name of peace' (Megoran et al. 2014), we also demonstrate the value of approaching the geopolitical by beginning with and foregrounding questions of peace, resistance, and justice. After all, as a discipline committed to examining practices, connections and unevenness across different sites, scales and bodies, geography is well placed to explore peace (Williams 2014), resistance, activism, and practices of 'pushing back'. Such practices are never singular.

On the contrary, they are multifaceted, always in process, emerging and undertaken by diverse peoples, young and old. Objects, materials, gases, and technologies also play their own role here in both enabling and disabling practices of peace, resistance, and protest. From smartphones to tear gas, the non-human is disruptive, disobedient, and disciplining, shifting and shaping power relations in protest contexts, and constructing the conditions for peace – but also for violence. These practices take place on a range of scales, from the everyday, to the national and global. Protest and resistance can, like fire, spread across borders, disrupting the structures of the state and oppressive regimes of power as it travels. Resistance (and its constituent parts of activism and protest) are multiple and plural (loud and quiet, offline and online), and our work and thinking on these terms should reflect this.

Summary

- Political geography is a discipline that has, in the past, been largely focussed on war and conflict. This is beginning to change as practices of peace and resistance receive increasing attention.
- Peace is not simply understood as an absence of war but as a practice that takes many forms across multiple scales and contexts. Peace has its own politics – who gets to name it? Who experiences it?
- Resistance often takes place in the face of violence. Activism and protest are practices through which alternative futures are enacted and brought into being.
- Activists take many forms and the practices of activism take place across multiple contexts. From quiet everyday activisms to deliberately loud protests, change is brought about in a range of ways.
- Geographers also engage in the practices of peace, resistance, and activism through their research. Research, whether in an undergraduate dissertation or academic paper, can be a tool of peace and activism when undertaken carefully.

Follow-on Resources

Organisation and associated social movements for climate change action: The National Association of Professional Environmentalists (NAPE) is an 'action organisation committed to sustainable solutions to Uganda's most challenging environmental and economic growth problems'. You can read more about NAPE here: www.nape.or.ug/. You can also read an associated discussion of the wider eco-feminist movement in Uganda discussed in *Wired* (2021) 'Eco-feminists are tackling climate change head on' available at www.wired.co.uk/article/eco-feminists-climate-change

The artists bringing activism into and beyond gallery spaces: This *New York Times* article raises important questions about the role of activism, alongside the space and actors that are important within it. See www.nytimes.com/2021/10/01/t-magazine/art-activism-forensic-architecture.html

Tear gas: An investigation by Amnesty International on 'what tear gas is, how it is abused and why you should care'. Note how non-human agencies are enrolled into resistant practices. See https://teargas.amnesty.org/#top

References

Amnesty International (2019). Scott Warren found not guilty in court. Available at: www.amnesty.org.uk/scott-warren-found-not-guilty-court (accessed 21 September 2022).

Askins, K. (2013). Activists. In K. Dodds, M. Kuus and J. Sharp (eds), *The Ashgate Research Companion to Critical Geopolitics* (pp. 527–541). Farnham: Ashgate.

Askins, K. (2014). A quiet politics of being together: Miriamand Rose. *Area, 46*(4), 353–354.

Askins, K. (2015). Being together: Everyday geographies and the quiet politics of belonging. *ACME: An International E-Journal for Critical Geographies, 14*(2), 470–478.

Awcock, H. (2019). The geographies of protest and public space in mid-nineteenth-century London: The Hyde Park railings affair. *Historical Geography, 47*, 194–217.

Awcock, H. (2021a). Stickin' it to the man: The geographies of protest stickers. *Area, 53*, 522–530.

Awcock, H. (2021b). Debating Covid-19 in public space: Covid conspiracy stickers. *Geography Directions*. Available at: https://blog.geographydirections.com/2021/06/14/debating-covid-19-in-public-space-covid-conspiracy-stickers/ (accessed 5 December 2022).

BBC News (2021). US–Mexico border migrant detention levels reach 21-year high, *BBC News*, 13 August. Available at: www.bbc.co.uk/news/world-us-canada-58207124 (accessed 4 March 2022).

Bhattacharyya, R. (2015). Understanding the spatialities of sexual assault against Indian women in India. *Gender, Place & Culture, 22*(9), 1340–1356.

Cain, S. (2017). 'Youthquake' named 2017 word of the year by Oxford Dictionaries. *The Guardian*, 15 December. Available at: www.theguardian.com/books/2017/dec/15/youthquake-named-2017-word-of-the-year-by-oxford-dictionaries (accessed 10 November 2022).

Chatterton, P. and Pickerill, J. (2010). Everyday activism and transitions towards post-capitalist worlds. *Transactions of the Institute of British Geographers, 35*, 475–490.

CNN (2021). Border Patrol tallies record 557 migrant deaths on US–Mexico border in 2021 fiscal year. *CNN Politics*, 29 October. Available at: https://edition.cnn.com/2021/10/29/politics/border-patrol-record-border-deaths-fiscal-year-2021/index.html (accessed 19 November 2022).

Customs and Border Protection (n.d.). Southwest land border encounters. Available at: www.cbp.gov/newsroom/stats/southwest-land-border-encounters (accessed 1 June 2022).

Dewan, D. (2021). How women in India reclaimed the protest power of ripped jeans. *The Conversation*, 25 March. Available at: https://theconversation.com/how-women-in-india-reclaimed-the-protest-power-of-ripped-jeans-157666 (accessed 7 May 2022).

Fox, S. and Bell, A. (2016). Urban geography and protest mobilization in Africa. *Political Geography, 53*, 54–64.

Hail, C. R. (2019). The activist as geographer: Nonviolent direct action in Cold War Germany and postcolonial Ghana. *The Journal of Historical Geography, 64*, 36–46.

Hall, S. M. (2020). The personal is political: Feminist geographies of/in austerity. *Geoforum, 110*, 242–251.

Hartocollis, A. and Alcindor, Y. (2017). Women's March highlights as huge crowds protest Trump: 'We're not going away'. *The New York Times*, 21 January. Available at: www.nytimes.com/2017/01/21/us/womens-march.html (accessed 17 June 2022).

Haynes, S. (2019). Students from 1,600 cities just walked out of school to protest climate change. It could be Greta Thunberg's biggest strike yet. *Time*, 24 May. Available at: https://time.com/5595365/global-climate-strikes-greta-thunberg/ (accessed 2 December 2022).

Heynen, N. (2009). Bending the bars of Empire from every ghetto for survival: The Black Panther Party's radical antihunger politics of social reproduction and scale. *Annals of the Association of American Geographers, 99*(2), 406–422.

Hooman, N. (2022). The protests in Iran are part of a long history of women's resistance. *The Conversation*, 23 October. Available at: https://theconversation.com/the-protests-in-iran-are-part-of-a-long-history-of-womens-resistance-191551 (accessed 29 November 2022).

Horton, J. and Kraft, P. (2009). Small acts, kind words and 'not too much fuss': Implicit activisms. *Emotion, Space and Society, 2*(1), 14–23.

Hou, J. (2020). 'Lennon Walls' herald a sticky-note revolution in Hong Kong. *The Conversation*, 17 January. Available at: https://theconversation.com/lennon-walls-herald-a-sticky-note-revolution-in-hong-kong-129740 (accessed 2 March 2022).

Hughes, S. M. (2020). On resistance in human geography. *Progress in Human Geography, 44*(6), 1141–1160.

Katz, C. (2001). On the grounds of globalisation: A topography of feminist political engagement. *Signs: Journal of Women in Culture and Society, 26*(4), 1213–1234.

Kobayashi, A. (2009). Geographies of peace and armed conflict: Introduction. *Annals of the Association of American Geographers, 99*(5), 819–826.

Koopman, S. (2011). Let's take peace to pieces. *Political Geography, 30*(4), 193–194.

Koopman, S. (2016). Beware: Your research may be weaponized. *Annals of the American Association of Geographers, 106*(3), 530–535.

Koopman, S. (2017). Geographies of peace. *Oxford Bibliographies*. Available at: www.oxfordbibliographies.com/view/document/obo-9780199874002/obo-9780199874002-0148.xml (accessed 1 October 2022).

Loyd, J. M. (2012). Geographies of peace and antiviolence. *Geography Compass, 6*(8), 477–489.

Lundberg, B. and Heidenblad, D. L. (2021). Greta Thunberg emerged from five decades of environmental youth activism in Sweden. *The Conversation*, 4 November. Available at: https://theconversation.com/greta-thunberg-emerged-from-five-decades-of-environmental-youth-activism-in-sweden-171043 (accessed 17 March 2022).

MacLeavy, J., Fannin, M. and Larner, W. (2021). Feminism and futurity: Geographies of resistance, resilience and reworking. *Progress in Human Geography*, *45*(6), 1558–1579.

Megoran, N. (2011). War and peace? An agenda for peace research and practice in geography. *Political Geography*, *30*(4), 178–189.

Megoran, N. (2013). Violence and peace. In K. Dodds, M. Kuus, M. and J. Sharp (eds), *The Ashgate Research Companion to Critical Geopolitics* (pp. 190–207). Farnham: Ashgate.

Megoran, N., Williams, P. and McConnell, F. (2014). Geographies of peace, geographies for peace. In F. McConnell, N. Megoran and P. Williams (eds), *Geographies of peace*. London, UK: I. B. Tauris & Co. Ltd.

Mott, C. (2016). Feminist geography. *Oxford Bibliographies*. Available at: www.oxfordbibliographies.com/display/document/obo-9780199874002/obo-9780199874002-0123.xml (accessed 10 August 2022).

NPR (2019). Jury acquits aid worker accused of helping border-crossing migrants in Arizona. Available at: www.npr.org/2019/11/21/781658800/jury-acquits-aid-worker-accused-of-helping-border-crossing-migrants-in-arizona (accessed 2 February 2022).

Oliver, C. (2021). Vegan world-making in meat-centric society: The embodied geographies of veganism. *Social & Cultural Geography*, *24*(5), 831–850.

Pandey, G. (2021). Why India is talking about ripped jeans and knees. *BBC News*, 22 March. Available at: www.bbc.co.uk/news/world-asia-india-56453929 (accessed 1 August 2022).

Panelli, R. (2009). More-than-human social geographies: Posthuman and other possibilities. *Progress in Human Geography*, *34*(1), 79–87.

Pew Research Center (2021). Migrant encounters at US–Mexico border are at a 21-year high. Available at: www.pewresearch.org/fact-tank/2021/08/13/migrant-encounters-at-u-s-mexico-border-are-at-a-21-year-high/ (accessed 2 April 2022).

Riethof, M. (2019). Chile protests escalate as widespread dissatisfaction shakes foundations of country's economic success story. *The Conversation*, 25 October. Available at: https://theconversation.com/chile-protests-escalate-as-widespread-dissatisfaction-shakes-foundations-of-countrys-economic-success-story-125628 (accessed 2 April 2022).

Routledge, P. (2009a). Activist geographies. In R. Kitchin and N. Thrift (eds), *International encyclopaedia of human geography* (pp. 7–14). Amsterdam: Elsevier.

Routledge, P. (2009b). Protest. In D. Gregory, R. Johnston, G. Pratt, M. Watts and S. Whatmore (eds), *The Dictionary of Human Geography* (5th edn). London: Wiley-Blackwell.

Routledge, P. (2009c). Activism. In D. Gregory, R. Johnston, G. Pratt, M. Watts and S. Whatmore (eds), *The Dictionary of Human Geography* (5th edn). London: Wiley-Blackwell.

Salmenkari, T. (2009). Geography of protest: Places of demonstration in Buenos Aires and Seoul. *Urban Geography*, *30*(3), 239–260.

Salmon, U. (2021). Risk and resistance strategies in the cleaning industry. *Interdisciplinary Perspectives on Equality and Diversity*, *7*(1).

Saunders, R. A. (2019). (Profitable) imaginaries of Black Power: The popular and political geographies of *Black Panther*. *Political Geography*, *69*, 139–149.

Skovdal, M. and Benwell, M. C. (2021). Young people's everyday climate crisis activism: New terrains for research, analysis and action. *Children's Geographies, 19*(3), 259–266.

Sparke, M. (2008). Political geography – political geographies of globalization III: Resistance. *Progress in Human Geography, 32*(3), 423–440.

Steele, W., MacCallum, D., Houston, D., Bryne, J. and Hillier, J. (2021). Ordinary people, extraordinary change: Addressing the climate emergency through 'quiet activism'. *The Conversation*, 24 August. Available at: https://theconversation.com/ordinary-people-extraordinary-change-addressing-the-climate-emergency-through-quiet-activism-160548 (accessed 11 September 2023).

Takahashi, L. M. (2009). Activism. In R. Kitchin and N. Thrift (eds), *International encyclopaedia of human geography* (pp. 1–6). Amsterdam: Elsevier.

Tyner, J. A. (2006). 'Defend the ghetto': Space and the urban politics of the Black Panther Party. *Annals of the Association of American Geographers, 96*(1), 105–118.

Victoria and Albert Museum (n.d.). Closed Exhibition – Disobedient Objects. Available at: www.vam.ac.uk/content/exhibitions/disobedient-objects/ (accessed 20 June 2023).

Ward, K. (2007). Geography and public policy: Activist, participatory, and policy geographies. *Progress in Human Geography, 31*(5), 695–705.

Williams, P. (2014). The geography of peace? *Queen Mary*, 27 August. Available at: www.qmul.ac.uk/geog/news/2014/items/the-geography-of-peace.html (accessed 15 October 2022).

Williams, P. and McConnell, F. (2011). Critical geographies of peace. *Antipode, 43*(4), 927–931.

Williams, P., Megoran, N. and McConnell, F. (2014). Introduction: Geographical approaches to peace. In F. McConnell, N. Megoran and P. Williams (eds), *Geographies of peace*. London, UK: I. B. Tauris & Co. Ltd.

Workneh, L. and Finley, T. (2018). 27 important facts everyone should know about the Black Panthers. *The Huffington Post*, 18 February. Available at: www.huffingtonpost.co.uk/entry/27-important-facts-everyone-should-know-about-the-black-panthers_us_56c4d853e4b08ffac1276462 (accessed 6 November 2022).

THIRTEEN

SURVEILLANCE: GEOGRAPHIES OF DIGITAL SPACE AND LIFE

Chapter Overview

Digital devices, processes, and systems increasingly shape our everyday lives, worlds, and spaces. This chapter introduces and interrogates the 'digital'. It examines how geographers have approached digital devices, spaces, and practices as they are deployed and experienced by states, corporations, and citizens alike. The chapter highlights that encounters with the digital are uneven, amplifying existing forms of inequality and marginalisation. However, it also demonstrates that the digital can be empowering, enabling, and afford a range of caring, resistant, and community-building relations and relationships.

Learning Objectives

1. To understand why it is important for political geographers to consider digital devices, spaces, practices, and experiences.
2. To gain insight into the digital as it acts and is encountered across multiple spaces and scales.
3. To develop a critical awareness around digital spaces and experiences as uneven, and to recognise the digital as both potentially harmful and empowering.

Read with: Chapter 5 (Non-human Worlds), Chapter 3 (Feminist Geopolitics), Chapter 12 (Peace and Resistance), Chapter 11 (Violence)

From smartphone communications to GPS navigations, to growing use of AI, digital technologies have become 'a central feature' of our everyday lives (Cuomo and Dolci 2021: 224). As the digital becomes increasingly significant in the management and governance of economics, cities, and politics, there remains 'almost no area untouched by digital technologies, logics, or devices' (Ash et al. 2019: 1). Within political geography and beyond, we 'are in a dynamic moment of thinking and re-thinking geography's encounters with the digital' (Elwood and Leszczynski 2018: 629). The digital can be understood as both technologies and the effects 'resulting from our engagement with digital mediums' (Ash et al. 2018: 26). In other words, the 'digital' does not refer only to 'material digital objects (the hardware, software, devices, content, code and algorithms)', but also to the ways in which they shape our worlds and lives (Ash et al. 2019: 3). This includes virtual spaces (Ferreira and Vale 2021) alongside wider technologies that underpin our lives in so many ways. There is no single 'digital' here with Ash et al. (2019: 3–4) urging geographers to always think in plural terms – with 'digital geograph*ies*', rather than digital geography.

KEY TERMS: DIGITAL

Geographers understand 'the digital' as object or thing, and impact and effect. The digital includes devices and their underpinning systems (software and hardware, data and algorithms), as well as their 'affective, political, economic, social and physical effects' (Gieseking 2019: 85). Digital devices, practices, and spaces are experienced differently, reflecting and 'encoding' 'structural oppressions and systems of power' within wider society (Gieseking 2019: 85), but they can also be empowering too.

An important consideration in digital geographies is that the 'human and technical are co-constituted'. In other words, they establish each other (Kinsley 2011: n.p.). For philosopher Bernard Stiegler, this process occurs through 'individuation', and the ways we 'come to know the world' (Kinsley 2011: n.p.). Here, 'the digital' is understood as a 'pharmakon', namely something with 'both curative and poisonous potential' (Kinsley et al. 2020: 1). In other words, while we make worlds with technology, the effects of this technology can be both positive and harmful. The term 'pharmakon' is therefore used to recognise the 'slipperiness' and 'ambiguity' of the digital as something that can both empower and discriminate (Kinsley et al. 2020: 1). As will be explored, feminist geographers have further explored both the ways in which digital technologies can discriminate and exclude, and the importance of thinking 'otherwise' about the digital to explore its more democratising, creative, and radical mobilisations (Elwood 2021). To contextualise this, it is worth noting that we can understand different contexts as being produced *through* and *by* the digital (Ash et al. 2018: 27).

Geographies Produced by the Digital

This refers to the idea that the digital produces spatial experience (Ash et al. 2018: 29). Work in this vein recognises digital technologies as shaping the everyday, 'mediating tasks such as work, travel, consumption, production, and leisure' and as having 'profound' spatial and social effects in doing so (Ash et al. 2018: 26, 29). One example concerns the growing 'infusion and mediation' of everyday life by software (Kitchin and Dodge 2011: 3). As Kitchin and Dodge (2011: 3) argue, software (such as email software, office suites, databases, internet browsers, and communication apps) 'produces new ways of doing things, speeds up/automates existing practices, reshapes information exchange, and transforms social and economic relations' (Kitchin and Dodge 2011: 3). As such, we can understand code and space as 'mutually constituted' (Ash et al. 2018: 31). Importantly, this is not an even process. On the contrary, software's production of space is 'uneven', 'creating particular power geometries' that differently impact diverse communities and individuals (Ash et al. 2018: 26, 30). We'll explore this further later in the chapter.

Geographies of the Digital

Whilst the digital can produce geography in different ways, digital technologies also have their own geographies in the ways their effects unfold, in the ways they are used, and through the processes by which they are developed (Zook and McCanless 2022: 25). Work on this theme involves exploring 'the digital as a geographical domain with its own logics and structures' (Ash et al. 2018: 32). It responds to the idea that digital technologies are commonly presented as 'black boxes' (with inputs and outputs but the workings inside 'mystified'), so instead pays attention to 'technology from the inside' (Layton 1977: 198). It also draws attention to user relationships between 'body and screen' or device to highlight how the digital can 'alter spatial understandings, embodied knowledge' and social and political 'relationships' (Ash et al. 2018: 33). In exploring the 'spatialities of video games', for example, Ash (2010: 654) undertook an ethnography at a videogame company to explore the 'process of designing and testing' a game. He argued that the designers work to create particular forms of 'encounters' to 'capture and hold the attention' of gamers (Ash 2010: 654, Ash et al. 2018: 33).

This chapter is thus interested in digital objects or things, the systems and networks that support them, and their uneven impacts and effects. It will grapple with these complexities by exploring the digital across a range of devices, spaces, practices, and experiences, first in relation to states, and then at the scale of everyday life.

Over to You: Digital Encounters

Take a moment to think about what the digital means to you. Make notes on the following questions:

- What comes to mind when you hear the word 'digital'?
- Where and how do you encounter the digital in your day-to-day life?
- How does digital technology impact your life?
- Can you think of any issues or critical questions that the digital technologies you've described might raise for political geographers?

Return to these questions at the end of the chapter and see if there is anything you need to add.

Digital States: (Mass) Surveillance

Technology and digital devices are mentioned in many of this textbook's chapters. It is clear that they play a significant role in practices of state governance. In Chapter 8 (Borders) we saw the role of digital biometric and algorithmic technology in the governance of citizens at the border. As Amoore (2021: 1) writes of 'deep neural network algorithms' in/as bordering, algorithms 'reorder what the border means' and 'how the boundaries of political community can be imagined'. The 'deep border' is 'inscribed in the body, it generates racialised bodies in novel forms that extend the reach of state violence' (Amoore 2021: 1). Just as Amoore's work aptly demonstrates the role of algorithms in state intervention at the border, others have highlighted their increasing importance in the functioning of states, with 'voting, legislation, regulation, and other political spaces mediated by algorithmic infrastructure' (Blankenship, 2020: n.p.). Computation, then, continues to enable 'new forms of governance, the production of new vulnerabilities' and the subjection of citizens to 'new forms' of digitally-mediated 'authority' (O'Grady and Dwyer 2020: n.p.).

To hone our attention to the state's engagement with the digital, this section turns to (mass) surveillance, defined as 'the observation or monitoring of social behaviour by individuals and institutions' with the aim of 'managing' it (Gregory et al. 2009: 733). Thinking back to the forms of relational thinking explored in Chapter 5 (Non-humans), surveillance functions as an 'ensemble' bringing together humans and non-humans (CCTV cameras, drones, or biometrics) in 'practices and techniques' of monitoring (Klauser 2013: 275; see Figure 13.1).

Surveillance is both undertaken by a range of state actors (including militaries, national security agencies, and police forces) and non-state actors (including corporations), and represents a growing and 'troubling' economy (Crampton et al. 2014: 196).

Figure 13.1 CCTV in operation sign

Credit: Rich Smith (Free to use under Unsplash License) https://unsplash.com/photos/b-0GqwAktDM

KEY TERMS: (GEO)SURVEILLANCE

Surveillance refers to the act of observing, monitoring, and gathering data on an individual or group. It is conducted by a range of actors, including militaries, police, and private security. Attention to the geographical dimensions of surveillance (or geosurveillance) draws on Foucault's conception of the 'panopticon' (see below) to argue that surveillance aims to discipline and control the bodies in its midst.

(Geo)surveillance is a disciplining practice with behavioural implications. The notion of the 'panopticon' is a useful entry point to explore this further. Designed by architect, Jeremy Bentham, the panopticon is a 'circular building, with the prisoners' cells arranged around the outer wall and the central point dominated by an inspection tower' (Bentham Project n.d.). Importantly, this design meant that the prison guard would be able to 'look into the cells at any time', while the prisoners 'would never be able to see the inspector' (Bentham Project n.d.). French philosopher Michel Foucault understood Bentham's design as significant as it highlights the disciplining potential of surveillance. Foucault (1995: 200) argued that this design 'imposes an axial' or asymmetrical 'visibility', where the prisoner 'is seen, but he does not see; he is the object of information, never a subject in communication'. Because the prisoner does not know whether they're being watched they assume 'permanent visibility' and thus adjust their behaviour, policing themselves (Foucault 1995: 201). The principle of the panopticon continues to be discussed in relation to contemporary digital surveillance. For example, Fyfe and Bannister (1996: 39) argue that the growth and normalisation of CCTV 'meets Bentham's principle that power should be visible yet unverifiable'. As Webster (2019: n.p.) writes, the UK is often understood as the 'most surveilled country on the planet', with 'millions of surveillance cameras' located in public spaces, as well as in 'private buildings and homes'. As Webster (2019: n.p.) continues, CCTV cameras are also changing through the (experimental) integration of facial recognition, which he describes as a 'quantum leap away from the old CCTV cameras with which we are familiar'. In this vein, others describe contemporary urban environments as 'super-panopticons' comprised of a variety of computational and digital technologies, 'storing and recombining large quantities of information in near real-time' through surveillance 'without walls, windows, towers or guards' and demonstrating 'a quantitative change in the state's ability to govern via direct surveillance' (Luque-Ayala 2019: 27).

One particularly relevant manifestation in recent years is that of mass surveillance. Mass surveillance can be understood as the 'large scale monitoring of populations' (Lyon 2014: 2). While occurring in a number of countries, it is particularly evident in the USA through the example of the US Patriot Act, essentially 'enabling secretive surveillance laws in the wake of 9/11' (Klomp and van Gorp 2022: 1600). However, the 2013 leaks of US National Security Agency (NSA) data by former contractor Edward Snowden exposed extensive state-led surveillance of digital spaces and 'communication data of citizens and institutions' both in and beyond the USA (Klomp and van Gorp 2022: 1599). While the

NSA 'dismissed' claims that its surveillance was unconstitutional (*The Guardian* 2013), the leaked material suggested that data from our everyday digital devices and interactions may be gathered to build a 'pattern of life', namely a 'detailed profile of a target and anyone associated with them' (*The Guardian* 2013: n.p.). Significantly, it suggested that the NSA was permitted to travel 'three hops' from its targets, i.e. 'people who talk to people who talk to people who talk to you' (*The Guardian* 2013: n.p.). If you have 500 friends on Facebook, this radius could equate to over 120,000,000 friends of friends of friends (*The Guardian* 2013: n.p.). Importantly, such practices 'don't affect everyone equally' (Amoore and de Goede 2021: 426). While the NSA repeated the dictum that 'if you have nothing to hide, you have nothing to fear', the revelations of the scale of mass surveillance prompted debate around both privacy and the 'socio-technical character' of surveillance more widely (Lyon 2014: 1).

Such revelations also raised wider questions about the role of non-human infrastructure. As we saw in Chapter 5 (Non-humans), non-humans co-create our worlds. While in thinking of surveillance we might imagine smartphones, such digital devices also rely on submarine fibre-optic cables. These cables were also revealed as crucial points in/of mass surveillance in the leaked documents which suggested that the NSA had its own 'cable-intercept programs tapping traffic flowing into and across the US', in a practice known as 'upstream collection' (*The Guardian* 2013: n.p.). Here we see fibre-optic cables as key in both the enabling of the digital, and as digital materiality 'enrolled in socio-spatial process of power' (Zook and McCanless 2022: 24, 25).

Collectively, such disclosures raise critical questions for political geographers about the spaces, materialities and practices of politics in the digital age. We also see these questions emerge in different contexts of state-led surveillance too. For example, in launching the 'Social Credit System' (SCS), China's government introduced wide-scale surveillance with the aim of 'raising the awareness of integrity and the level of trustworthiness of Chinese society' (Zeng 2018: n.p.). The SCS works through generating and enforcing a 'standardised reward and punishment system based on a citizen's credit score' (Zeng 2018: n.p.). This score is derived from a range of sources, such as social media activity, consumer behaviour and legal convictions, and while citizens are 'rewarded' if they do 'good deeds' (e.g., charity work, recycling), their scores and lives are punished if they do not (Caprotti and Liu 2020, Zeng 2018: n.p.). Actions such as jaywalking or failing 'to pay a court bill' may result in their 'travel and access to public services being restricted' (Zeng 2018: n.p.). While understood as 'globally, the most comprehensive attempt to capture digital sources of data about citizens and to reconcile them within a single social credit score' (Caprotti and Liu 2020: 3), the context is important. As Zeng (2018: n.p.) notes, the use of the word 'credit' is significant. In Chinese culture the word historically refers to a 'moral concept that indicates one's honesty and trustworthiness', a meaning that has since been 'extended to include financial creditworthiness'. Further, others have drawn attention to the ways citizens have creatively mobilised the SCS to showcase 'government officials on the blacklists' too (Zeng 2018: n.p.).

> ## Case Study: (Self/ie-)Surveillance in India During the Covid-19 Pandemic
>
> Ayona Datta (2020: 234) explores the 'role of the selfie' as a 'central' aspect of the 'management' of the pandemic in India. Datta (2020: 234) notes that in March 2020 'the Indian state announced a complete lockdown' to limit the spread of Covid-19, introducing 'strict quarantine and containment measures'. Alongside the role of 'smart technologies' such as CCTV and drones in the 'management of monitoring of quarantined and infected persons', Datta (2020: 234) describes the emergence of 'contact tracing and quarantine apps' such as 'Quarantine Watch'. Here, quarantined individuals had to upload their 'GPS tagged selfie once every hour, with a break from 10 pm to 7 am for sleep', and the authorities were then alleged to check these images using 'facial recognition software' (Datta 2020: 235). If an individual 'fails to upload on time' or the image is deemed to be of someone else, 'further checks' were undertaken (Datta 2020: 235). Such 'self(ie) surveillance' demonstrates a disciplining capacity. Further, Datta (2020: 237) argues that such practices can be understood as 'intimate surveillance' seeking to 'extend' state reach into the 'domestic spaces' and relations of home.

Everyday Encounters with the Digital: Online Spaces, Digital Homes, and Bodies

So far, the chapter has explored state mobilisations of the digital. In this section, following calls for further attention to both non-state actor engagements with digital technologies (Jackman and Brickell 2022) and the 'space and time of everyday life' (Gieseking 2019: 87), everyday encounters with the digital are foregrounded. These 'ordinary and often taken-for-granted digital objects, practices, productions and sites' have significant political and social implications and thus warrant further attention (Leszczynski 2020: 1194). These complexities are explored first through online spaces and social media worlds, foregrounding diverse and uneven experiences of the digital. We demonstrate that digital spaces can both amplify discrimination and afford opportunities for coming together and community building. It then turns attention to different sites and scales of digitality, exploring both the home and body as scales of digital encounter and experience. Lastly, it explores calls within digital geographies for further attention to how digital devices and technologies are not always used as intended, but rather are resisted, reimagined, and reworked in interesting ways. It introduces the notion of the 'glitch' as a concept urging us to think otherwise about digital spaces, technologies, and futures.

Online Spaces and Social Media Worlds

Warf (2013: 1) argues that the digital and everyday lives 'have become so thoroughly fused that it is difficult, if not impossible, to disentangle them'. Further, Warf (2013: 1)

Figure 13.2 Man on smartphone

Credit: Jonus Leupe (Free to use under Unsplash License) https://unsplash.com/photos/WargGLQW_Yk

continues, digital activity online – emailing, digital banking, and social media – has 'profound effects on social relations, everyday life, culture and politics' (see Figure 13.2). For example, the new forms of geography social media create can '(re)produce iniquities' and inequalities (Kinsley et al. 2020: 2).

A particular challenge lies in how anonymity on the internet can 'give free reign' to different forms of discrimination (Kinsley et al. 2020: 2), disproportionately disadvantaging and harming marginalised communities. 'Digitality' is thus 'deeply implicated in sociospatial processes of exclusion' and 'differentiation' (Elwood 2021: 209, 211). This takes place across a range of digital spaces and platforms. For example, writing in the context of the US housing market, Fields (2022: 160) turns to the example of the 'automated landlord', that is the smartphone-mediated 'management of tenants and properties'. Fields (2022: 160) argues that 'digital technologies' play an important role in housing, but can also be understood as 'comprising a crucial terrain of struggle'. This relates to how racism has been shown to 'operate' during the process of securing housing (Rosen et al. 2021: 789). While the 'screening' of potential tenants has long-included 'explicit' forms of 'racial bias', it now also increasingly features more 'covert' forms of bias enacted through 'digital technologies' (Rosen et al. 2021: 789).

For example, drawing attention to evolution and digitisation of 'landlord tech', McElroy and So (2021: n.p.) describe examples such as 'tenant screening services that provide reports about prospective tenants to landlords so that landlords can determine if the tenant is '"good enough" to move in', as well as 'eviction and debt-recovery apps, property management apps' and more. These technologies are 'tied up in processes of gentrification and racial dispossession' (McElroy 2020: n.p.). McElroy (2020: n.p.) continues that while 'charting the harms' of such technology is key, it is crucially important for research to 'reframe' analysis to centre 'tenant perspectives' and to facilitate 'housing justice-oriented knowledge'.

Geographies of digitality and difference have also been explored in the context of social media influencers. As Willment (2020: 392) observes, 'social networking sites and blogs' enable users to form novel 'networked connections', variously reshaping how people work. For example, the global influencer market has skyrocketed, with 'some 300,000 people aged 18-26 already using content creation as their sole income source' (Willment 2022: n.p.). However, while the lifestyles social media influencers display online appear 'enticing', different forms of precarity and exclusion underpín this digital work (Willment 2022: n.p.). Drawing on research with 'travel influencers and content creators', Willment (2022: n.p.) details both 'pay inequality based' on gender, sexuality, race, and disability, and the significance of algorithms in 'determining which posts are shown, in which order' and to which users. Digital experience is thus not even nor visible for all.

Beyond the harms embedded in the digital, digital spaces also contain 'contradictory possibilities', that is the digital also enables caring, compassionate, resistant, and community-building relations (Kinsley et al. 2020). For example, Jenzen's (2017: 1626) work on 'trans and gender questioning youth' draws attention to trans youth as both 'social media users and producers' and highlights a range of digital strategies they deploy 'in order to cope and thrive'. Jenzen (2017: 1626) argues that 'in the face of rampant transphobia and cis coded online paradigms', trans youth develop and deploy both 'critical and creative' practices, enacting 'self-expression and community formation'. Thus, while 'mainstream' (digital) culture can variously 'disempower' trans life, so too are digital platforms and online spaces 'a crucial lifeline' (Jenzen 2017: 1638).

Case Study: Indigenous Social Media Networks of Care

Hate speech, racist abuse, and cyberbullying are rife on social media in ways that disproportionately impact marginalised peoples (Frazer et al. 2022: 1). Frazer et al. (2022: 1) turn to the context of 'Indigenous people in the continent now referred to as Australia' to reconsider social media as a space of 'support, care and trust'. They are interested in 'how, in a context of ongoing settler-colonial marginalisation and widespread distrust of settler health services', Indigenous peoples maintain networks of care via the 'less formal connections social media make possible' (Frazer et al. 2022: 4).

Following the 'barriers' surrounding 'access to formal help in times of need', Frazer et al. (2022: 4, 6) describe the online responses of 'Aboriginal and Torres Strait Islander people'. These include social media use for the direct provision of digital 'emotional support' and care, and to provide more 'general and indirect' forms of care by making online spaces 'more positive, hopeful and encouraging for friends and family' (Frazer et al. 2022: 5, 6). Recognition of this diversity of practices is important, Frazer et al. (2022: 1) argue, because Indigenous people are commonly represented as 'recipients of care', rather than as agents forming care-full networks and practising care. These examples also demonstrate digital spaces and practices that exceed and go 'against and outside settler geographies' Indigenous communities encounter (Frazer et al. 2022: 1). Indigenous social media usage here thus acts to 'alter, challenge and transform dominant geographies of settler colonialism' (Frazer et al. 2022: 1).

The digital is also important when thinking through questions of peace and resistance (see Chapter 12). The 'oppositional voices' of political bloggers in Russia provide a clear example here (Wolfe 2021: 1251). While the 'Russian state has clamped down on internet activities', bloggers have mobilised online spaces as resistant, 'revealing new geographies of contestation against state strategies' (Wolfe 2021: 1251). We can also think here about the emergence and mobilisation of the hashtag #GambiaHasDecided following the 2016 elections in the Gambia, wherein an 'autocratic' president who 'kept the west African country under an iron grip for more than two decades' was voted out in a 'shock election' (Maclean and Graham-Harrison 2016: n.p.). However, 'former president Yahya Jammeh refused to vacate his office and hand over power after suffering electoral defeat' (Mourdoukoutas 2018: n.p.). As Mourdoukoutas (2018: n.p.) writes, in response 'young people's political activism' sought to 'safeguard the integrity of the election' by using the hashtag. The role of social media and digital space was key here in the 'anti-Jammeh campaign' and, it is argued, demonstrates how 'social media has forever changed the dynamics of politics in Africa' (Diab in Mourdoukoutas 2018: n.p.) (we explore these themes further in Chapter 12).

Lastly, geographers have also urged consideration of the wider spatial implications and feedbacks of the digital into our landscapes. For example, in exploring the digital as a site in which 'sexual minorities' can find each other for communication, friendship, or sexual encounters, Miles (2021: 203) highlights that smartphones are changing and 'disrupting' traditional 'understandings of space and place'. Highlighting that online dating apps such as 'Grindr, Tinder, and Blued' act to 'reconfigure any street, park, or home into a queer space' of encounter, Miles (2021: 203) argues that we need to think further about what these digital interactions mean for 'already-existing queer spaces'. These apps, Miles (2021: 203) argues, can be understood as a 'terrain that can sidestep' 'established gay neighbourhood', spaces which have traditionally and historically played an important role in 'brokering social and sexual connection for sexual minorities'.

Sites and Scales of Digitality: Homes and Bodies

While state-led surveillance is significant, the 'monitoring and administration of everyday life reaches far beyond' this (Klauser 2013: 275). This is evidenced through the proliferation of 'smart home' devices. Falling under the broad definition of the Internet of Things, such devices include home 'heating systems, webcams', televisions, and voice assistants (O'Grady and Dwyer 2020: n.p.). Seeking to 'sense' our homes to provide tailored 'services' (Gram-Hassen and Darby 2018: 94), these devices raise questions around both the data they collect about our everyday 'activities and desires' (Richardson 2018: 91) and the ways non-human digital technologies variously 'remake domestic life' (Goulden 2021: 904).

SURVEILLANCE | 213

KEY TERMS: INTERNET OF THINGS

This refers to a range of devices in the home, from heating systems that you control through apps to smart TVs and digital assistants such as Amazon's Alexa, 'that have become Internet-enabled and connected' (O'Grady and Dwyer 2020: n.p.). These devices are growing in popularity and raise a range of questions for political geographers around privacy and surveillance as well as (cyber) security.

The drone as a (smart) home security technology is a useful example here. Jackman and Brickell (2022: 163) explore the example of a drone-enabled autonomous home security system, patrolling the perimeters of its user's home in order to 'learn your property's routines' and 'alert you to unusual behaviour'. Here the system's motion detection flags 'perceived transgressions' while rendering visible heat maps of detected movement on the user's smartphone screen (Jackman and Brickell 2022). This home security drone raises questions for political geographers around how 'unusual behaviour' is defined and determined, and the 'kinds of power relationships that might be enacted in an uneven targeting and subjugation of individuals below' such systems (Jackman and Brickell 2022: 165). The authors continue that these practices remain bound to questions around discrimination, with digital determinations of behaviour and 'criminality' often disproportionately impacting marginalised groups (West et al. 2019: 3). As 'drone capitalism' continues (Richardson 2018), political geographers should thus further attend to the uneven social relations and embodied experiences such technologies usher in.

Such practices and sensibilities can also be scaled down further to the scale of the body, with self-tracking devices as a prime example. Self-tracking refers to 'practices in which people knowingly and purposively collect information about themselves which they then review and consider applying to the conduct of their lives' (Lupton in Fletcher 2022: 11). Fitness watches (see Figure 13.3) are a case in point but there are other manifestations of this too (such as smart clothing and implantables). Here, much existing work returns to Foucault's discussion of the panopticon, as introduced earlier. Such accounts draw attention to the 'involuntary aspects of surveillance inherent' in forms of 'pushed' self-tracking technologies, namely those where 'the impetus to self-track comes from another actor in a position of authority' such as a workplace, with the aim 'to regulate, manage and discipline people' (Fletcher 2022: 13). This work also highlights the 'internalised disciplinary gaze' of fitness tracking, stating that 'prompts' lead users to internalise and 'turn the gaze upon themselves' (Fletcher 2022: 13).

However, contemporary digital technologies and practice can also 'complicate the panoptic metaphor' (Fletcher 2022). As Fletcher (2022: 13) argues, it is important to explore how such technologies might move beyond Foucault's initial meaning which was not 'intended to be used to describe every situation in which surveillance is present'. As such, Fletcher (2022: 11) considers digital fitness tracking in different terms, reflecting on 'social surveillance' through a physical activity tracking app in the context of the Covid-19 pandemic. Drawing upon digital interviews with app users, Fletcher (2022: 11)

Figure 13.3 Fitness watch

Credit: Onur Binay (Free to use under Unsplash License) https://unsplash.com/photos/bwFW9PTJZx8

highlights both that bodies are 'fleshy and digital', and that during the pandemic, 'these apps offered a form of connection' in a time of 'isolation'.

In further thinking about the intersection of bodies and the digital, geographers have explored the 'different ways in which different bodies experience' digital practice and space (Luque-Ayala 2019: 31). Gender is a key consideration here with menstruation tracking apps offering a further example of the collision of the everyday, personal, and political. Such apps are increasingly popular, enabling users to track their 'reproductive cycle, sex life and health in order to provide them with algorithmically derived insights into their body' (Shipp and Blasco Alis 2020: 491). As Bhimani (2020: n.p.) writes of 'period tracker apps (PTAs)' as a 'part of a fast growing Femtech product market', PTAs 'can be used to monitor menstruation as well as produce workout patterns, nutritional regimes and family planning tailored to body cycles' and their 'home screens usually display a numerical countdown and/or graphic illustrations of the number of days to the beginning of the next period or ovulation'. These apps raise questions about the politics of bodily data and the 'extent to which it is possible to trust private corporations' with the 'sensitive and intimate data' such apps capture (Shipp and Blasco Alis 2020: 491). As such engagements with the digital demonstrate, studying 'digital phenomena' is challenging because they are 'constantly evolving practices, actants, and geographies' (Zook and McCanless 2022: 23).

In the Field with Laura Shipp: Menstrual-Tracking Apps

Laura Shipp is an interdisciplinary scholar exploring period tracking apps, Femtech and the intersection between cyber security and bodies.

(Continued)

Why are you interested in researching menstrual tracking apps?

They intersect bodies and technologies, but also pose different questions and issues from other kinds of self-tracking technologies out there. They help people to manage their cycle, learn about their bodies, prevent or plan pregnancy, demonstrating they have an important role in the relationships people have with their bodies. They also belong to an expanding industry of technologies, called Femtech, which aim to sell technological solutions to (largely) women. From this industry there are a host of new interesting forms and applications for this technology.

What methods have you used to explore menstrual tracking apps?

I conducted interviews and focus groups with app users where we discussed how they used the apps, and how the technology impacted their relationship with their body. I also undertook an ethnography of the Femtech industry that makes apps. I went to industry events and interviewed stakeholders in the sector. I also did an analysis of how the apps looked after people's data, including autoethnographically using an app myself.

Do you have any top tips for students interested in researching technologies and their interactions with/relations to bodies?

Keep your interaction with the topic human. Just because you're researching technology does not mean it's any less human in its origin and impact. When using social methods, I found it important to use the same language as my participants. For example, I did learn some technical terms from my ethnography which I used when speaking to those involved in Femtech, but I wouldn't use these when talking to app users.

Over to You: Your Body and the Digital

Think about any digital devices you use in your day-to-day life. Perhaps you have a smartphone nearby or are wearing a smart watch. Select a device and reflect on:

1. How does your digital device involve or engage your body?
2. Is your digital device designed for particular types of body, or does it make any assumptions about your body in the uses it is designed for?
3. Can you imagine another body who may not experience your digital device in the same way as you do?

Conclusions: Thinking otherwise About the Digital

By way of conclusion, it is important to note that digital technologies do not always function to plan, and they are variously resisted, reimagined and reworked. Feminist geographers argue that when we write about digital technologies, the most common 'orientation' remains 'technodystopian' (Elwood 2021: 211), that is we tend to think about how technologies may enact or amplify suffering or injustice in (future) worlds. While asserting that attention to 'digital mediations of domination' are crucial, so too are there opportunities to 'theorize beyond' this (Elwood 2021: 211). Here, Legacy Russell's (2012) notion of the 'glitch' has been mobilised. While the word 'glitch' commonly implies 'error', Russell (2012) reframes this as an opportunity for 'correction to a system' (Leszczynski 2020: 191). Using this concept, feminist geographers argue that we can make space for the everyday ways in which people mundanely, hopefully, and creatively intervene in and comprise digital space (Leszczynski 2020: 191). In recognising such 'small-scale' actions, glitch thinking at once raises questions of 'who is legible' in our accounts of the digital, and affords attention to their 'everyday possibilities for politics' (Leszczynski and Elwood 2022: 1, Mahmoudi and Sabatino 2022: 3). Further, to think about digital spaces and practices of 'survival and thriving' as much as violence invites 'exciting possibilities of building more intersectional feminist digital geographies futures' (Elwood and Leszczynski 2018: 637).

Summary

- This chapter demonstrates the centrality of the digital in shaping contemporary worlds and lives.
- In exploring the digital as a site of politics, it foregrounds attention to both state practices and more everyday experiences of the digital.
- It highlights the complexity of exploring the digital, as digital devices, spaces, and practices vary and are unevenly experienced, '(re)producing existing socio-spatial inequalities along lines of race, gender, class, sexuality, age, ability and more' (Elwood and Leszczynski 2018: 630).
- It demonstrates that the digital is 'ambiguous', both potentially oppressive and discriminatory, and empowering and enabling (Kinsley et al. 2020: 2).

Follow-on Resources

The Anti-Eviction Mapping Project: This website captures research at the 'intersection of racist surveillance and housing injustice, both before and during Covid-19' (McElroy and So 2021: n.p.). The project includes a 'website, survey and map' entitled 'Landlord Tech Watch' which details and explores 'landlord technologies, or the systems, platforms, hardware, software, algorithms, and data collection that landlords and property managers use to automate landlordism' and renders visible the uneven effects of this iteration of contemporary surveillance (McElroy and So 2021: n.p.).

Lo and Behold, Reveries of the Connected World: This is a documentary film, directed by Werner Herzog (2016). It explores the advent of the internet, tracing a range of its effects. See www.imdb.com/title/tt5275828/

Influencerpaygap: This is a space for social media influencers to 'anonymously share stories about their experiences of collaborating with brands. In addition to racial disparities, the account exposes pay gaps experienced by disabled and LGBTQ+ influencers' (Willment 2022: n.p.).

References

Amoore, L. (2021). The deep border. *Political Geography*, 102547.

Amoore, L. and de Goede, M. (2021). Datawars: Reflections twenty years after 9/11. *Critical Studies on Terrorism, 14*(4), 425–429.

Ash, J. (2010). Architectures of affect: Anticipating and manipulating the event in practices of videogame design and testing. *Environment and Planning D: Society and Space, 28*(4), 653–671.

Ash, J., Kitchin, R. and Leszczynski, A. (2018). Digital turn, digital geographies? *Progress in Human Geography, 42*(1), 25–43.

Ash, J., Kitchin, R. and Leszczynski, A. (2019). Introducing digital geographies. In J. Ash, R. Kitchin and A. Leszczynski (eds), *Digital geographies* (pp.1–10). London: Sage.

Bentham Project (n.d.). The Panopticon. Available at: www.ucl.ac.uk/bentham-project/who-was-jeremy-bentham/panopticon (accessed 1 December 2022).

Bhimani, A. (2020). Period-tracking apps: How femtech creates value for users and platforms. *LSE blogs,* 4 May. Available at: https://blogs.lse.ac.uk/businessreview/2020/05/04/period-tracking-apps-how-femtech-creates-value-for-users-and-platforms/ (accessed 2 November 2022).

Blankenship, J. (2020). Algorithmic governance. In A. Kobayashi (ed.), *Encyclopaedia of human geography* (2nd edn). Elsevier Science and Technology (accessed online). Available at: www.elsevier.com/books/international-encyclopedia-of-human-geography/kobayashi/978-0-08-102295-5 (accessed 19 October 2022).

Caprotti, F. and Liu, D. (2020). Emerging platform urbanism in China: Reconfigurations of data, citizenship and materialities. *Technological Forecasting and Social Change, 151,* 119690.

Crampton, J., Roberts, S. M. and Poorthuis, A. (2014). The new political economy of geographical intelligence. *Annals of the Association of American Geographers, 104*(1), 196–214.

Cuomo, D. and Dolci, N. (2021). New tools, old abuse: Technology-Enabled Coercive Control (TECC). *Geoforum, 126,* 223–232.

Datta, A. (2020). Self(ie)-governance: Technologies of intimate surveillance in India under COVID-19. *Dialogues in Human Geography, 10*(2), 234–237.

Elwood, S. (2021). Digital geographies, feminist relationality, Black and queer code studies: Thriving otherwise. *Progress in Human Geography, 45*(2), 209–228.

Elwood, S. and Leszczynski, A. (2018). Feminist digital geographies. *Gender, Place & Culture, 25*(5), 629–644.

Ferreira, D. and Vale, M. (2021). From cyberspace to cyberspatialities? *Fennia, 199*(1), 113–117.

Fields, D. (2022). Automated landlord: Digital technologies and post-crisis financial accumulation. *EPA: Economy and Space, 54*(1), 160–181.

Fletcher, O. (2022). 'Friendly' and 'noisy surveillance' through MapMyRun during the COVID-19 pandemic. *Geoforum, 133*, 11–19.

Foucault, M. (1995). *Discipline and punish: The birth of the prison*, 2nd edn (A. Sheridan, trans.). New York: Random House.

Frazer, R., Carlson, B. and Farrelly, T. (2022). Indigenous articulations of social media and digital assemblages of care. *Digital Geography and Society, 3*, 1000038.

Fyfe, N. R. and Bannister, J. (1996). City watching: Closed circuit television surveillance in public spaces. *Area, 28*(1), 37–46.

Gieseking, J. J. (2019). Digital. In T. Jazeel, A. Kent, K. McKittrick, N. Theodore, S. Chari, P. Chatterton, V. Gidwani, N. Heynen, W. Larner, J. Peck, J. Pickerill, M. Werner and M. W. Wright (eds), *Keywords in radical geography: Antipode at 50*. Oxford: Wiley.

Goulden, M. (2021). 'Delete the family': Platform families and the colonisation of the smart home. *Information, Communication & Society, 24*(7), 903–920.

Gram-Hanssen, K. and Darby, S. J. (2018). 'Home is where the smart is?' Evaluating smart home research and approaches against the concept of home. *Energy Research & Social Science, 37*, 94–101.

Gregory, D., Johnston, R., Pratt, G., Watts, M. J. and Whatmore, S. (2009). *The dictionary of human geography* (5th edn). London: Wiley-Blackwell.

Jackman, A. and Brickell, K. (2022). 'Everyday droning': Towards a feminist geopolitics of the drone-home. *Progress in Human Geography, 46*(1), 156–178.

Jenzen, O. (2017). Trans youth and social media: Moving between counterpublics and the wider web. *Gender, Place and Culture, 24*(11), 1626–1641.

Kinsley, S. (2011). Reading Bernard Stiegler. *Spatial Machinations*, 1 November. Available at: www.samkinsley.com/2011/11/01/reading-bernard-stiegler/ (accessed 10 September 2022).

Kinsley, S., McLean, J. and Maalsen, S. (2020). Editorial. *Digital Geography and Society, 1*, 100002.

Kitchin, R. and Dodge, M. (2011). *Code/space: Software and everyday life*. Cambridge, MA: MIT Press. Available at: https://direct.mit.edu/books/book/5039/Code-SpaceSoftware-and-Everyday-Life (accessed 15 November 2022).

Klauser, F. R. (2013). Political geographies of surveillance. *Geoforum, 49*, 275–278.

Klomp, L. and van Gorp, B. (2022). Setting the Standard? Revisiting the unfolding discourse in American and British online news on the Snowden revelations. *Geopolitics, 27*(5), 1599–1621.

Layton, E. (1977). Conditions of technological development. In I. Spiegel-Rosing and D. J. deSolla Price (eds), *Science, technology, and society*. London: Sage.

Leszczynski, A. (2020). Digital methods III: The digital mundane. *Progress in Human Geography, 44*(6), 1194–1201.

Leszczynski, A. and Elwood, S. (2022). Glitch epistemologies for computational cities. *Dialogues in Human Geography, 12*(3), 1–18.

Luque-Ayala, A. (2019). Urban. In J. Ash, R. Kitchin and A. Leszczynski (eds), *Digital geographies* (pp. 24–35). London: Sage.

Lyon, D. (2014). Surveillance, Snowden, and Big Data: Capacities, consequences, critique. *Big Data and Society*, 1–13.

Maclean, R. and Graham-Harrison, E. (2016). The Gambia's President Jammeh concedes defeat in election. *The Guardian,* 2 December. Available at: www.theguardian.com/world/2016/dec/02/the-gambia-president-jammeh-concede-defeat-in-election (accessed 18 November 2022).

Mahmoudi, D. and Sabatino, A. (2022). Witches as glitches: A response to Leszczynski and Elwood. *Dialogues in Human Geography, 12*(3), 1–4.

McElroy, E. (2020). Landlord tech and racial technocapitalism in the times of Covid-19. *UCHRI*. Available at: https://uchri.org/foundry/landlord-tech-and-racial-technocapitalism-in-the-times-of-covid-19/ (accessed 15 November 2022).

McElroy, E. and So, W. (2021). Landlord tech in Covid-19 times. *Metropolitics*, 30 March. Available at: https://metropolitics.org/Landlord-Tech-in-Covid-19-Times.html (accessed 22 November 2022).

Miles, S. (2021). Let's (not) go outside: Grindr, hybrid space, and digital queer neighborhoods. In A Bitterman and D. Baldwin Hess (eds), *The life and afterlife of gay neighbourhoods: Renaissance and resurgence* (pp. 203–220). Switzerland: Springer.

Mourdoukoutas, E. (2018). The hashtag revolution gaining ground. *Africa Renewal,* April–July. Available at: www.un.org/africarenewal/magazine/april-2018-july-2018/hashtag-revolution-gaining-ground (accessed 26 November 2022).

O'Grady, N. and Dwyer, A. C. (2020). Cyber security. In A. Kobayashi (ed.), *International encyclopedia of human geography* (2nd edn). Elsevier Science and Technology. Available at: www.sciencedirect.com/referencework/9780081022962/international-encyclopedia-of-human-geography

Richardson, M. (2018). Drone capitalism. *Transformations, 31,* 79–98.

Rosen, E., Garboden, P. M. E. and Cosseyleon, J. E. (2021). Racial discrimination in housing: How landlords use algorithms and home visits to screen tenants. *American Sociological Review, 86*(5), 787–822.

Russell, L. (2012). Digital dualism and the glitch feminist manifesto. *The Society Pages,* 10 December. Available at: https://thesocietypages.org/cyborgology/2012/12/10/digital-dualism-and-the-glitch-feminism-manifesto/ (accessed 25 October 2022).

Shipp, L. and Blasco Alis, J. (2020). How private is your period? A systematic analysis of menstrual app privacy polices. *Proceedings on Privacy Enhancing Technologies, 4,* 491–510.

The Guardian (2013). NSA files: Decoded. Available at: www.theguardian.com/world/interactive/2013/nov/01/snowden-nsa-files-surveillance-revelations-decoded (accessed 7 July 2022).

Warf, B. (2013). *Global geographies of the internet*. London: Springer.

Webster, D. (2019). Surveillance cameras will soon be unrecognisable – time for an urgent public conversation. *The Conversation*, 18 June. Available at: https://theconversation.com/surveillance-cameras-will-soon-be-unrecognisable-time-for-an-urgent-public-conversation-118931 (accessed 1 December 2022).

West, S. M., Whittaker, M. and Crawford, K. (2019). Discriminating systems: Gender, race and power in AI. *AI Now Institute*, 1 April. Available at: https://ainowinstitute.org/discriminatingsystems.html (accessed 3 September 2022).

Willment, N. (2020). The travel blogger as digital nomad: (Re)imagining workplace performances of digital nomadism within travel blogging work. *Information Technology & Tourism*, *22*, 391–416.

Willment, N. (2022). 'Influencer' is now a popular career choice for young people – here's what you should know about the creator economy's dark side. *The Conversation*, 28 June. Available at: https://theconversation.com/influencer-is-now-a-popular-career-choice-for-young-people-heres-what-you-should-know-about-the-creator-economys-dark-side-185806 (accessed 25 November 2022).

Wolfe, S. D. (2021). Blogging the virtual: New geographies of domination and resistance in and beyond Russia. *Antipode*, *53*(4), 1251–1269.

Zeng, J. (2018). China's Social Credit System puts its people under pressure to be model citizens. *The Conversation*, 23 January. Available at: https://theconversation.com/chinas-social-credit-system-puts-its-people-under-pressure-to-be-model-citizens-89963 (accessed 14 August 2022).

Zook, M. and McCanless, M. (2022). Mapping the uneven geographies of digital phenomena: The case of blockchain. *The Canadian Geographer*, *66*(1), 23–36.

FOURTEEN

CRISIS AND HOPE: THINKING WITH GEOPOLITICAL FUTURES

Overview

From terrorism and climate change to global pandemics, how we imagine and respond to potential and unfolding futures is inherently geopolitical. This chapter introduces futures thinking as a lens to explore and interrogate potential futures. In the contexts of data, outer space, and climate change futures, it applies this thinking to explore how practices of imagining and anticipating futures unevenly impact different people and spaces. While thinking with crises, we also explore reactions to this – from direct action and hopeful practices of storytelling – to highlight the agencies of diverse and hopeful peoples in the face of future crises, and the ways we can and might reimagine and reshape geopolitical futures.

Learning Objectives

1. To introduce geopolitical thinking on futures.
2. To apply futures thinking as a lens to explore different geopolitical phenomena, from data to climate change futures.
3. To reflect on enacting hope in the face of crisis, and to explore how such responses can and might reshape geopolitical futures.

Read with: Chapter 8 (Borders), Chapter 10 (Mobilities), Chapter 12 (Peace and Resistance)

Whether 'in relation to terrorism, climate change or trans-species epidemics, acting in advance of the future is an integral part of life' (Anderson 2010: 777) futures 'take on' a 'form of presence' in the here-and-now (Anderson and Adey 2012: 1529). These relations, and the conundrums that surround them, are the focus of work exploring geopolitical futures.

While the future is yet to happen, futures are nonetheless envisioned, imagined, and prepared for. As Anderson and Adey (2012: 1529) write, 'questions of what the future might be animate the contemporary condition'. Such work explores actions in the present as different actors aim, design, and prepare for particular desired futures. A core concept within this thinking is 'anticipatory action', referring to the ways we practise and perform potential futures (Anderson 2010: 777). We might, for example, think carefully about 'style' (the 'statements' we make about the future), the practices that 'give content to specific futures' (such as 'calculating or imagining'), and the logics underpinning and justifying 'which actions' are undertaken 'in the present' (Anderson 2010: 778–779). Attention to such factors enables a consideration of the kinds of 'geographies' that are 'made and remade' when we anticipate potential futures (Anderson 2010: 777).

KEY TERMS: FUTURES

Geopolitical work on futures is interested in how different actors envision and anticipate potential futures, the actions they take to design and prepare for these, and the potential implications and inequalities of desired futures.

Military drone strikes provide an example of anticipatory action. A growing number of global militaries possess or are developing armed drones, capable of wide-reaching surveillance and the delivery of missiles. 'Targeted killing' involves the 'intentional, premediated and deliberate use of lethal force' against an 'individual who is not in the physical custody of the perpetrator' of the strike (United Nations 2010: 3). In the case of US-led drone strikes, the 'right to anticipatory self defence' to protect itself from an 'imminent threat' is invoked (Boyle 2015: 111). Drone strikes have been criticised as a 'target' is considered not in relation to 'crimes already committed' but rather in relation to their 'potential to become dangerous' (Weizman 2014: 368). Drone strikes thus demonstrate 'anticipatory action' in practice, as a 'target's' potential future is anticipated and acted upon in the present, to lethal effect. Notably, this form of 'governing the future' does not occur evenly (Anderson and Adey 2012: 1530), the drone's gaze disproportionately targets people along spatial and racialized lines (see Chapter 11).

Futures in Times of Crisis

Anderson and Adey (2012: 1529) write that in 'thinking about the future', we should start with a 'problem'. This enables us to reflect on how particular issues are narrated as crises, and the ways in which their potential 'futures are made present, given presence, or even give presence' (Anderson and Adey 2012: 1529). The next section employs futures thinking to explore two particular 'problems' or crises people around the world are facing and fearing the futures of. We first explore data futures as technologies attempt to pre-empt

CRISIS AND HOPE | 223

and mitigate terrorism, and second, climate change and after-earth futures, examining climate crisis as an ongoing form of colonialism.

Terror and Data Futures

While terrorism remains a 'contested term', geographical attention to terrorism grew in the aftermath of the 11 September 2001 attacks in the US (Mustafa and Shaw 2013: n.p.). Attention particularly lies in the 'spectacular violence' of terrorism, such as attacks 'destroying places of everyday existence' including 'cafés, markets, and transportation networks' (Mustafa and Shaw 2013: n.p.). The 'everyday felt experiences of urban terrorism' in the aftermath of such events (Fregonese and Laketa 2022: 1) have also garnered significant attention. In addition to 'physical interventions altering the mobility, continuity and openness of urban space', counter-terrorism measures such as the declaration of a 'state of emergency' also 'alter the felt experience of a city' in important and uneven ways (Fregonese and Laketa 2022: 1).

Given that geographies 'are made and lived in the name of pre-empting, preparing for, or preventing threats', 'prediction' plays an important role in the policing and attempted mitigation of terrorism (Anderson 2010: 777, Anderson and Adey 2012). As Chapter 8 demonstrates, borders are important sites through which modes and practices of prediction circulate. They are also the sites of increasingly 'sophisticated technological innovations' aiming to monitor and 'control mobile human bodies' in the 'name of security' (Paasi 2022: 19). Here, technologies such as biometrics assign bodies in relation to calculable 'risk' (Amoore 2006), informing whether and how people can move. These technologies are also evolving. To this end, Amoore (2021: 1) introduces the 'deep border', referring to the growing involvement of 'deep neural network algorithms' in bordering. Amoore (2021: 1) and understands algorithms as both 'bordering devices that classify, divide and demarcate', and technologies extending the reach of the biometrics. While biometrics 'inscribe' the border 'in the body', the deep border 'generates the racialized body' (Amoore 2021: 1). It works by understanding us 'as clusters of attributes' and locating us within 'lines of best fit' (Amoore 2021: 1). To demonstrate the deep border in action, Amoore (2021: 1) turns to the case of a 'Muslim American woman, Amara Majeed', who found 'her image circulating globally on social media'. Sri Lankan authorities published a photograph of her 'among the images of others wanted in connection with the Easter Sunday bombings' (Amoore 2021: 1). Amara responded that she has 'been falsely identified' (Amoore 2021: 1). Yet, while police issued a 'correction', revealing their 'facial recognition algorithm' incorrectly identified Amara as a 'person of interest', Amara nonetheless 'received racist abuse and death threats' (Amoore 2021: 1). These technologies are also evolving (see Figure 14.1).

We might consider this an example of the racialised failings of facial recognition. Several years prior, Amara 'wrote an open letter to then presidential candidate Donald Trump', in which she identified herself as an 'activist and feminist', while accusing him of 'creating an atmosphere' of hate around Islam (Amoore 2021: 2). While the 'biometric algorithm misrecognized' Amara's face, the 'deep border rendered her

Figure 14.1 Facial recognition

Credit: teguhjatipras (Creative Commons CC0 1.0 Universal Public Domain) https://commons.wikimedia.org/wiki/File:Face_Recognition_3252983.png

recognizable to the state, knowable as a cluster of attributes' (Amoore 2021: 2). Drawing from Amara's 'digital writing', it 'disaggregated her' into particular 'derivatives' – 'feminist', 'activist', 'Muslim' which were 'translated as threats to the state' (Amoore 2021: 2). The deep border is thus concerned not only with our faces, but with our 'past' and 'everyday' activities online, those it uses to predict how we might act in the future (Amoore 2021: 2).

How future 'risks' are imagined and embedded in technologies, who these forms of futures governance serve, and who they subjugate, are thus key questions moving forward.

Over to You: Facial Recognition Futures?

Find your own example of a state that uses, or is considering deploying, facial recognition as a tool of policing.

- How are 'risky' futures imagined or described?
- How is facial recognition understood to respond to, or mitigate against, these risks?
- Does facial recognition impact everyone evenly?
- Does this example fit with, extend, or complicate particular themes in the textbook? (You might consider, for example, bodies, the state, or borders.)

Climate Change and After-earth Futures

Our climate is in crisis. From heatwaves to droughts and flood, climate change is 'the most serious threat to life on this planet' (Jubb and McLaughlin 2022: n.p.). It is also geopolitical at its core, concerned as it is with space, power, and agency. The Anthropocene refers to the current era in which 'human action is shaping the future of the earth's climate system' at a scale which poses considerable threat (Dalby 2013: 39). In recognition that 'Anthropocene thinking' is underscored by a 'perceived need for anticipatory governance' (Derickson 2018: 425), efforts in the present seek to respond to the future impacts of climate change. These include international discussions at events such as 'COP27', the 2022 iteration of the United Nations climate change summit. They also include climate change 'adaptations' across multiple scales, including 'processes of adjustment, planning, and transformation to global environmental change' (Eisenhauer 2016: 207). While providing 'useful and useable information which can help close the persistent gap between knowledge about climate and the action to address it', such approaches are also critiqued as they remain focused 'on the narrow technical question of what is being adapted, rather than the goals and values behind adaptation' (Eisenhauer 2016: 208). In critiquing adaptation as a 'pliable grand vision', it is also argued that such approaches don't adequately attend to the wide-ranging 'alternative adaptations' taking place on the ground (Smith 2022: 2), particularly by the communities most harmed by the climate crisis.

KEY TERMS: ANTHROPOCENE

The Anthropocene refers to the 'emergence of a new geological epoch' or period 'characterized by human impacts on the geology of the planet' (Derickson 2018: 425). Notions of the Anthropocene simultaneously 'locate contemporary human experience in relation to deep time' and geological pasts, while actions in response (such as adaptation) are underpinned by climate changed futures (Derickson 2018: 426).

Here it's useful to introduce 'critical approaches to climate justice', which foreground 'climate injustices and their underlying causes' (Sultana 2021: 449). In recognition that climate change encompasses 'unequal and uneven burdens', such approaches turn attention to questions of exposure, vulnerability, ethics, and responsibility (Sultana 2022a: 118). The pursuit of climate justice involves attending to diverse 'Indigenous or broadly non-Western practices' that are traditionally excluded in adaptation discourse, and rethinking the framing of these issues from 'nations where vulnerabilities occur' to questions of which 'visions' of climate justice are recognised and 'how and by whom decisions should be made' (Smith 2022: 2).

Geography, then, is 'undergoing a reckoning', grappling with 'contemporary ecological crisis' and its entanglement with 'histories of genocide, enslavement, and

POLITICAL GEOGRAPHY

White supremacy' (Vasudevan et al. 2022: 3). This entanglement is powerfully examined in work on climate coloniality. Sultana (2022b: 1) argues that to understand climate change, it is crucial to approach it through the lens of colonialism, 'forcing a relocation of how, why, and who is responsible'. 'Climate coloniality' refers to both the ongoing impacts of the 'racial domination and hierarchical power relations established during active colonialism' and their resultant 'ecological degradations' (Sultana 2022b: 4). These degradations and their impacts shape everyday lives, spaces, opportunities, and possibilities, in uneven ways. In response, we need to work to 'decolonize climate' through both interrogating relationships between empire and capital, and addressing their 'material outcomes' (Sultana 2022b: 6). This work, she describes, is at once tough and inspiring. After all, and as we'll explore later, 'precarity, vulnerability' and crisis 'co-exist with connectedness, kinship' and hope (Sultana 2022b: 4).

Case Study: Anthropocene Islands

Islands are central to discussions around anthropogenic climate change and climate (in)justice. Chandler and Pugh (2021: 410) argue that islands are not 'simply illustrative figures for the Anthropocene' but rather they are important and 'generative' in how we think about the Anthropocene. Given their centrality to issues such as 'global warming, rising sea levels, the legacies of colonialism, the effects of mainland Western consumerism, nuclear fallout, climate migration, intensified hurricanes, and ocean acidification', islands have emerged as increasingly important sites for understanding 'relational entanglements' (Chandler and Pugh 2021: 396, 395) between humans, non-humans, and environments in the Anthropocene.

Writing in response to Chandler and Pugh, Perez (2021) offers an alternative perspective on thinking about Anthropocene islands. Perez (2021: 429) introduces their position as an Indigenous academic from 'Guåhan (Guam)' in the Pacific. Perez (2021: 429) continues that when growing up, they didn't see their home represented on maps – their archipelago was 'too small to matter'. Perez (2021: 429) reflects on the significance of the 'new visibility of Pacific islands and islanders' in the context of climate crisis. While noting the value of visibility in awareness-raising, Perez (2021: 429) also cautions against 'reductionist representations of the Pacific'. Pacific islands are repeatedly 'depicted as vulnerable, disappearing, sinking' (Perez 2021: 430). While raising visibility, such representations can also 'be leveraged for exploitation', by 'green and blue' corporations 'hoping to profit' from activities to 'save the vulnerable islands', to eco-tourism and deep-sea mining alike (Perez 2021: 430). Similarly, while representations of Pacific Islanders as 'drowning victims' raise awareness of the 'existential threats' such communities face, they also obscure the 'agency, complexity, and subjectivity' of islanders (Perez 2021: 431, 429). Perez (221: 432) thus urges attention to the islands and islanders as multiple, at once complicit in producing, as well as resisting, climate change.

After-earth Futures

A further response to planetary climate crisis has been to look to outer space. Geographers are turning increasing attention to the ways outer space is being imagined in the context of 'near-term earthly apocalypse', with key 'contemporary discourses' of outer space including 'humans polluting the earth beyond repair', growing 'resource scarcity', and the solution of 'colonizing outer space' as an expanse with an 'infinite quantity of resources and possibilities' (Kilnger in Dunnett et al. 2019: 320).

These discourses are (re)produced in initiatives investing in inhabiting outer space and exploring and exploiting it as a site of resources. Corporations such as SpaceX, Virgin Galactic and Blue Origin are 'competing to claim the right to colonise' outer space, 'Mars, the moon and even asteroids' (Squire et al. 2021: n.p.). Work is 'underway here on Earth' to 'prepare these corporations' as 'gatekeepers to the heavens' (Squire et al. 2021: n.p.).

Such desires are also echoed in visions of the 'first lunar civilisations', through initiatives such as the National Aeronautics and Space Administration's Artemis program (Brookes 2021: n.p.). While framed as 'innovative solutions' to 'escape unfolding earthly crises', attempts to 'colonise' outer space raise important questions (Squire et al. 2021: n.p.). They are visions put forward by 'a capitalist, masculine and patriarchal class' motivated by 'frontier profiteering' rather than a 'commons for the benefit of all' (Squire et al. 2021: n.p.). The recognition that it is possible to 'imagine' outer space 'worlds otherwise' and to ask critical questions of 'who such futures are for, who is imagining them and foreclosing others, who is able to participate, and what happens to those left behind' is pertinent when you consider Elon Musk's (SpaceX) proposal that 'regular people' may participate in space travel if they take out a 'loan that they can then pay off by working on Mars' (Squire et al. 2021: n.p.). Such statements raise questions of whether such

Figure 14.2 SpaceX SN8 flight

Credit: Ron Frazier (Attribution 2.0 Generic (CC BY 2.0) www.flickr.com/photos/tomronworldwide/50840168402/

228 | POLITICAL GEOGRAPHY

'settlers' would 'have their passports removed until they pay off these debts, or be unable to access transport home', and risk extending existing earthly 'settler-colonial appropriations and violences' beyond earth (Squire et al. 2021: n.p.).

Here, Smiles' (2020: n.p.) work arguing that contemporary 'space exploration' is rooted in the 'logics of settler colonialism' is notable. In the context of the US, settler colonialism refers to a 'form of colonialism based upon the permanent presence of colonists upon land' (Smiles 2020: n.p.) (see Chapter 11). The US 'was built upon' problematic notions of 'terra nullius (no man's land)', which 'proceeded upon a project of cultural and physical genocide, with lasting effects' (Smiles 2020: n.p.). Troublingly, 'similar language is being used' in the context 'of American power being extended to space' (Smiles 2020: n.p.). We can, however, 'look to Indigenous conceptions of space' as a way to 'foil these colonial logics' (Smiles 2020: n.p.). While there exists a 'long history of colonial disrespect of Indigenous people and Indigenous spaces in the name of science', Smiles (2020: n.p.) highlights diverse Indigenous engagements with space. By foregrounding 'Indigenous thinkers who are already deeply immersed into explorations of Indigenous space here on Earth' we can learn about how 'Indigenous peoples make and remake space' and reflect on how such 'practices might provide another blueprint to engage with space beyond Earth' (Smiles 2020: n.p.).

In the Field with Deondre Smiles: Researching Space Futures

Deondre Smiles is an Assistant Professor at the University of Victoria, Canada. Deondre is an Indigenous geographer whose research interests include Indigenous geographies/epistemologies, science and technology studies, and tribal cultural resource preservation/protection.

Why are you interested in outer space futures?

I've been a big fan of learning about space since I was a young child! But my current interests stem from rhetoric used by former US President Donald Trump, who when speaking about outer space exploration in 2020 used a lot of colonial language that has also been used to justify colonisation here on Earth, which is what I mainly study. I realized there is a deep connection between the ways we've viewed colonisation here on Earth, as well as in space. As we get closer to potential manned voyages to places like Mars, I feel it's important to fully think about why we go to space – and how we can avoid the same mistakes and missteps we've taken here on Earth.

Your work highlights the ways in which Indigenous knowledges are overlooked. How might geographers be more open to diverse knowledges and experiences?

Historically, any types of spatial knowledge that are not centred in Western/European thought or intellectual traditions have been pushed out to the margins of geography.

(Continued)

CRISIS AND HOPE | 229

Being willing to listen to, and perhaps embrace the benefits of other relationships with space and place is one recommendation I have. Openness to these perspectives can unlock new ways of thinking about and solving the most pressing issues facing us today.

What are some of the challenges of researching geopolitical futures?

Probably the biggest challenge is that there is no one 'geopolitical future' – futures, in my mind, are best understood through the desires and dreams of the groups and communities that are thinking about these futures. So, when researching geopolitical futures, you have to be willing to accept that you may be encountering widely different futures, that may even contradict each other! But, that is OK – that is what happens when we dream – they fit to our own individual or communal circumstances.

We also see an 'earthly logic of resource extraction' extended and deployed as a justification of outer space colonisation (Squire et al. 2021: n.p.). A 'New Space Economy', referring to the growing interest and 'involvement of private sector' actors in 'outer space operations' (Jones 2021: n.p.), is emerging, driven by the anticipation of outer space as a site for future resource extraction. Such visions also raise critical questions around 'ownership, rights, and whose future this industry speaks of, for, and mobilises' (Jones 2021: n.p.). These questions are pertinent in light of the passing of the 'SPACE Act' or the 'Commercial Space Launch Competitiveness Act' by the US in 2015, a 'potentially watershed moment in the legal status of off-world resources, which were previously protected from private or national exploitation' (Lockhart et al. 2021: n.p.). Other countries have followed suit, leading to a wider 'opening up of space regulation' and a growth in 'space exploration and colonisation programmes' (Lockhart et al. 2021: n.p.). While we confront climate crisis on earth, we should also remain aware and critical of growing attention to outer space as a site of future expansions and exploitations.

Over to You: The Space Force

While we have reflected on outer space inhabitation and resource extraction futures, we can also consider outer space as the site of potential military interest. In 1996 the former US 'commander-in-chief of the North American Aerospace Defense Command, famously said: "We're going to fight in space. We're going to fight from space and we're going to fight into space"' (Chen 2022: n.p.). In the years since, we have witnessed the development of 'weapons that can interfere with, disrupt or destroy space assets' and the 'establishment of the US Space Force' (Chen 2022: n.p.), a separate and distinct branch of the armed services.

(Continued)

- Search for more information on the US Space Force. What are its aims? What is it doing?
- What visions of earth and conflict futures is the Space Force imagining and anticipating?
- Who is served by, at the centre of, or left out from these visions?

(Re)imagining and (Re)building Geopolitical Futures

This section draws attention to how citizens are confronting, resisting, and adapting in the face of multiple crises. Consider Covid-19. While it 'ruptured our global society', it also 'created space for radical politics of mutual aid' (Mould et al. 2021: 865). From 'concerned neighbours, members of local volunteer groups, faith networks, schools, mental health services, or food banks' to organising around housing insecurity (Mould et al. 2021: 869, 872), 'everyday acts of care and compassion radiated in spite of the pandemic' (Springer 2020: 112). Considering mutual aid in Covid times might also aid us in better understanding and 'tackling the root causes of' the 'climate catastrophe' (Mould et al. 2021: 867). We can adopt a 'more radical view of vulnerability', one that is not just passive but rather is a 'site of possibility and connection' (Mould et al. 2021: 867). While Covid introduced many who were 'not normally subject to socio-political shocks' to new vulnerability, so too did it reveal different forms of 'care' (Mould et al. 2021: 868), such as the 'community larder' converted phone box where people give as they can and take what they need (pictured in Figure 14.3), the likes of which could be mobilised in the face of climate crisis.

If the 'silver lining' to the pandemic is that 'we are reawakening to our fundamental connections to one another' (Springer 2020: 115), so too might we reimagine our connection to the planet. Hope remains a 'powerful antidote to fear' (Springer 2020: 642).

KEY TERMS: GEOGRAPHIES OF HOPE

Geographers have explored hope as orientation, form, and relation. To be hopeful is not only to have a 'positive orientation to the future', but is to disrupt conditions of hopelessness and 'create conditions of possibility' (Joronen and Griffiths 2019: 69). Hopeful practice is diverse, from protests to storytelling, each imagining and enacting alternative geopolitical futures.

Hope is an orientation, form, and relation. It is 'not simply a positive orientation to the future', but 'an experience' that 'ties hopeful waiting' to 'practices that disrupt' present hopelessness, creating 'conditions of possibility' (Joronen and Griffiths 2019: 69). It is also something that takes many forms, from 'individual action' to 'collective' solidarities (Mostafanezhad 2017: 70). Hope as 'solidarity' takes diverse forms, from 'meetings and

Figure 14.3 'Community larder' in West End of Newcastle (August 2021, permission granted)

marches, to collective organising' (Fernandes 2022: 1). The goal of hopeful action is to 'produce alternative' social relations, configurations and 'territories' resisting dominant forces (Fernandes 2022: 1). Hope also has the capacity to engender different ways of living and relating.

Hopeful Engagements with Climate Change and Earth Futures

While experiences and anticipations of climate change are linked to diverse emotions such as 'sadness, distress, anger, fear, helplessness, and hopelessness', 'emotions like hope offer the strength needed to face such threats' (Klocker et al. 2021: 2). From direct action in the streets to imagining climate futures otherwise, political geography can offer an avenue for hopeful interventions. Climate activism aims to 'mobilise knowledge about the dangers and impacts of anthropogenic climate change, catalyse action' and hold to account governments across different scales on how they 'implement and monitor climate policy' (Kythreotis et al. 2021: 70). As the climate crisis accelerates, new 'local forms of climate activism' have emerged (Kythreotis et al. 2021: 69). Notably, of the roughly '7.6 million people participating in global climate strikes' across '4,500 actions in 150 countries' in 2019, many were 'youth-led' (Dewi 2022: n.p.). This is perhaps unsurprising given that a 2021 study in *The Lancet* surveying 10,000 16–25-year-olds across ten countries demonstrated the 'extent climate fear has taken hold in younger generations' (Buchholz 2022: n.p.). Almost 70% stated that 'they were either extremely worried or very worried about climate change', with responses higher in the Global South (e.g., 84% Philippines, 78% India) (Buchholz 2022: n.p.). While underscoring that children and young people are political forces, such research highlights the importance of inclusive climate action attentive to diverse and marginalised voices.

Yet, while climate activism remains 'bound up with the disproportionate racialized and classed impacts of environmental damage' (Bowman 2020: 2), debates continue about inclusive environmentalism. Issues around the Whitewashing of climate activism were highlighted when Ugandan climate activist Vanessa Nakate was 'cropped out of a photo featuring prominent climate activists including Greta Thunberg, Loukina Tille, Luisa Neubauer and Isabelle Axelsson' by the Associated Press (Evelyn 2020: n.p.). While further attention is needed to the ways that climate activism can 'alienate BAME people' (Bell and Bevan 2021: 1205), efforts are underway to raise the visibility of the ongoing work of activists of colour. This includes projects such as 'Climate Reframe' which highlights 'some of the best Black, Brown, Asian, People of Colour and UK based Indigenous Peoples who are climate experts, campaigners and advocates' (Climate Reframe n.d.). Climate activism is, after all, a 'polyphonic' movement (Bowman 2020: 1).

Over to You: Youth Action and Climate Change

Alongside reflection on the role and agencies of young people in the context of climate crisis, it's also important to recognise the Whitewashing that can occur in relation to climate activism, adaptation efforts, and media reportage on this. Search for a climate activist group or initiative led by a person or community of colour. Reflect on:

- What are the goals of your activist group or initiative?
- What kinds of climate future are they imagining, confronted with, and seeking to respond to?
- How are they responding? Can you identify practices of hope or care?
- How do their goals or practices fit with this chapter's discussions of climate and the future?

While youth-led action is one response to climate crisis, there are of course other actors responding by 'rupturing, resisting and reworking' its 'fissures' (Sultana 2022b: 9). Following that 'climate change hurts – not just physically but also emotionally', growing numbers of people are 'experiencing intense emotional burdens' in response (González-Hidalgo 2022: 1). To this end, González-Hidalgo et al. (2022: 2, 1) turn attention to communities in Mexico, Colombia, and Spain that are 'exposed to long-lasting environmental and climate inequalities' and three collectives therein 'who are developing healing strategies to emotionally support local communities'. Collective activities include addressing 'individual and collective traumas' (Mexico), exploring wellbeing practice (Colombia), and foregrounding the 'emotional implications of opposed visions and responsibilities regarding climate change' (Spain) (González-Hidalgo 2022: 2). They argue that such 'healing practice' can be understood as both 'political' practice and an alternative form of climate change adaptation (González-Hidalgo 2022: 2). Community-led responses are also accompanied by state-led ones that both seek to creatively respond, and raise wider questions of the concept of the state in the context of climate crisis.

Case Study: Creative Reimaginings of Climate Crisis Futures

As we saw in this chapter's earlier case study (Anthropocene islands), the Pacific islands are particularly vulnerable to the effects of climate crisis. It is predicted that 'several Pacific Island nations will become uninhabitable', and for countries such as Tuvalu, this may 'happen in the next two to three decades' (*Time* 2022: n.p.). While small-island states are typically presented with climate change adaptations such as 'planned resettlement' (an authority-led form of 'mobility' determining 'why, where, and how people move') (Rogers and Wilmsen 2020: 256, 258), Pacific Island nations are pursuing creative responses.

Speaking at the UN Climate Change Conference COP27, Tuvalu's Minister of Justice, Communication and Foreign Affairs announced that the 'Pacific island had begun to create a Digital Nation in the metaverse' in response to 'the reality of rising sea levels' (Long 2022: n.p.) and a future in which the state may be submerged. The metaverse refers to an online world containing digital features and experiences that act as, and offer an alternative to, the physical world. Tuvalu's metaverse project is set to start with 'its smallest island of Teafualiku Islet' before beginning a wider 'cataloguing, mapping, recording and saving' of 'historical documents, records of cultural practice, family albums and traditional songs' (Long 2022: n.p.). Aiming to 'capture as much of Tuvaluan island life as possible', the Minister described the project of 'becoming the world's first digital nation' as a response to 'our land disappearing' (Long 2022: n.p.).

Lastly, in reflecting further on creative responses, storytelling is also a means of engaging with climate futures. Drawing attention to 'climate change cartoons' and the ways they 'work to communicate geopolitical visions', Manzo (2012: 481) argues that 'visuality is integral to climate change communication' as media such as cartoons make 'climate change feel real'. Analysing cartoons 'submitted to an international political cartoon competition', Manzo (2012: 481) explores both 'different geopolitical visions of climate change' and how cartoons depict and grapple with the 'geopolitics of climate change itself'. While we can also explore storytelling through popular media (see Chapter 6), it's also important to 'value storytelling' of different kinds and to explore it as 'decolonial climate action' (Sultana 2022b: 9). Here, Vasudevan et al.'s (2022: 3, 1) work on storytelling as both a way people 'make sense of the world and our place in it' and an 'alternative mode of theorising' understandings of 'contemporary planetary crisis within longer histories and plural understandings of our relations with earth', is instructive. Vasudevan et al. (2022: 1) argue that our imaginations of the 'figure of the human' is commonly a 'White, cis male, bourgeois and propertied' person. This is significant as it 'reproduces a story' that normalises particular relations of domination and extractivism, between people and land (Vasudevan et al. 2022: 1). In response, Vasudevan et al. (2022: 1) turn to 'anticolonial feminist storytelling' as a tool to 'open a space of possibility, to tell stories otherwise' and to reflect on how we are a 'node within a relational network of human and non-human kin'.

Over to You: Poetry and Climate Change Futures

Storytelling is a way climate change is narrated, understood, and communicated. Poetry is also a powerful medium through which climate change hopes, fears, and futures are recounted and shared. Search online and find two poems about climate change futures. To explore different forms of poetry, include terms such as 'Indigenous climate change poetry'.

- How is climate change presented in the poems you've found?
- What visions does the author(s) have of the future?
- What hopes or fears are communicated?
- How does the poetry you've selected fit with, extend, or challenge the themes explored in this chapter?

Conclusions: Political Geography Futures?

This textbook has introduced and grappled with different concepts and approaches, demonstrating the importance of attending to and thinking between different scales. In this final chapter, the concept of the future is introduced as a tool to consider how particular futures are imagined (who by, who for) and the ways 'futures are made' and folded into the 'present' with real effect (Anderson and Adey 2012: 1533). We applied this thinking to demonstrate both the power imbalances of future imaginations of climate crisis, their uneven effects, and a range of hopeful responses to these.

Such an investigation, however, prompts us to think back over the textbook as a whole. As Afinson (2022: 138) writes of climate change, it 'remakes the politics of violence', 'opening new arenas for struggle'. So too does climate change urge us to rethink our conceptualisations of borders. After all, climate migration is and will see 'climate refugees' forced to 'uproot, relocate and live through' climate-related hardship (Baldwin 2014: 516). As is evident in the case study of Tuvalu's creation of a Digital Nation in the metaverse, climate change also presses us to reconsider state-led responses to changing climatic conditions, as well as the concept of the state itself. As we've seen across the chapter's discussion of embodiment, climate change also necessitates sharpened attention to how 'differences or oppressions' such as 'gender, race/ethnicity, class, disability, age, sexuality, religion, caste, livelihood and migrant status' inform and (re)create inequitable experiences of climate change (Sultana 2021: 449).

To think of geopolitical futures in the context of the climate crisis is thus to grapple with its effects on 'all manner of geographical categories' and concepts (Baldwin 2014: 516). In thinking about both geopolitical futures and the futures of political geography, we must be willing to participate in an ongoing reflection of the sub-discipline's core concepts and approaches, asking critical questions about 'how the future of the "geo" is being shaped, by whom and whose interests' (Dalby in Agnew et al. 2020: 1213). Whilst this is a daunting agenda for geopolitics scholars, there is little choice but to grapple with the sub-discipline's complexities in a time characterised by crisis. Political geography, concerned as it is with power, place and people at multiple scales, is well placed to meet this challenge, to offer critical perspectives, and to envision more just, equitable, and hopeful futures.

Summary

- This chapter introduced geopolitical thinking on futures.
- Through the examples of data and climate change futures, it highlighted the ways in which 'the future' is imagined and acted upon in the present, and how these practices unevenly impact different people, spaces, and populations.
- It also demonstrated the significance of hope in the face of futures punctuated by crisis, exploring multiple actors responding to and reshaping geopolitical futures.

Follow-on Resources

Everyday stories of climate change: Gemma Sou, Adeeba Nuraina Risha, and Gina Ziervogel's research on the climate crisis is represented in a comic. It begins, 'when we talk about climate change, we often use abstract ideas such as the "planet is warming". But, how do these changes actually impact the daily lives of "ordinary" families across the world?'. This comic 'travels to five countries to explore everyday' experiences. See https://gemmasou.com/everyday-stories-of-climate-change/

Politics of care in pandemic time: This research project spanning universities in the UK and India explores how 'solidarity networks emerged during the pandemic and how they provided care to vulnerable communities'. See www.ucl.ac.uk/bartlett/development/research-projects/2022/nov/politics-care-pandemic-time

Fridays for Future: This is a 'youth-led and organised global climate strike movement'. Their website details the growth of the movement, provides climate crisis resources, and reminds us of the importance of student-led activism. See https://fridaysforfuture.org/take-action/

References

Afinson, K. (2022). Climate change and the new politics of violence. *New Political Science, 44*(1), 138–152.

Agnew, A., Dalby, S., Flint, C., Mamadouh, V., Newman, D. and Schofield, R. (2020). Geopolitics at 25: An editorial journey through the journal's history. *Geopolitics, 25*(5), 1199–1227.

Amoore, L. (2006). Biometric borders: Governing mobilities in the war on terror. *Political Geography, 25*(3), 336–351.

Amoore, L. (2021). The deep border. *Political Geography*. Available at: https://doi.org/10.1016/j.polgeo.2021.102547 (accessed 10 December 2022).

Anderson, B. (2010). Preemption, precaution, preparedness: Anticipatory action and future geographies. *Progress in Human Geography, 34*, 777–798.

Anderson, B. and Adey, P. (2012). Guest editorial: Future geographies. *Environment and Planning A, 44*, 1529–1535.

Baldwin, A. (2014). Pluralising climate change and migration: An argument in favour of open futures. *Geography Compass, 8*(8), 516–528.

Bell, K. and Bevan, G. (2021). Beyond inclusion? Perceptions of the extent to which Extinction Rebellion speaks to, and for, Black, Asian and Minority Ethnic (BAME) and working-class communities. *Local Environment, 26*(10), 1205–1220.

Bowman, B. (2020). 'They don't quite understand the importance of what we're doing today': The young people's climate strikes as subaltern activism. *Sustainable Earth, 3*(16), 1–13.

Boyle, M. J. (2015). The legal and ethical implications of drone warfare. *The International Journal of Human Rights, 19*(2), 105–126.

Brookes, E. (2021). Space architectures: Living under the dome. *Society and Space*, 24 May. Available at: www.societyandspace.org/articles/space-architectures-living-under-the-dome (accessed 4 January 2023).

Buchholz, K. (2022). This chart shows global youth perspectives on climate change. *World Economic Forum*, 26 October. Available at: www.weforum.org/agenda/2022/10/chart-shows-global-youth-perspectives-on-climate-change/#:⊠:text=Among%20the%2010%2C000%2016%E2%80%9325,to%20climate%20change%2Drelated%20destruction (accessed 3 December 2022).

Chandler, D. and Pugh, J. (2021). Anthropocene islands: There are only islands after the end of the world. *Dialogues in Human Geography, 11*(3), 395–415.

Chen, K. W. (2022). Amid tensions on Earth, the United States claims that 'conflict in space is not inevitable'. *The Conversation*, 1 May. Available at: https://theconversation.com/amid-tensions-on-earth-the-united-states-claims-that-conflict-in-space-is-not-inevitable-181993 (accessed 4 January 2023).

Climate Reframe (n.d.). Climate Reframe. Available at: https://climatereframe.co.uk/ (accessed 4 January 2023).

Dalby, S. (2013). The geopolitics of climate change. *Political Geography, 37*, 38–47.

Derickson, K. (2018). Urban geography III: Anthropocene urbanism. *Progress in Human Geography, 42*(3), 425–435.

Dewi, S. N. (2022). Youth climate movement in the Global south: Reaching the critical mass we need. Available at: https://th.boell.org/en/2022/06/20/youth-climate-movement (accessed 4 December 2022).

Dunnett, O., Maclaren, A. S., Klinger, J., Lane, K. M. D. and Sages, D. (2019). Geographies of outer space: Progress and new opportunities. *Progress in Human Geography, 43*(2), 314–336.

Eisenhauer, D. C. (2016). Pathways to climate change adaptation: Making climate change action political. *Geography Compass, 10*(5), 207–221.

Evelyn, K. (2020). Outrage at Whites-only image as Ugandan climate activist cropped from photo. *The Guardian,* 24 January. Available at: www.theguardian.com/world/2020/jan/24/whites-only-photo-uganda-climate-activist-vanessa-nakate (accessed 8 November 2022).

Fernandes, B. M. (2022). Territories of hope: A human geography of agrarian politics in Brazil. *Environment and Planning E: Nature and Space, 0,* 1–16.

Fregonese, S. and Laketa, S. (2022). Urban atmospheres of terror. *Political Geography, 96*(102569), 1–12.

González-Hidalgo, M., Del Bene, D., Iniesta-Arandia, I. and Piñeirode, C. (2022). Emotional healing as part of environmental and climate justice processes: Frameworks and community-based experiences in times of environmental suffering. *Political Geography, 98,* 102721, 1–11.

Jones, C. H. (2021). Enclosing the cosmos: Privatising outer space and voices of resistance. *Society and Space,* 24 May. Available at: www.societyandspace.org/articles/enclosing-the-cosmos-privatising-outer-space-and-voices-of-resistance (accessed 4 January 2023).

Joronen, M. and Griffiths, M. (2019). The moment to come: Geographies of hope in the hyperprecarious sites of occupied Palestine. *Geografiska Annaler: Series B, Human Geography, 101*(2), 69–83.

Jubb, R. and McLaughlin, A. (2022). Climate activism has so far been fairly peaceful: Here's why that might change. *The Conversation,* 7 July. Available at: https://theconversation.com/climate-activism-has-so-far-been-fairly-peaceful-heres-why-that-might-change-185625 (accessed 5 December 2022).

Klocker, N., Gillon, C., Gibbs, L., Atchison, J. and Waitt, G. (2021). Hope and grief in the human geography classroom. *Journal of Geography in Higher Education.* Available at: https://doi.org/10.1080/03098265.2021.1977915 (accessed 5 June 2023).

Kythreotis, A. P., Howarth, C., Mercer, T. G., Awcock, H. and Jonas, A. E. G. (2021). Re-evaluating the changing geographies of climate activism and the state in the post-climate emergency era in the build-up to COP26. *Journal of the British Academy, 9*(s5), 69–93.

Lockhart, A., While, A. and Marvin, S. (2021). Automation, robotics and off-world frontier-making. *Society and Space,* 24 June. Available at: www.societyandspace.org/

articles/automation-robotics-and-off-world-frontier-making (accessed 4 January 2023).

Long, D. (2022). Tuvalu creates digital nation in the metaverse as climate change threatens the Pacific nation island. *The Drum,* 21 November. Available at: www.thedrum.com/news/2022/11/21/tuvalu-creates-digital-nation-the-metaverse-climate-change-threatens-the-pacific (accessed 5 January 2023).

Manzo, K. (2012). Earthworks: The geopolitical visions of climate change cartoons. *Political Geography, 31*(8), 481–494.

Mostafanezhad, M. (2017). Celebrity humanitarianism and the popular geopolitics of hope along the Thai–Burma border. *Political Geography, 58,* 67–76.

Mould, O., Cole, J., Badger, D. and Brown, P. (2021). Solidarity, not charity: Learning the lessons of the COVID-19 pandemic to reconceptualise the radicality of mutual aid. *Transactions of the Institute of British Geographers, 7,* 866–879.

Mustafa, D. and Shaw, J. R. (2013). Geography of terrorism. *Oxford Bibliographies.* Available at: www.oxfordbibliographies.com/view/document/obo-9780199874002/obo-9780199874002-0066.xml (accessed 1 December 2022).

Paasi, A. (2022). Examining the persistence of bounded spaces: Remarks on regions, territories, and the practices of bordering. *Geografiska Annaler: Series B, Human Geography, 104*(1), 9–26.

Perez, C. S. (2021). Thinking (and feeling) with Anthropocene (Pacific) islands. *Dialogues in Human Geography, 11*(3), 429–433.

Rogers, S. and Wilmsen, B. (2020). Towards a critical geography of resettlement. *Progress in Human Geography, 44*(2), 256–275.

Smiles, D. (2020). The settler logics of (outer) space. *Society and Space,* 26 October. Available at: www.societyandspace.org/articles/the-settler-logics-of-outer-space (accessed 2 November 2022).

Smith, W. (2022). Climates of control: Violent adaptation and climate change in the Philippines. *Political Geography, 102740,* 1–10.

Springer, S. (2020). Caring geographies: The COVID-19 interregnum and a return to mutual aid. *Dialogues in Human Geography, 10*(2), 112–115.

Squire, R., Mould, O. and Adey, P. (2021). The final frontier? The enclosure of a commons of outer space. *Society and Space,* 24 May. Available at: www.societyandspace.org/forums/the-final-frontier-the-enclosure-of-a-commons-of-outer-space (accessed 7 November 2022).

Sultana, F. (2021). Climate change, COVID-19, and the co-production of injustices: A feminist reading of overlapping crises. *Social & Cultural Geography, 22*(4), 447–460.

Sultana, F. (2022a). Critical climate justice. *The Geographical Journal, 188,* 118–124.

Sultana, F. (2022b). The unbearable heaviness of climate coloniality. *Political Geography, 102638,* 1–14.

Time (2022). The climate crisis is making the Pacific islands uninhabitable. Who will help preserve our nations? *Time,* 28 September. Available at: https://time.com/6217104/climate-crisis-pacific-islands-uninhabitable/ (accessed 5 January 2023).

United Nations (2010). Report of the Special Rapporteur on extrajudicial, summary or arbitrary executions. Study on targeted killings. *General Assembly*, 28 May. Available at: www2.ohchr.org/english/bodies/hrcouncil/docs/14session/A.HRC.14.24.Add6.pdf (accessed 10 October 2022).

Vasudevan, P., Marietta Ramírez, M., González Mendoza, Y. and Daigle, M. (2022). Storytelling earth and body. *Annals of the American Association of Geographers.* Available at: https://doi.org/10.1080/24694452.2022.2139658 (accessed 5 June 2023).

Weizman, E. (2014) Introduction, Part II: Matter against memory. In Forensic Architecture Collective (eds), *Forensis: The architecture of public truth* (pp. 361–379). London: Sternberg Press.

INDEX

Abortion, 29–30
Activism, 187, 189–191, 193, 195, 198, 212, 231–2
Activist, 91, 107, 110, 158, 191–4, 196, 198, 223, 232
Actor Network Theory (ANT), 61–2, 74
Adey, Peter, 68, 150, 152–6, 157, 160–1, 221–2, 234
Afghanistan, 28, 34, 89, 172, 176
Africa, 10, 12, 47, 48–50, 66, 126, 143, 146, 153, 161, 170, 175, 189, 212,
Agnew, John, 7, 15–16
Air, 32, 68, 101, 108–110,150, 154–156
  Space, 108–9
  Travel, 154–6
  Pollution, 109
  Port, 122, 150, 153, 156, 161
Algorithm, 121, 204, 206, 211, 214, 216
Anderson, Ben, 60, 221–3, 234
Anderson, Benedict, 133–135
Animal, 52, 59–62, 69–72, 74, 91
Anthropocene, 71, 225–6
Anticipatory action, 222

Amoore, Louise, 121–2, 124, 206, 208, 223–4
App, 213–5
Arctic, 63–4
Affect, 67, 82, 92, 135–9, 142, 146, 155, 204
Assemblage, 62–4, 68, 74, 100, 125
Atmosphere, 134, 135–7, 139, 223
Awcock, Hannah, 190, 195–6

Benwell, Matt, 68, 101, 139–140, 192–3
Billig, Michael, 138–9
Biometric, 121–4, 128, 129, 206, 223
Biomimetic, 64, 69
Black
  Geographies, 44, 46, 47–50, 57, 120–1
  Lives Matter, 31, 47, 67
  Panther, 189–190
  Women, 32, 101, 120–1
Blog, 82, 94, 151, 211
Body, 1, 3, 23, 25, 27–30, 32, 36, 47–48, 56, 59, 67, 69, 72, 86, 110, 115, 119–122, 124–125, 140, 143, 152, 156, 161,169, 171–172, 176, 179, 185, 187, 205–206, 209, 213–215, 223

Embodiment, 27, 235
Embodied, 23, 27–8, 31–2, 89, 91, 92, 105,
  107, 115, 117, 124, 129, 150–151, 156,
  157, 158, 161, 168, 169, 170, 174, 175,
  179, 189, 191, 205, 213
Disembodied, 24, 108
Border, 1–3, 8, 33–35, 49, 52, 60, 65, 70–72, 74,
  82, 87–88, 91, 98, 100, 104–105, 115–129,
  141, 144, 149–151, 153, 156, 159–160,
  162, 194, 198, 206, 223–224, 234
Bordering, 115, 116–122, 125, 127–8, 160,
  194, 206, 223
Borderscapes, 115, 117
Offshoring, 116, 124–7, 129
Bos, Daniel, 80, 81–2, 90, 92
Brickell, Katherine, 25–6, 31, 171, 175, 178–9,
  209, 213
Bush, George, 83, 119, 141–2

Call of Duty, 90–1,
Care, 125, 144, 146, 211, 230, 235
Camp, 124, 144–146, 149, 157–158, 160–161
  Calais, 160
  Detention centres and sites, 85, 88, 149, 157
  Refugee, 102, 124, 144–5, 157, 161
  Migrant, 119, 149,
  Protest, 158
Canada, 10, 51–2, 174
Carter, Sean, 82, 83, 84, 89
CCTV, 65, 67, 74, 206–7, 209
Childs, John, 73, 74
Chile, 194–5
China, 10, 91, 102, 106, 196, 208,
Citizen, 9, 34, 98, 100, 102, 106, 117, 118, 137,
  140–1, 185, 189, 196, 203, 206, 207–8
Citizenship, 27, 34, 101,138, 144, 156, 170
Civilian, 28, 90, 172
Class, 18, 24, 25, 32, 34, 42, 62, 120, 156,
  158, 187, 216, 235
Climate
  Activists, 110, 191, 192, 193, 232,
  Change, 24–5, 93, 129, 149, 193, 198, 221,
    223, 225–6, 231–5
  Coloniality, 226
  Crisis, 192–3, 223, 225, 226, 227, 229,
    230–3, 235
  Emergency, 33, 97, 110
  Justice, 110, 225–6
  Protest, 110, 193
Closs, Angharad, 135–8
Cold War, 10, 15–6, 20, 80, 83, 128
Colonialism, 8, 12, 20, 27, 41–44, 50–52, 54,
  167, 172–174, 179–180, 223, 226, 228,
  Colonial, 8, 27, 41–44, 46–47, 49, 50–56,
    66, 86, 91, 104, 107, 120, 169–170,
    172–174, 228
  Settler, 52, 167, 172–4, 179, 180, 211, 228
Cook, Simon, 149, 151–2

Covid-19, 1, 25, 31, 37, 60, 91, 98, 116, 119,
  150, 152, 156, 195, 209, 213, 216, 230
  Lockdown, 25–6, 150, 195, 209
  Pandemic, 25–6, 31, 37, 60, 74, 91, 98, 116,
    119, 152, 209, 213–4, 230, 235
Crenshaw, Kimberlé, 32
Crisis, 4, 60, 118–119, 125, 143–145, 158,
  161, 192–193, 221–223, 225–227,
  229–235
Critical Geopolitics, 16–20, 23, 35, 51, 80, 94
Critical Military Geographies, 169, 171
Cuomo, Dana, 26, 171, 177, 178, 179, 204

Daigle, Michelle, 47, 51–3
Dalby, Simon, 16, 68, 225, 235
Data, 45, 100, 101, 102, 121, 122, 124–5, 180,
  204, 207–8, 212, 214–6, 221, 223, 235
Datta, Ayona, 177, 209
Decolonising, 7, 41, 43–46, 50, 55–57, 94
  Decolonial, 42, 43, 46, 54, 55, 61, 107, 234
Deep Sea Mining, 73, 226
de Leeuw, Sarah, 172–4
Derickson, Kate, 31, 225
Desai, Vandana, 43–4, 45–5, 49, 55, 56
Dickinson, Hannah, 64, 69, 70, 71–2
Digital
  Geographies, 203–5,
  Technologies, 88, 195, 203, 206. 208,
    212–6, 233
  Space, 88, 189, 191, 203, 207, 209–11, 233
  States, 206–9
Direct action, 189–90, 221, 231
Dittmer, Jason, 60, 62, 64, 80–82, 93
Dodds, Klaus, 8, 16, 17, 18, 80–1, 83, 93
Dreading the Map, 49–50
Drone, 25, 52, 64, 66, 159–160, 170, 206, 209,
  213, 222

Elden, Stuart, 104, 108
Elements, 59–61, 63, 68, 74
  Elemental, 60–1, 68–9, 74
Emotion, 17, 24, 26, 30, 32–35, 82,
  120, 135, 144, 175, 177, 178, 211,
  231–3
Empire, 7, 8–11, 20, 41–2, 48, 69, 128, 226
Environmental Determinism, 8, 9, 10, 11, 60
Esson, James, 41, 42, 43, 44, 45, 46
Europe, 10, 12, 93, 158,
EU, 71, 125–6, 128, 158
Everyday, 1–2, 7, 15, 18, 23–27, 30–34, 36–37,
  44, 47, 49, 52, 57, 60. 64, 66–67, 74,
  79–83, 86, 89–90, 93, 98, 100–102, 104–
  105, 110–111, 115, 117–121, 124–125,
  127, 133, 136–140, 143, 145–146, 149,
  151–152, 154, 161, 167, 169, 171–2,
  176–179, 185–187, 189 , 191–193, 195,
  198, 203–205, 208–210, 212, 214, 216,
  223–224, 226, 230, 235

Facial recognition, 207, 209, 223, 224
Fear, 15, 17, 25, 33–4, 51, 65, 108, 124, 133, 142, 155–6, 157, 172, 177, 179, 191, 208, 222, 230, 232, 234
Feminist Geopolitics, 3, 23–25, 27–28, 32, 35, 36, 83,111, 171
  Approaches, 3, 117, 120, 133, 143, 146, 179
Femicide, 175
Flag, 62, 72, 83,
Flint, Colin, 15, 186, 100, 133–5, 138–9
Fluri, Jennifer, 30, 168, 175, 176
Forsyth, Isla, 69, 169, 170
Freeman, Cordelia, 29–30, 88
Frontex, 159
Future, 2, 4–5, 79–81, 83, 93, 97, 110, 143, 145, 188, 190, 198, 209, 216, 221–223, 225, 227–235

Gas, 63, 152, 161
Geographical Pivot of History, 10
Geopolitical imagination, 10, 18, 80, 82, 88, 89, 91, 93, 94, 104, 115
Gender, 18, 24–25, 29–32, 37, 47, 55, 62, 66, 86, 88–89, 120–121, 124, 153, 156, 161, 169, 171, 175, 177–178, 180,187, 190–191, 211, 214, 216, 235
Germany, 7, 10, 12–4, 128
Gilmore, Ruth Wilson, 32
Global, 1, 24–25, 29, 34, 36–37, 44, 50–51, 60, 71, 74, 80, 85, 91,98, 110, 111, 118, 217, 137, 145, 150, 152, 155, 160–161,169, 175, 176, 189, 193, 198, 211, 221, 222, 225, 230–232, 235
Globalisation, 97, 98, 110, 116, 129, 155
God's Eye View, 8, 10, 16, 18, 108
Gregory, Derek, 155, 170–1, 172, 179, 206

Halvorsen, Sam, 104–5
Hitler, Adolf, 12–5
Home, 23, 24, 25–7, 34, 26, 60, 63, 72, 79, 87, 88, 103, 111, 120, 144, 151, 169, 172, 174, 177, 179, 193, 207, 209, 212–14, 226, 228
Hong Kong, 67, 91, 108, 196–7
Hope, 33, 35, 67, 86, 128, 156, 190, 211, 216, 221, 226, 230–1, 232, 234, 235
Hospitality, 133, 135, 143, 145
Huang, Yan, 104, 106
Hughes, Sarah, 64, 88, 187–8, 191
Hyndman, Jennifer, 4, 19, 23, 24–5, 28, 36, 153

Imagination, 10, 17, 18, 60, 66, 79, 80–1, 82, 84, 88, 89, 91, 93, 94, 103, 104, 109, 115, 117, 128, 234
Immigrant, 32–34, 87, 121, 154
Immigration, 97–88, 94, 116, 125–127, 142, 157, 191

Indigenous, 30, 42–3, 45–7, 51–2, 53, 54, 56, 63, 72–3, 74, 86, 94, 104, 106–7, 172–5, 179, 180, 211, 225, 226, 228, 232, 234
India, 10, 25, 44, 102–3, 143, 171, 174, 177, 191, 209, 232, 235
Intellectuals of statecraft, 16, 17
Internet of Things, 212–13
Intersectional, 3, 18, 32, 55, 62, 94, 117, 161, 192, 216
  Intersectionality, 18, 32, 55, 62, 94, 177, 161, 192, 216
Intimate, 25, 31, 35, 72, 120–121, 143, 172, 175, 177, 193, 209, 214
  Bordering, 120–1
  Geopolitics, 35, 72, 172, 177, 193, 209, 214
  Scales, 25, 143
Invisible beings, 54, 59, 73, 74
Iran, 122, 123, 188
Iraq, 28, 34, 85, 89, 98

Jazeel, Tariq, 43, 46, 54, 55
Jeffrey, Alex, 98, 100
Johnson, Elizabeth, 64, 69
Jones, Reece, 101, 117, 118–19, 125, 135, 139–40, 141

Klinke, Ian, 11–13, 14–15
Koopman, Sara, 17, 18, 19, 24, 28, 36, 18–7

Lacoste, Yves, 169
Lebensraum, 12–3, 15
LGBTQ+, 88, 94,175, 217
Ludic Geopolitics, 89, 94

Mahan, Alfred, 11
MacKinder, Halford, 7, 8–11, 12, 15, 16, 20, 42, 128
McConnell, Fiona, 98, 102–3, 189
Map, 10, 16, 17, 49–50, 97, 99, 103, 104, 106, 108, 115, 117, 128, 129, 139, 150, 160, 162, 174, 213, 216, 226, 233
Mason, Olivia, 27–28
Massaro, Vanessa, 16–19, 24–25, 36, 71
Material(ity), 12, 14, 27, 33, 37, 47, 51, 59–62, 64, 68, 71, 73, 88, 97, 100, 102, 107, 110, 118, 124, 135, 141, 144, 146, 150, 152, 156–157, 159, 168, 172, 177, 195–196, 198, 204, 208, 226
  Turn, 59–61, 62, 64, 68
McKittrick, Katherine, 32
Mediterranean, 118–9, 125–6, 129, 144, 158–9, 162
Megoran, Nick, 115–6, 118, 124, 128–9, 186–7, 189, 197
Mexico, 70, 74, 87, 106, 116, 127, 175, 194, 233

Migrant, 33, 49, 87, 94, 105, 117–121,
125–127, 129, 137, 141, 149, 157, 159,
160–162, 194, 235
Crisis, 158–60, 161
Military, 9, 14, 28, 31, 35, 51, 64, 66, 69–70,
80, 83–4, 89, 90, 91, 92–3, 101, 105, 106,
109, 169–72, 176, 178, 179
Mobility, 27, 60, 65, 68, 82, 117, 121–122,
125,139, 149–162,191, 223, 233
Everyday, 150, 151–2
Material, 150, 152
Spatialised, 150, 153
Uneven, 150, 153
Immobility, 117, 148, 157, 160–1, 162
Mountz, Alison, 27, 29, 31, 100, 102, 167
Music, 64, 79–80, 85–6, 87–8, 93, 94, 101,
120, 135, 196

Nation, 9, 11, 13, 24, 31, 48–49, 51–52, 66,
98, 117–118, 129, 133–135, 138–144, 146,
156, 172–173, 197, 225, 233–234
Nationalism, 38, 69, 81, 128, 133–146, 171
Banal, 138, 171
Everyday, 134, 136, 138–40, 143, 146
Nazi, 7, 12–15, 20
Non-human, 52, 59–62, 64, 69, 72, 73–4, 107,
152, 157, 161, 170, 185, 195, 198, 199,
206, 208, 212, 234
Noxolo, Patricia, 41, 42, 43, 44, 47, 48–50, 54, 55

Object, 3, 33, 52–53, 59–62, 64–68, 74, 80,
88–89, 92, 100, 110, 115, 129, 134–135,
138–139, 143, 150, 159, 171, 195–196,
198, 204–205, 207, 209
Disobedient, 66–67, 74, 195, 198
Olympic games, 134, 135–6, 137–8
Othering, 44, 118, 142
Orientalism, 142
O'Tuathail, Gerard, 16–7, 18, 169
Outer Space, 221, 227–9

Paasi, Anssi, 98, 100, 116, 125, 223
Pain, Rachel, 26–7, 30, 31, 32, 33–4, 169,
175, 177
Painter, Joe, 97, 98, 100, 101–2
Pandemic, 1, 25, 26, 31, 37, 60, 74, 91, 99, 116,
119, 152, 209, 213, 214, 221, 230, 235
Palestine, 35, 36, 108, 109
Palestinian, 35, 36, 67, 108, 145, 157
Panopticon, 207, 213
Passport, 60, 102, 118, 122–3, 128, 156, 161,
228
Peace, 31, 33, 51, 185–189, 197–198, 212
Peaceful, 31, 185, 186, 187
Perez, Craig Santos, 226
Pharmakon, 204
Pipeline, 68, 152, 173

Play, 89–91, 92, 93
Police, 31, 108, 142, 153, 159, 174, 177, 180,
188, 206, 207, 223
Popular Geopolitics, 18, 79, 80–2, 86, 89, 91,
92–4
Postcolonial, 54, 91, 154, 172
Post-human, 61, 62, 72, 74
Power, 1–2, 8–11, 13, 16–17, 24–30, 32, 36,
42–44, 46–47, 49–50, 52, 54, 56, 61–62,
64–67, 72–74, 81–84, 86–89, 97–98, 101,
104–106, 108–112, 116, 119–121, 124,
128, 134, 136, 140–141, 143, 146, 149,
151, 153–154, 156–161, 168–170,
173–174, 179, 185–191, 195, 198,
204–205, 208, 212–213, 225–226, 228,
234–235
Power container, 98, 11, 116
Positionality, 24, 42, 46, 47, 54, 92, 118
Protest, 30, 31, 37, 47, 67, 87, 100, 108, 110,
149, 157–8, 161, 173, 185, 188, 189–91,
193, 195–6, 198, 230
Protestor, 31, 64, 67, 109, 158, 188, 191
Stickers, 195–6

Race, 10–11, 18, 24–25, 28, 30, 32, 42–43, 45,
47, 49, 57, 62, 86, 101, 118, 120, 142,
153, 161, 169, 211, 216, 235
Racism, 32, 41–44, 46–48, 49–50, 109,
142–143, 168, 210
Radcliffe, Sarah A, 42, 46, 174
Ratzel, Frederich, 11–12, 14–15
Rech, Matthew, 64, 66, 169, 171
Refugee, 32, 49, 102, 117–118, 124, 127,
140–141, 143–146, 150, 156, 161–162,
193, 234
Resilience, 160, 187
Resistance, 2, 30–31, 48–49, 52, 67, 86–87,
109, 117, 120, 157–158, 161, 176, 179,
185–189, 191,193, 195, 197–198, 212,
Resources, 9, 11, 17, 42, 61, 63, 66, 73, 83,
90, 98, 104, 108, 118, 128, 168, 174, 190,
227, 229
Royal Geographical Society, 9, 20, 45, 49–50
Running, 27, 151–152
Russia, 10, 14, 25, 98, 127, 143, 185, 212

Sea, 10, 15, 17, 63, 68–70, 73–74, 106, 108,
111, 119, 125–127, 129,145, 158–160,
162
South China, 106
Mediterranean, 118–119, 125–126, 144,
158–159, 162
Seafarer, 160
Security, 24, 30, 33–34, 49, 57, 68, 71, 87,
116, 125, 153, 155–156, 168, 187, 197,
206–207, 213–214, 230
Insecurity, 49, 57, 152, 230,

September 11th (9/11), 33–34, 50–51, 83–84, 119, 121, 141–143, 158, 207, 223,
Sexuality, 18, 47, 62, 88. 190, 211, 216, 235
Sharp, Jo, 18–19, 23–24, 26, 34, 50–51, 55, 80–81, 85,
Sidaway, James, 17–18,
Smiles, Deondre, 172, 174
Smith, Sara, 25, 27, 32–34, 120, 124, 134, 141, 225
Social Media, 82, 91–93, 137, 167, 171, 191, 195, 208–212, 217, 223
Soldier, 28–29, 69, 90, 150, 170–172
Sovereignty, 52, 71, 98, 104, 106, 108, 110, 111, 173
Space Force, 229–230
Spirits, 53, 59–60, 72–73, 174
  Spiritual, 53, 72–74,134, 175
  Spirituality, 73, 175
Staeheli, Lynn, 26, 30–31, 175, 177
State, 1, 4, 8–12, 14–17, 19, 23–25, 27–29, 34, 36, 43, 49, 52, 54, 64–67, 72–73, 85–86, 88, 91, 93, 97–98, 100–112, 115–119, 122–125, 127–129, 133–134,138–141, 143–145, 156–157, 159, 169–170, 174, 176–177, 188–189, 191, 197, 203, 205–210, 212, 216, 224, 233, 235
  Statecraft, 9, 16–17
  State of exception, 119
Subaltern, 50–51,
Sultana, Farhana, 25, 225–226, 232, 234–235
Sundberg, Juanita, 24, 61, 70–73
Surveillance, 48–49, 67, 108, 126, 153–154, 156, 170, 176, 203, 206–209, 212–213, 216, 222
  (geo), 207

Teargas, 32, 67, 108, 195, 196, 198, 199
Technology, 2, 4, 9, 29, 88, 104, 121, 170, 204–206, 213, 215, 228
Territory, 8, 11–12, 27, 52–53, 86, 97–98, 103–111, 116, 125, 134, 140–141
Terrorism, 33, 85, 143, 153, 172, 221, 223
Theriault, Noah, 54, 72–73
Tibet, 102–103
  Tibetan Government in Exile, 102–103, 111
Time space convergence, 155
Toal, Gerard, 8–11, 15,
Toy(s), 2, 79–81, 89

Trump, Donald, 188, 223, 228,
Tyner, James, 31, 168, 189–190

Ukraine, 14, 98, 127, 143, 150, 187
United Nations (UN), 25, 33, 37, 98, 124, 126, 222, 225
United States/USA, 14, 31, 34, 46, 52, 62, 65, 67, 81, 83, 87, 116, 138, 153, 154, 157, 172, 173, 188, 189, 191, 207
USSR, 81

van Houtum, Henk, 115, 116
Video Games, 18, 89–93, 205
Violence
  Domestic, 26–7, 169, 177–9
  Gendered, 31, 32, 175, 177
  Racialised, 49, 86, 153, 168
  Sexual, 26, 120–1, 159, 171, 177, 191
  Settler colonialism, 52, 167, 172–4, 179, 180, 211, 228
Violent, 7–8, 27, 30, 34, 43–44, 46, 52, 56, 90, 98, 107, 110, 116, 118–121, 127–129, 161, 167, 168–169, 172, 176, 179, 185, 190
  Borders, 98, 118–9, 121
Virus, 60, 150, 152, 161
Volume, 97, 108, 110, 111

Walking, 27–8, 150, 151, 171, 195 , 208
War, 1, 10, 12–16, 20, 28, 33, 66, 69, 81, 83, 89–94, 119–120, 128, 134, 150, 167, 169–172, 179–180, 185–187, 198, 229
  Warfare, 15, 26, 64, 66, 69, 72, 90, 91, 169–70, 179, 197
  War on Terror, 28, 33–4, 83–4, 92, 121, 142, 169, 172
Weclome, 133, 143–5, 146
Weizman, Eyal, 108, 222
West Bank, 108
Williams, Alison, 25, 64, 108
Williams, Jill, 16, 17, 18, 19, 24, 25, 32, 33, 34, 36, 71
Woodyer, Tara, 89, 94
Woon, Chih Yuan, 33, 34, 172

Youthquake, 192

Zurita, María de Lourdes Melo, 105–6

Printed in the USA
CPSIA information can be obtained
at www.ICGtesting.com
JSHW051353010824
67246JS00005B/50

9 781526 498854